THE GOD OF THE MACHINE

The Library of Conservative Thought
Michael Henry, Series Editor
Russell Kirk, Founding Series Editor

America's British Culture, by Russell Kirk
Authority and the Liberal Tradition, by Robert Heineman
A Better Guide than Reason, by M.E. Bradford
Burke Street, by George Scott-Moncrieff
The Case for Conservatism, by Francis Graham Wilson
Céline, by Milton Hindus
Character and Culture, by Irving Babbitt
Collected Letters of John Randolph of Roanoke to
John Brockenbrough, 1812–1833, edited by Kenneth Shorey
A Critical Examination of Socialism, by William Hurrell Mallock
Edmund Burke: Appraisals and Applications, edited by Daniel E. Ritchie
Edmund Burke: The Enlightenment and Revolution, by Peter J. Stanlis
The Essential Calhoun, by John C. Calhoun
Foundations of Political Science, by John W. Burgess
Ghosts on the Roof, by Whittaker Chambers
The God of the Machine, by Isabel Paterson
A Historian and His World, A Life of Christopher Dawson 1889–1970,
by Christina Scott
Historical Consciousness, by John Lukacs
I Chose Freedom, by Victor A. Kravchenko
I Chose Justice, by Victor A. Kravchenko
Irving Babbitt, Literature, and the Democratic Culture, by Milton Hindus
The Jewish East Side, edited by Milton Hindus
Lord George Bentinck, by Benjamin Disraeli
The Moral Foundations of Civil Society, by Wilhelm Roepke
Natural Law, by Alexander Passerin d'Entréves
On Divorce, by Louis de Bonald
Orestes Brownson: Selected Political Essays, edited by Russell Kirk
The Phantom Public, by Walter Lippmann
*The Politics of the Center, Juste Milieu in Theory and Practice, France and
England, 1815–1848*, by Vincent E. Starzinger
Regionalism and Nationalism in the United States, by Donald Davidson
Rousseau and Romanticism, by Irving Babbitt
The Social Crisis of Our Time, by Wilhelm Roepke
Tensions of Order and Freedom, by Béla Menczer
We the People, by Forrest McDonald

THE GOD OF THE MACHINE

ISABEL PATERSON

*With a New Introduction
by Stephen Cox*

Transaction Publishers
New Brunswick (U.S.A.) and London (U.K.)

Eighth printing 2009
New material this edition copyright © 1993 by Transaction Publishers, New
Brunswick, New Jersey 08903. Originally published in 1943 by G.P. Putnam.

This book is printed on acid-free paper that meets the American National
Standard for Permanence of Paper for Printed Library Materials.

Library of Congress Catalog Number: 92-32935
ISBN: 978-1-56000-666-4
Printed in the United States of America

             Library of Congress Cataloging-in-Publication Data
Paterson, Isabel.
   The god of the machine / Isabel Paterson; with a new introduction by Stephen
Cox.
       p. cm.—(Library of conservative thought)
   ISBN 1-56000-666-8 (pbk.)
     1. Political science. 2. Economic policy. 3. United States— Civilization.
   I. Title. II. Series.

JC251.P3   1993
320—dc20   92-32935

I wish to acknowledge a considerable obligation to Professor Thomas T. Read, E.M., Ph.D., for acute and cogent critical comments on the manuscript of this book, which were most helpful toward clarifying the presentation of the theme. This does not imply that Professor Read necessarily agrees with all or any of the ideas and conclusions expressed, for which the author is responsible.

Isabel Paterson.

Contents

Introduction to the Transaction Edition

The God of the Machine is remarkable in many ways.

It presents one of the few original theories of history that have been developed in America, and one of the very few historical theories that have discovered patterns and principles in human events but not a system of determining forces. It offers ideas for progress, derived from a commitment to traditional values; a concept of a just and well structured society, based on an ideal of individual freedom; and a critique of ideological materialism, expressed in language normally employed in the study of material processes. *The God of the Machine* is a political and economic defense of free enterprise, devised by a literary intellectual who took no active part in politics and who struggled hard just to earn a decent living.

On its publication in 1943, *The God of the Machine* appeared hopelessly old-fashioned. Today, it appears prophetic. It exposes the moral and practical failures of collectivism, failures that are now almost universally acknowledged but are still far from universally understood; and it identifies problems that continue to threaten the destruction of free societies.

The God of the Machine contains principles congenial both to modern conservatism and to traditional liberalism. But so clearly is this book stamped with the individual character of its author that it resists classification as a typical product of any intellectual movement or combination of movements. A work of creative imagination brought to bear on fact, it challenges readers to see, as if for the first time, the shape of the world in which they live—to envision its history, examine its values, and decide its future.

I

The author of *The God of the Machine* was as remarkable as her book.

Isabel Bowler Paterson was born on 22 January, 1886, in the little community of Tehkummah, Manitoulin Island, Ontario, Canada, one of nine children of Francis (Frank) and Margaret Bowler. She was probably born in a log house that stood just up the hill from a grist mill built by her father.[1] Her family soon moved to the Upper Peninsula of Michigan. All her life she would remember the town of Newberry, where the beech trees were "vocal with squirrels" and where raspberries ripened along a narrow-gauge track that ran out to a lumber camp. When Isabel was six, the Bowlers moved again, much farther to the west. They farmed or ranched in Utah and Alberta. Her girlhood, she said, "was rather dull, being spent in the Wild West."[2]

It was not only "dull" but poor. The family lived for a long time in tents.[3] Paterson, who believed without good reason that she was an especially plain woman, would attribute much of her supposed plainness to uneven growth caused by malnutrition in her youth.[4] She did the hard work of a farm child, making soap, helping the hay pitchers, taking care of livestock. She "spent—lavished, one might say"—about two years in a log schoolhouse in the Glacier Park district near Alberta's border with Montana.[5]

That concluded her formal education. But she read whatever she could get her hands on: newspapers, the Bible, the fiction of Dickens and Dumas, Charles Taze Russell's *Millennial Dawn*, Shakespeare's *Antony and Cleopatra*. Often she "sat in an obscure corner perusing 'The Police Gazette'" and listening to her uncles and aunts tell their private histories.[6] She loved poetry; many years afterward, she could quote by the acre the verse of Swinburne that she had discovered in her youth.

Older worlds lingered, not too far away. The Blood Band of the Blackfoot Indians were neighbors of the Bowler family, and Isabel was a guest at their Sun Dance. In some mysterious way, as she remarked, her values would always be connected with salient images of those early days: an Indian hunter arriving with a sackful of fuzzy wolf pups; a little grey sand-lizard discovered under a sagebrush; the first, uncanny sight of an automobile "scurrying along the horizon" like "a large black beetle." She was sixteen when she saw her first electric light, and she thought it might kill her if she touched it to turn it off.[7]

In later life, she was fond of saying that she had seen both the stone age and the air age. A girlhood in which she "witnessed the obliteration of the last fringe of the frontier" gave her a dramatic sense of history, the sense of a world constantly transforming itself in astonishing ways. From the impressions of her youth she received both an expectation of progress and a fear of tragic loss.

> Haven't we personally been torn from three countries before we grew up? The Michigan woods, the sage and mountains of Utah, and the prairies of the Northwest. Since then we have loved and lost, above all, the north Pacific coast. All Americans are in the same situation, even if they have moved much less in space. Time has bereaved them.[8]

The novels that Paterson wrote in middle age would often be concerned with the emotions of people who feel themselves bereaved by time. In one of these works, a woman remembers the "wild land" of the West and imagines herself as belonging "to a sunken continent; lost Atlantis. . . . Europeans think Americans are young; we're two thousand years older than they. . . . They've read their history. We've been through it all ourselves."[9] Although Paterson did not become a citizen of the United States until 1928, her feeling for the American experience long antedated that event. She said it was an experience "so various, rich and strange" that no "school of fiction has done it justice or could do so."[10] *The God of the Machine* is one result of her own long attempt to do imaginative justice to American history.

At about eighteen years of age, she went to work for pay. She held a variety of jobs, including those of a waitress, stenographer, and bookkeeper. She knew what it was like to earn as little as $20 a month, for working ten or twelve hours a day, including Sundays.[11] But she was independent and intensely proud of her ability to stay that way. She once remarked to Muriel Welles Hall, a young journalist: "'Listen, my girl, your paycheck is your mother and your father'; in other words, respect it." Paterson was always outspokenly contemptuous of well-born or well-subsidized intellectuals who presumed to lecture working people about the evils of a society dominated by the "bourgeois class."

Her experience helped her to a thoroughly individualist view of "class." The notion of "class" that mattered to her grew out of the enormous respect she developed, during the course of a long working life, for the determinedly competent individuals of every "economic class" who keep society going, who (in the workers' own colloquial expression) maintain the basic "set-up." Paterson devoted her political and economic writing to defending these people's interests. Prosperity, she thought,

> depends entirely upon a minority being allowed to function. We do not mean a class, but a certain type of mind. It exists in various degrees and forms—business men and farmers and foremen and housewives, the people who will always somehow get things done, get some practicable result from whatever material is at hand and whatever other people they must work with. They are self-starters. And they are seldom conspicuous.

> The self-starters are never college professors nor politicians. Neither do we mean inventors, intellectuals, artists or writers—the creative artist [e.g., Paterson herself!] is naturally anti-social. The self-starters, of course, use what more original minds discover, and

their particular function is to hold everything together. One can't always see how they do it. . . .

In an effort to regulate everything those people may easily be eliminated. They have been very nearly exterminated in Russia. Bureaucracy smothers them. And the set-up goes with them. [12]

The God of the Machine would show more respect for inventors and intellectuals. But it would retain the concept of the "self-starters," the productive class whose interests are naturally antagonistic to those of the class of nonproducers and regulators of other people's production. In *The God of the Machine*, the best possible "set-up" is identified as free-enterprise capitalism.

Isabel Bowler eventually got a job doing secretarial work for R. B. Bennett, a Calgary, Alberta, lawyer who in 1930 became premier of Canada. Paterson would remember Bennett as "a good egg," despite the sharp divergence of their political views. He offered to have her articled as a law student in his office, but she declined, preferring to maintain her freedom from the obligations of a profession. [13] And she had no more desire to become a writer than she had to become a lawyer. As a girl, she had contributed items to the newspaper, but merely because she would "get bored playing poker with the rest of [her] large family on winter evenings" and wanted something else to do. She had "vague notions" of becoming an actress or marrying a millionaire. [14]

On 13 April, 1910, at Calgary, she married Kenneth Birrell Paterson. It is safe to say that Kenneth Paterson was not a millionaire, but practically nothing is known about him or the marriage, except that it was unsuccessful. Correspondence of 1918 suggests that by that time Isabel Paterson no longer knew where her husband was. She continued to bear his orthographically troublesome surname, which, according to her, was spelled with only one "t" because his family was too cheap to use two of them. By the mid-1920s, she was known to most people as "Pat." [15] But she was not in the habit of discussing her husband,

and he remains a mysterious figure, one of the reasons why "prospective biographers of Mrs. Paterson," as an interviewer once commented, "will probably end in Bellevue."[16]

To her own surprise, Paterson had begun to write for a living. While visiting Spokane in 1910, she was offered a job as secretary to the publisher of a local paper, the *Inland Herald*. She reacted so strongly to his mangling of English syntax, as she took dictation, that he hired a more tolerant secretary and put Paterson to work writing editorials. She later wrote for two papers in Vancouver, for one of which she contributed dramatic criticism. In 1913 she is reported in New York, where she worked on the *World* and the *American*. During the Great War, she considered going to France with the Red Cross. She is said to have moved several times back and forth across North America.[17] In late 1917 and 1918, for instance, she found herself in San Francisco. By that time, she had begun her career as a novelist.

She was led toward that career by a friend who

thought we needed encouragement, and required us to bring her one chapter a week. We thought it was a strange craving, but to please a dear friend, we wrote our first novel. It was simply awful.

When we read it over, we could see that it lacked everything a novel should have. This roused our curiosity. We began pondering, what should a novel be like? We got to brooding over it. . . . We've never had a carefree moment since we began learning to write.[18]

Paterson's first published novel, *The Shadow Riders*, appeared in 1916; her second, *The Magpie's Nest*, which was completed somewhat earlier (certainly by late 1914), appeared in 1917.[19] Although Paterson was dissatisfied with these early works,[20] they have considerable literary interest. They contain some arresting imagery and complex studies of character. They provide strong and detailed pictures of the upstart towns of the

North American West and the lives of young women starting out in them.

Living on the east coast after the war, Paterson worked for Gutzon Borglum, the sculptor of Stone Mountain and Mount Rushmore, whom she considered "the finest craftsman of this age."[21] Meanwhile, she did her best to read through the holdings of the New York Public Library. In 1921, a friend introduced her to Burton Rascoe, an editor of *McCall's* who early the next year became literary editor of the New York *Tribune*. Rascoe had taken "a violent dislike to Mrs. Paterson." Nevertheless, she got herself hired as his assistant, after a brief but decisive campaign:

> She said bluntly that she wanted the job. . . . I told her my budget would not allow me to pay what she was worth. She said she would work for whatever I was prepared to pay. I said the pay was forty dollars a week. She said, "I'll work for that."
>
> I was afraid not to hire her.[22]

The *Tribune* soon became the *Herald Tribune*. For its weekly *Books* section, a respected journal with a nationwide circulation, Paterson wrote reviews and a column that appeared from late 1924 until early 1949.

II

Paterson's column was perhaps intended simply as a department of literary news and anecdotes, but it didn't stay that way. Almost anything could find its way in, from a one-line note on a recently published book to an 1800-word essay on philosophy, economics, natural history, politics, the American character, Paterson's sense of life, or all of the above. Paterson jokingly but accurately observed that the "peculiar charm" of her column came from its "personal element": "The books are a mere pretext."[23]

The column's only unifying feature was the alternately wry and bemused, confiding and commanding personality of "I.M.P." ("Isabel Mary Paterson"), who signed each of the 1200 weekly offerings and in whom Paterson created one of the most distinctive literary projections of the era. Through the notorious I.M.P., Paterson managed to say just what she thought about whatever concerned her. Her readers, says a contemporary source, "seem to be divided into two camps—those who love her and those who take her as their Sunday morning hair shirt—but everybody reads her."[24]

Some of I.M.P.'s concerns, of course, were literary; but on this subject it is hard to generalize about her attitudes. Rascoe, a lively young man with self-consciously advanced views of literature, thought that "Mrs. Paterson, by expressing the conservative point of view . . . would be something of a counterbalance" to himself. Paterson's conservatism was qualified, however, by her sympathy for Rascoe's fight against "the genteel Victorian tradition."[25] After the unpleasant start of their relationship, Paterson and Rascoe warmed to each other. She also got along well with her next boss, Stuart Sherman, a leader of the conservative forces who was drifting toward the other side. But she never joined a specific critical or cultural sect.

> The saddest spectacle imaginable to us is an anxious youth endeavoring to like only what the current intellectual mode approves.[26]

Paterson laughed about the conservative New Humanism when it became a subject of popular debate. She also laughed about attempts to devise a "proletarian" theory of literature; such adventures reminded her, she said, of "the cowboy who got himself a brand before he had any cattle."[27]

Essentially self-educated, Paterson could afford to feel contemptuous of all supposed beneficiaries of expensive formal educations who had never bothered to acquaint themselves with the seminal works of the Western tradition. But she was not a committed literary traditionalist. "The support of a great tradition," she wrote in a cheeky, partly self-mocking mood, "is no doubt a good thing for those who need it, but we can get along on our own. After all, there have been a great many traditions, and they are transitory and contradictory and foreign; but there's only one of us."[28] It's worth noting, however, that this was not the attitude she took toward the American moral and political tradition, which seemed anything but transitory or foreign to her. That was the tradition, she thought, that enabled individuals to develop on their own in every other respect.

Paterson's critical method was consonant with her individualism. It might, perhaps, be called a commonsense Aristotelianism. She did not try to prescribe the literary projects that writers should choose, but she did try to assess each writer's skill in using the literary tools appropriate to the project of his or her choice.

> Joseph Conrad expressed on behalf of all novelists the whole purpose of fiction, perhaps of literature: "It is to make you see, to make you feel." But there are as many modes of conveying the image and the emotion as there are writers, and all of them are right so far as they are effective.[29]

Effectiveness can be judged by the vitality with which artistic intentions are realized:

> The first, last and continuous duty of a writer is to be interesting. Far too much latitude is allowed to bores in all walks of life. It is assumed that a bore must mean well. Even if he does, what of it? Good intentions are a bad excuse.[30]

If Paterson found classic works of literature lacking in vitality, she felt no compunction about saying so. When someone asked her to screw up her courage and "tell the truth about 'Moby Dick,'" she replied, "Why, that doesn't require any courage. Every one knows that 'Moby Dick' is a prodigiously boring book, with a murky streak of genius buried in it."[31] By remembering that streak of genius, however murky, Paterson preserved a sense of vitality in her own remarks.

John O'Hara spoke for numerous other authors when, on the publication day of his *Appointment in Samarra*, he confessed, "I'm very much afraid of Isabel Paterson."[32] As it turned out, Paterson enjoyed O'Hara's novel. But he had reason to be afraid of her. If she did not enjoy someone's novel, she might say, "It's a sad story. The style alone would bring tears to your eyes."[33] Or she might say that an author "arrives at her meanings by a process almost as distressing to the sensibilities as the spectacle of a cat being pulled backward by the tail."[34]

Paterson declared that "a sincere dislike is also a basis of enjoyment,"[35] and she especially enjoyed disliking authors whom she regarded as pretentious nonentities:

> Gertrude Stein, author of "The Autobiography of Alice B. Toklas," is coming over soon for a lecture tour. One of her lecture topics will be "The History of English Literature as I Understand It." That should be a very brief lecture.[36]

> Babies are complete egotists, and they possess a naive charm. If a baby could write a book it would resemble "The Autobiography of Alice B. Toklas."[37]

Of the members of "The Lost Generation," Paterson wrote: "Their essential docility, underneath the surface revolt, was complete and touching. . . . They felt themselves persecuted by 'The Saturday Evening Post.'"[38]

But Paterson preferred to be pleased by what she read. She made cautious but respectful estimations of Faulkner and Hemingway and was willing to be interested, at least, by the phenomenon of D. H. Lawrence and his cult following. She enjoyed Mencken, even though she regretted his influence on would-be imitators. Among her contemporaries, Yeats was the author she most greatly esteemed; he was "not only a great poet, but perhaps the only great man in the world."[39] She also appreciated writers as diverse as Virginia Woolf, Thornton Wilder, Willa Cather, Allen Tate, Ford Madox Ford, Elinor Wylie, Sinclair Lewis, James Branch Cabell, Nevil Shute, Wil-

liam Saroyan, Margaret Mitchell, Richard Hughes, P. G.
Wodehouse, William Carlos Williams, and Ellen Glasgow.

A number of these authors became Paterson's friends; several,
in fact, owed much of their success with the American public to
her loud advertisements. Besides demanding that her audience
attend to significant poetry and fiction, she made an effort to
popularize meritorious biographies, histories, and works on
technical and scientific subjects, especially the kind of works
that might otherwise escape attention. She was an advocate of
such important works of foreign literature as *The Tale of Genji*
and the memoirs of the French enlightenment. Meanwhile, she
noticed, without condescension, many light, admittedly
ephemeral contemporary works. Her appreciation for even a
modest show of literary skill made her vulnerable to such an-
tagonists as Mary McCarthy, who cut her journalistic teeth on
Paterson's supposedly lax standards of evaluation.[40]

Paterson at times had literary proteges, two of whom played
particularly large roles in her life. She befriended the shy,
intensely neurotic humorist Will Cuppy, recognized his talent,
supported him emotionally while he was preparing his books (to
which she contributed some of the jokes), and promoted him
mercilessly in her columns. Her other protege, Ayn Rand, was
as different from the unassuming Cuppy as anyone could possibly be. Rand, a formidable personality, was supremely proud
of her intellectual independence, but she was strongly influenced
by her relationship with Paterson. Rand was one of the friendly
"assistants" who joined Paterson on Monday nights while she
checked the proofs of *Herald Tribune "Books"* as it went to
press. During this period, Rand (who was nineteen years
younger than Paterson) has been described as "sitting at the
master's feet" while Paterson instructed her.[41]

Rand was not especially well read; Paterson read everything,
and she seems to have been responsible for much of what Rand
knew about economics, philosophy, history, and government,
especially American history and government. Paterson seems

also to have exerted a substantial effect on the individualist philosophy that Rand was evolving; no one else, certainly, had so great an influence on it as Paterson. *The Fountainhead,* Rand's breakthrough work of philosophical fiction, appeared in the same month as *The God of the Machine.* In Paterson's copy of the novel, Rand inscribed: "You have been the one encounter in my life that can never be repeated."

Paterson used her column to keep *The Fountainhead* and its author before the public. But Rand and Paterson found themselves at odds with each other over such issues as Paterson's religious belief (she was a deist, while Rand was a crusading atheist), Rand's attempt to develop her own systematic philosophy, and Paterson's failure to acknowledge intellectual debts that Rand considered owing to her. Agreeing in the intransigence with which they held their opinions, Rand and Paterson finally stopped speaking to each other.

During the *Herald Tribune* period, Paterson continued her own career as novelist by publishing three historical and three modern works. *The Singing Season* (1924), which is set in fourteenth-century Spain, has some political interest. It sketches a number of conflicts between liberty and authority, including the struggle of industrious merchants against an exploitative state. *The Fourth Queen* (1926), a story of romantic love in Renaissance England, resulted from Paterson's fascination with Queen Elizabeth, whose political shrewdness she greatly admired. The unlikely subject of *The Road of the Gods* (1930) is the life of Germanic tribesmen in the first century before Christ. This subject allows Paterson to develop a theme that will become important in *The God of the Machine*: the shaping of each human culture by its distinctive moral premises and by the particular set of "engineering" practices that order social relationships within it.

Never Ask the End (1933) uses a stream-of-consciousness method to explore the experience of several characters of Paterson's generation as they recall their past, assess their present, speculate on their future, and try to find the shape and meaning of their lives. It is the kind of novel that Paterson the critic would call "the modern type . . . not built on a story. It is not linear but radial."[42] In a sense, however, it is another of Paterson's historical novels. It is a series of meditations on the transformation of North Americans from inhabitants of the frontier to outwardly sophisticated but inwardly bewildered cosmopolitans.

Never Ask the End concludes on the eve of the great depression. Paterson's next novel, *The Golden Vanity* (1934), considers the meaning of that event as viewed from the perspectives of three women who are related to one another but occupy quite different positions on the social spectrum. Paterson's political and economic views are introduced, but she remains faithful to her conviction that novels, as distinguished from newspaper columns, should avoid becoming mere vehicles for messages. The foreground of *The Golden Vanity* is occupied by the characters' emotions, not their author's opinions. The novel is clean and spare, edged with gentle satire; its characters are substantial, adroitly analyzed, and exactly proportioned to their social environments. The novel is one of the depression era's most distinguished works of fiction.

But Paterson would publish only one more novel. *If It Prove Fair Weather* (1940) appeared at a time when she was intensely concerned with political issues. Here, however, she is more intent than ever on keeping her fiction from turning into a polemic. She sets out to write "a love story," period. As one might expect, this is a story of frustrated love. A woman college professor involves herself with a married businessman; there are practical barriers to the relationship, but the barriers that Paterson emphasizes are those that arise in the characters' sensibilities. Paterson contrives the kind of situation that allows her to study the basic moral and psychological dilemmas that she regards as typical of intimate relationships. Of her chief male character, Paterson remarked that "there was no way for him to behave well. He had only a choice of behaving badly in different ways."[43]

Paterson's novels of the 1920s and 1930s sold well. At least two of them, *The Singing Season* and *Never Ask the End,* qualified as best sellers. And Paterson was well regarded by fellow authors. She had started late, but by her fiftieth year she had made a place for herself in American letters.

III

Paterson was a slight woman, 5' 3" tall, very nearsighted, a lover of pretty and slightly eccentric clothes, fond of delicate foods, a light drinker, a devotee of nature who could spend all day watching a tree grow, but also a devoted watcher of heavy machinery. She was friendly with the operators of the Moran tugboats and sometimes went for rides around Manhattan on a company boat. In youth and middle age, before she was made lonely by her political opinions, she enjoyed going to parties and mixing in society; for a while in the 1920s she was part of a social group that attended the festive gatherings of Lee Meader, a wealthy architect. But she refused to thrust herself forward:

> What we'd most like is to be something like the First, Second or Third Citizen in the big play. To get in on things without having to make any of the orations. To be independent and active and have some sort of invisible passport that would admit us wherever we had a notion to go.[44]

Paterson's life was dominated by work. Her job as a critic required her to read hundreds of books a year; and, as she often testified, she actually read those books. Although she wrote her newspaper columns very rapidly once she got going (she was a skilled procrastinator), her novels were the products of slow and often agonizing writing and rewriting. "Only the world's worst writers," as she put it, "ever feel inspired and enjoy writing." [45]

In conversation as well as in print, Paterson was accustomed to expressing herself in precise terms, no matter what. Rascoe reported that at his first meeting with her,

> I . . . said something with which she disagreed (knowing her later I am astonished that I had got as far as I did before that happened) and she made me feel instantly not only that I was in error, but that being in error was my habit of mind.

The poet Elinor Wylie said that Paterson looked "precisely like one of Jane Austen's heroines" but that she was "a woman of singularly pointed and ironical speech." Varying the literary metaphor, Rascoe described Paterson as having "a sort of Thackeray drawing-room air about her—when silent, at ten feet away." When, however, she was "aroused" by stupidity or pomposity, she dispatched it with "devastating thoroughness."[46]

Paterson was wryly, though not very ruefully, aware of her ability to dominate conversations. Informed that a certain author could discuss a great variety of topics, she responded, "Not in our presence. He will listen to the facts on those and other subjects. . . . Imparting information is our weakness."[47] It was a weakness she did nothing to correct.

One of Paterson's acquaintances observed, nevertheless, that "if people can stand her at all, they eventually become very fond of her."[48] Even in her very late middle age, it is said, she met men who found her "irresistibly attractive"—although she seems to have found no one permanently capable of engaging her both intellectually and romantically. One man whom we know she cared for was Nat Roberts, an American businessman resident in Europe, with whom she spent some time on a European trip in 1929, and who is the basis for the character Russ in *Never Ask the End*. But Roberts suffered a stroke in December 1929, and died on his voyage back to America in 1930. [49]

From 1922 to 1934, Paterson lived in a fifth-floor walk-up apartment at 508 W. 34th Street in Manhattan. Her near neighbors in what was called "Hell's Kitchen" were a factory, tenements, a rowdy political club, longshoremen, and many noisy young people. She often stayed up until the early morning hours, reading or writing, drinking Chinese tea brewed in the cup and smoking perpetual hand-rolled cigarets.[50] "He rolls his own" was one of her favorite complimentary expressions.

In 1934, when the *Herald Tribune* was paying her about $5,000 a year (not an inconsiderable sum, in those days), and her novels were earning substantial royalties, she built a house for herself in Hillcrest Park, Stamford, Connecticut. Her property had trees and a little stream and was visited by wild animals. Here Paterson and her cat Brainless entertained themselves with the changing seasons.

IV

The 1930s were Paterson's crucial decade, the period during which she attained and passed the peak of her success as a novelist and began her determined crusade for traditional American political values, a crusade that culminated in *The God of the Machine*.

Paterson was not a politician, and she ordinarily disliked politicians. One of the few she respected was Al Smith, for whom she voted in the presidential election of 1928. She never liked Herbert Hoover. The election of 1932 found her planning to vote for the Democrats, but only because they favored repeal of prohibition. When Roosevelt took office, she was already wishing that "Big Men would stop Saving Us. After four years of being Saved, where are we?" She did not take long to decide that the Roosevelt administration had no intention of calling the Big Men off. In 1936, she announced her support for the G.O.P., "whether it likes it or not." She supported the Republicans again in 1940, when their candidate was Wendell Willkie, who enjoyed her writing and sometimes dropped by her office.[51] After 1940 she declined even to vote.

Paterson seems never to have joined a political organization. She was not inclined to speak in public or to listen to speeches, and she detested committees of writers organized to support a cause. She held that "authors should not indulge in deliberate organized propaganda for the best cause under heaven," because in so doing they "destroy all faith and credit in the written word." Besides, she thought she should stay away from any group of people who supposedly agreed with her, in order to avoid being "thrown out as soon as we get down to cases."[52]

Nevertheless, she thought that authors should "write as individuals anything they hold to be true or important," and she lived up to her own advice. Throughout the 1930s, she eagerly attacked both fascism and "the queer and hideous creed of Communism," viewing them not as antithetical to each other but as the common products of "all the measures proposed by 'radical thinkers,' socialists and communists, for a hundred years past."[53] The possibility that America might imitate the collectivist "measures" of Europe filled her with horror and disgust, despite the fact that the current capitalist system treated her personally with something other than distinguished courtesy. The *Herald Tribune* gave her a large pay cut during the depression, her income as a novelist was naturally insecure, and her tax returns from 1930 to 1941 show losses of the immense sum, for her, of $30,000 on investments in stocks and bonds.

Still she retained her faith in free enterprise, while viewing with ever greater alarm the schemes of reformist planners to settle her affairs:

> We feel toward Planners as the heroine of the old-time melodrama felt toward the villain. After having pursued her through four acts with threats of a fate worse than death, which he emphasized by shooting at her, setting fire to her home, and tying her to the railroad track just before the down express was expected, he inquired reproachfully, "Nellie, why do you shrink from me?"[54]

Paterson's scornful preoccupation with the large-scale government interventions of the depression years and with the growth of collectivist ideologies among American intellectuals caused her political ideas to crystallize in definite, elaborate, and highly visible forms. But she had been developing them for a long time. In her youth she became suspicious of "Utopian political schemes" when she observed the way in which the government encouraged homesteaders to take up land that could not, in the long run, turn a profit. Her opposition to a "status society," a major emphasis of *The God of the Machine,* appears in remarks of the 1920s comparing the exploitation of women with the exploitation of "the 'lower orders'" by "the governing classes."[55] Never the conservative of the popular stereotype, she referred to Herbert Hoover as "the Fat Boy"[56] and was aggrieved by the failure of businessmen, especially big businessmen, to understand the free enterprise system on which depended their lives and everyone else's.

In *The Shadow Riders*, which is in some respects Paterson's most political novel, she had taken up the concern of Progressive-era reformers about the manipulation of politics by business. The novel describes the attempt of a syndicate of Canadian businessmen (the setting is Alberta) to turn the government's regulatory authority to the syndicate's own advantage and secure a lucrative municipal franchise. The novel takes a rather benign view of municipally owned utilities and even of a more "democratic" approach to land ownership. But it also takes a benign view of business. The leader of the syndicate is the novel's strongest character and one of its most admirable: "He would never miss the money lost; what he was after was the creative power." And *The Shadow Riders* is clear about the basic principle of free trade. The novel's discussion of the protective tariff, the great Canadian issue, focuses on the idea that "We *need* competition; competition in brains."[57]

The Singing Season emphasizes the predatory nature of a state (in this case, the monarchy of fourteenth-century Castile) that tries to aggrandize itself at the expense of productive enterprise.

Such a state must finally die a suicide, having refused to understand the true maxims of government:

> Keep the roads open, the ports clear; make of [yourself] a safe haven
> for the merchants of all nations. . . . It is better to make than take.
> [58]

The Singing Season describes a "status society" supporting itself by the exploitation of a commerce disdained by the rulers who feed on it. In her newspaper writings of the late 1920s, Paterson identifies an analogous problem in contemporary society, observing that "the salaries of safe jobs in the Civil Service must be paid by shrewd, vulgar traders and manufacturers" to whom people with safe positions feel themselves superior.[59]

Paterson's columns of the early 1930s include most of the other themes of *The God of the Machine:* her opposition to economic determinism, her critique of planning ("despotism tempered by imbecility"),[60] her belief that human values are not subject to calculation, her distaste for "altruists" urging schemes of social control, her insistence that production must precede philanthropy, her conviction that modern collectivist economies live parasitically on the inventiveness of free economies, her ideas about money, and her way of thinking about historical processes as movements of "energy."

Some of her columns at the end of the decade look like abstracts for *The God of the Machine.* The main connections between her idea of history and her idea of government are set forth, for instance, in her 16 July, 1939, column, which contains a long discussion of "dynamic" and "static" systems, the contrasting "political frameworks" of America and Europe, and the different responses of America and Europe to the release of human "energy," which, she argues, would best be accommodated by "the loose, almost imperceptible, limited, minimum" form of government originated in America. In her column of 15 December 1940 (to cite another example), she defines "the condition of the machine age" as "the increased extension of individual liberty, the strict limitation of government itself, according to the original American principle."

By early November 1941, *The God of the Machine* existed as an unfinished book that Paterson was anxious to get on with. On March 30 1942, criticisms of several manuscript chapters were returned to her by her friend Thomas T. Read, professor of mining engineering at Columbia University, whose advice she acknowledges in the published book. On 12 November, 1942, Paterson wrote to a new friend, historian Robert Selph Henry: "I have long been working on a book about what I call the long circuit of energy in production, and the political organization it calls for. That's as much as to say, about our own country, what is it and how come." She solicited Henry's advice on a number of points. On 17 March 1943, her publishers sent Henry a set of page proofs of the completed book.[61] *The God of the Machine* was published by G. P. Putnam's in May 1943.

V

The remainder of the 1940s was a time of emotional exhaustion for Paterson. She was sickened by the second world war, as she had been by the first; she was horrified by America's increasing centralization of political power, symbolized by Roosevelt's election to a third term; and she was discouraged by her increasingly obvious isolation from the mainstream, or even the principal eddies, of intellectual opinion.

In early 1949, Paterson left the *Herald Tribune*. Irita Van Doren, her editor, intimated to inquiring readers that Paterson had "been retired"; Paterson stated, more straightforwardly, that she had been fired because of her political views. In notes written some years later, she said that she had "no feud" with the *Herald Tribune*: "it is my considered conviction that if I had got on any other paper by chance (I got on the H. T. by chance) I think I would have been fired years before and furthermore, that I would not have been allowed to get in print one quarter what the H. T. printed of mine."[62]

She was given an annual pension of $1980, which the *Herald Tribune* reduced to $918 by subtracting from it an amount equal to her Social Security benefits. These benefits, however, were purely notional, because Paterson refused to accept them. She was opposed to the whole idea of the government's making itself responsible for people's security: "I will not subscribe to any such scheme, which anyone but a fool must know will ultimately contribute to the destruction of my country."[63] The Social Security card that was issued to her without her cooperation remained in an envelope marked "'Social Security' Swindle." She had invested modestly in real estate, and she intended to prove that she could provide for herself in spite of the costly and enforced benevolence of the state.

In 1942, she had moved from Stamford to a house that she built on Limestone Road in Ridgefield, Connecticut. There she lived for ten years, when she moved again, to an old house on a hundred acres of land on Canal Road near Princeton, New Jersey—"the house George Washington refused to sleep in." Meanwhile, she rented out a house in Greenwich, Connecticut. A good judge of properties, she would make enough on the sale of her Canal Road holdings in 1959 to enable her "to live more or less comfortably, at least until our government gets further along with its constant job of reducing our currency to waste paper."[64]

In retirement, Paterson amused herself by working in her garden, reading widely and annotating energetically, recording her speculations about philosophical problems posed by the physical sciences, trying unsuccessfully to sell her last novel, *Joyous Gard*, to a publishing world that considered her both annoying and passé, and writing an occasional article for William F. Buckley's *National Review*. She also quarreled with Buckley and other people. As Buckley has remarked, Paterson fought over principles;[65] and she had a lot of principles to fight over. It was characteristic of Paterson that after her embittered break with Rand she protested *National Review*'s bad notice of Rand's *Atlas Shrugged*—though Paterson thought, for her own reasons, that the novel was quite open to criticism.[66]

Paterson spent the last fifteen months of her life "between houses" but still eminently solvent, visiting (and, at her insistence, paying rent) at 101 S. Mountain Avenue, in Montclair, New Jersey, the home of her friends Ted and Muriel Welles Hall. She helped educate the Halls' young children, watched television coverage of the 1960 political conventions, maintained a select correspondence, and considered writing an autobiography. She suffered from gout and a variety of other ailments. On the day after Christmas 1960, she became acutely ill; on 10 January 1961, she died in her upstairs bedroom in the house on Mountain Avenue. She was buried on 11 January in the Welles family plot in St. Mary's (Episcopal) churchyard in Burlington, New Jersey.

Paterson's grave is unmarked. Her life is not. Its most prominent monument is *The God of the Machine*.

VI

There is reason for surprise, however, that *The God of the Machine* exists at all, given its author's views. The book presents a theory of history that is strongly influenced by a theory of economics. Yet Paterson harbored a violent skepticism about the theorizing intellect, and some of her most violent skepticism was directed against historical and economic theory.

Always sympathetic to the claims of empirical evidence, Paterson reacted vigorously against "a century during which, against all evidence, the Serious Thinkers held to the doctrine that the 'economic' nexus was the prime determinant throughout history." She asserted that "no 'explanation' covers human behavior in such quantity," because the people who are the subjects of explanation act from a multitude of motives in pursuit of a multitude of incommensurable goals. The results of history are literally incalculable: "The net, in terms of either personal conduct or social results, cannot be ascertained."[67]

The incalculability of human events and values is an important basis of the argument against collectivism in *The God of the Machine*. Because "there is no collective sum or equation of good," Paterson maintains, it is senseless for collectivists to claim that they can arrange a society that can achieve "the greatest good of the greatest number"—an essentially meaningless phrase, but vicious in its effects. When taken seriously, it justifies the tyranny of planning and the ruin of minorities for the "good" of the majority.[68]

But although Paterson warns that one should not expect history to develop according to somebody's conscious plan, she is certain that history does develop, and that the patterns of its development merit an attempt at explanation—in short, a theory. She had long felt that the historical event that cried most loudly for explanation, "the most extraordinary 'economic' result that ever occurred in this world . . . was the development of the United States and its industrial economy." This "economic" result was all the more interesting to her theorizing imagination because it transcended anything that theorizing imaginations could have predicted. It was unplanned and spontaneous; it was the effect of "political and idealistic principles the proponents of which never dreamed what was to grow from their planting."[69]

The development of the American republic was not planned, but there was something about its "political and idealistic principles"—its "engineering principles," if you will [94]—that permitted and encouraged the great historical movement from "the stone age" to "the air age" that Paterson herself had seen. *The God of the Machine* emphasizes two of these principles: an ethical and economic individualism based on the concept of inherent rights, including property rights; and the institutional complement of individualism, limited government. According to Paterson's antimaterialist theory, "ideas precede accomplishment" [53]. The two engineering principles had to be in place, or the astonishing growth of the machine age, which was the effect of economic individualism largely unfettered by government, could never have happened.

Notice, however, that the correct application of the two principles is understood as discreetly negative rather than directively positive. The individual's right, in Paterson's terms, is the right to be left alone, to develop in his or her own way; government should act to protect this right, not to pursue its own schemes of social betterment. The engineering principles themselves are the products of a long and mostly unplanned evolution. Paterson had essentially conservative intuitions about the indebtedness of the present to the many legacies of the past. Western civilization, as she thought, was able to arrive at the revolutionary principles embodied in American institutions only after it had passed a series of intellectual thresholds.

The first threshold was the Greek discovery of science, with its possible applications to the study and criticism of political principles. The second threshold was the Roman discovery of law, an abstract authority that can guarantee the individual's right against the state. The third threshold was the Christian discovery of the significance of the individual soul. At last, in the eighteenth century, "The three great ideas were brought together . . . without impediment; the individual and immortal soul, exercising self-government by law, and free of the universe to pursue knowledge by reason" [135].

But the great ideas could not work together to form the values of a modern individualist society until the "engineering" problems of political organization were mastered. Although immense creative energy could be released when the pursuit of knowledge was protected by law and by respect for the sanctity of the soul, energy was repeatedly short-circuited or grounded by institutions adapted to only a "low potential."

Greek democracy, for example, encouraged scientific inquiry, but the instability of democratic political life discouraged capital-intensive scientific applications [16-17]. Pytheas, Paterson's great example of the scientist-merchant-adventurer, sailed through the Straits of Gibraltar in defiance of the Phoenicians' restrictions on commerce, but his discoveries were not followed up. Roman law permitted the development of a vast trading area around the Mediterranean, but the Roman Empire collapsed as more and more of its economic energy was "diverted from production into the political mechanism" [39]. The successor societies of the middle ages grounded creative energy by permitting individuals only the roles appropriate to their "status."

It was reserved for the British colonies of North America to become the chief "object lesson and proving ground" of the free society. Because they were left more or less free to govern themselves, they took the liberty of the individual for granted: "Yet they prospered; people got along with one another, and with much less government than in Europe there was no more crime" [66]. The order that they achieved was spontaneous; it was the result of people's natural tendency to expand the circuit of their productive activities. Its survival was ensured by the founders of the American constitutional system, who engineered political structures that could accommodate individual freedom and a high potential and flow of energy. The American system was the fulfillment of the "active enterprise" displayed in the apparently fruitless explorations of Pytheas, who "could not know that he was looking toward America" [14].

VII

In Paterson's account, people often achieve more than they can know. Few of the actors in the great unscripted drama, the age-long development of a free society, can be expected to understand the full significance of their actions.

The drama is enacted before a series of backdrops. The first is the blue horizon of the ancient Mediterranean world, where the "solitary figure" of Pytheas appears "framed in light" in the gates of the Atlantic. Then the scene shifts to Rome, medieval England, and various periods of American history. But the reader can glimpse, behind these steadily more recent and, in Paterson's presentation, more detailed historical backdrops, the framework of the theater itself: the ultimate context of human action; the world of God, who created the "natural" tendencies from which the great processes of history result.

The God of the Machine offers no very elaborate religious theory. Although Paterson was a dedicated student of theology, she assented to no creed of historic Christianity. She was a deist, and the theology of deism may not be capable of great extension. Yet the title of her book should not be ignored. "In the social organization," she asserts, "man is the dynamo, in his productive capacity" [82]; but the human machinery has a God who is the author and authorizer of the proper conditions for its use. As Paterson had written, half-ironically, "There is an idea concealed somewhere on these premises."[70]

God is important to Paterson's understanding both of the nature of humanity and of the history of humanity's self-discovery. God, the source of this world's energy, created man as a being who must choose for himself how energy should be used. People cannot even "obey a command" without acting on their own volition [42]. The condition appropriate to a volitional being is freedom; and freedom implies the right to own property, without which one cannot act independently. Property is a "divine" as well as a "natural" right [180]. Paterson, who had been bothered by the suggestion that she was a philosophical anarchist,[71] stipulates that government is necessary to keep people from violating one another's rights. But government has no separate or higher authority. The nature of the machine that God invented indicates the nature of the government it needs, which is not a directing but an inhibiting device—a brake that stops the machine when its action becomes self-destructive but that does not presume to steer it [85-86].

At the crucial moment of human self-discovery, the moment when America affirmed the principles of individual freedom and "minimum government," the concept of God was rightly invoked. The American revolutionaries saw that

> men are neither wholly "noble" nor incorrigibly bad, but rather imperfect creatures gifted with the divine spark and so capable of improvement, perhaps in the long run of "perfectibility." This is essentially a secular application of the Christian doctrine of the individual soul, born to immortality, with the faculty of free-will, which includes the possibility of sin or error, yet equally enabled to strive toward salvation, its heritage. Let anyone who does not recognize the connection of these principles try to rewrite the Declaration of Independence without reference to a divine source of human rights. It cannot be done; the axiom is missing. [69-70]

Only disaster could result from the attempt of modern materialism to deny the connection between God and human freedom:

> A philosophy of materialism can admit no rights whatever; hence the most grinding despotism ever known resulted at once from the "experiment" of Marxist communism, which could posit nothing but a mechanistic process for its validation. [70]

The God of the Machine is not the God of a mere Mechanism. A mechanism is an object operated from the outside; one usually thinks of mechanisms as susceptible to being planned down to their minutest details. But the human dynamo, as Paterson imagines it, is always a subject gifted with free will, "a genuinely automatic machine, self-starting and self-acting" [84], and interacting with other subjects to unpredictable ends. Precisely because "ideas precede accomplishment," one should entertain a more exalted idea of humanity than that of an object amenable to the kind of measurements, plans, and experiments that are applied to material objects.

The early chapters of *The God of the Machine* demonstrate the weakness of historical theories derived from the premises of economic materialism, theories such as Paterson had been discussing for years in the *Herald Tribune*. She had asked the economic interpreters of history:

> Where do you get your economics to interpret? And how do you get them? Somebody had to create those economic conditions; they don't just happen, like the weather. The Marxian dictum that everything else depends on the modes of production takes no account of what the modes of production depend on. [72]

In *The God of the Machine*, she demands to know what "material factor" allowed Rome to eliminate its competitor Carthage. Did Rome win because it was superior in raw materials, economic development, or military fitness? No. "The materials were at hand" for Carthage as well as Rome [9]. Rome won because it had a better idea than Carthage of how to organize resources—or, to put this in terms more agreeable to Paterson's way of thinking, because Rome had a better idea of how to allow individuals to organize their own resources.

> A production system does not determine the moral relations of society. The moral relations create the production system. [275]

The Roman idea of law, and the corresponding idea of a government limited by law, set Romans free, for a time, to use resources with relative efficiency. Rome exemplified the general principle that in any contest between societies at similar levels of technical development, "that one in which government is most limited will win" [61]. By this point in Paterson's analysis, another thesis has also become evident: her idea that the societies in which government is most successfully limited are those in which technological development is most likely to proceed apace, that an understanding of literal machines develops along with an understanding of the great Machine.

VIII

In one of her many jobs, Paterson had proofread Marx's *Capital*: "and a dreary job it was."[73] The contrast between Marx, the arrogant friend of the working class, and Paterson, the working stiff, is always entertaining. Marx views the primary forces of history as material and concrete, and he expresses this view in the most abstractly intellectual terms available, the terms of German idealist philosophy. Paterson views the primary forces of history as intellectual and spiritual, and she appropriates the most concrete and "material" terms available, the terms of modern technology. She is even willing to make something of the word "mechanism," so long as it is understood in the context of her voluntaristic, antideterminist, and therefore nonmechanistic theory. A "mechanism," in this context, is the political and economic technology chosen and used by the human dynamo.

Thus, describing the "mechanism of production and therefore of power," Paterson says that

> personal liberty is the pre-condition of the release of energy. Private property is the inductor which initiates the flow. Real money is the transmission line; and the payment of debts comprises half the circuit. An empire is merely a long circuit energy-system. The possibility of a short circuit, ensuing leakage and breakdown or explosion, occurs in the hook-up of political organization to the productive processes. [62][74]

In defense of her terms, Paterson adds: "This is not a figure of speech or analogy, but a specific physical description of what happens" [62].

Paterson knows which aspect of her argument is most likely to strike the reader as purely fanciful, purely the product of a literary imagination; and she gives notice that she means to stick to her imagery, come what may. And she has reason for her claim that it is more than literary decoration. *The God of the Machine* makes a closer connection between images and objects than works of historical theory usually make. An empire is more often compared to an organism than to "a long circuit energy-system," but the first comparison is somewhat more distantly metaphorical than the second. Empires do not have bloodstreams or lymph glands, but they do have energy, which their economic institutions may either waste or transmit with some prospect of an increase in usefulness. No one willingly "releases" economic energy or parts with its products unless there is some prospect of recovering, in exchange, the products of other people's energy, usually "transmitted" by money. If an exchange of this kind is not, in concrete terms, an "energy circuit," it is pretty close to it. Equally concrete is Paterson's suggestion that a society cannot enjoy the benefits of a "high energy" economic system if it does not possess the institution of private property. How efficiently, she asks, can people generate energy if they must continually ask the state for permission to use the generating equipment?

Some of Paterson's language may seem strange merely because it is surprisingly *un*metaphorical. In discussing private property, for instance, she relies on no Lockean metaphors about mixing one's labor with material objects. She merely notices that "two bodies cannot occupy the same space at the same time" [180]. True, but what does that have to do with property rights? As it follows, everything. If I, as a being possessed of a physical body, am to do anything of importance, I must have a place of my own to do it in; and if I do not have a right to acquire that place, that private property, and to use it without depending on anyone else's permission, then I have none of the freedom appropriate to a volitional being: "How can a man speak freely if there is no spot on which he and his audience have the right to stand? How can he practice his religion if he has no right to own a religious edifice, or to his own person?" [184]

The commonsense nature of Paterson's approach is confirmed when one reflects on the ease with which any number of specific rights have been extinguished in Marxist countries by the simple expedient of forbidding private ownership of land. The right of religious freedom means nothing if one must beg a government official for license to occupy a space in which to exercise one's religious freedom. In this instance, as in several others, one notices the elegant negativity of Paterson's argument. She establishes the importance of the property right by observing that we cannot have a coherent conception of freedom without it.

She often makes her points with a minimum of argument merely by noticing certain concrete conditions that might easily escape a theorist's attention. She notices that "when any institution is not run for profit, it is necessarily at the cost of the producers" [222]; that "heavy government expenditure must always be taken from the workingman's wages" [212]; that when the state, endeavoring to stimulate enterprise, makes itself the only provider of a service, it also makes itself a monopoly [166-69]; that the organizations of free enterprise, unlike the organizations of the state, "are self-liquidating at the limit of their usefulness" because they cease to exist when they cease providing goods that people are willing to purchase [228].

This idea of a self-correcting system is particularly important. In Paterson's view, modern liberal advocates of a reform of free enterprise would reform something that will reform itself—if left alone. Attempts to change its spontaneous order can proceed only at the cost of massive coercion by "the governing classes." In this respect, the reforming and rationalizing spirit of the twentieth century is the enemy of right reason and true reform, even (or especially) when that spirit exerts itself in "humanitarian" causes.

The Soviet Union, of course, provides the strongest evidence for the connection that Paterson wants to make between "the humanitarian in theory" and "the terrorist in action" [242]. At a time when many other respected journalists were fooling themselves, or at least their readers, about what was happening among the Soviets, Paterson made herself a nuisance by announcing that the communist government was using starvation and slavery in pursuit of its "humanitarian" goals. Throughout the 1930s, she insisted that "the power to do things for people is also the power to do things to people—and you can guess for yourself which is likely to be done."[75]

Her dissection of "humanitarianism" becomes especially interesting, however, when one remembers that she herself was a humanitarian (by most neutral definitions of the term) and a persistent advocate of fundamental reforms in other people's attitudes. She was quite willing to tell people what was good for them. She expressed herself candidly on this point:

> The real motive of a reformer is to mind some one else's business. Quite a natural impulse, too—but less injurious when recognized and gratified as what it is, snooping and pestering.
>
> We do not speak as a scribe or a Pharisee. Snooping and pestering are our own favorite occupations, which we have all too few opportunities of indulging.[76]

After a lifetime of observing the behavior of humanitarians whose exuberance was unconstrained by her own degree of self-knowledge, Paterson was prepared to say that "nothing that well meaning people might do would surprise us." But just how well meaning are these people? Paterson had long entertained suspicions about the professional altruist: "The biggest pests are the people who use altruism as an alibi. What they passionately wish is to make themselves important."[77]

The God of the Machine is concerned with something worse than pests. It is concerned with the radical evil of the totalitarian mentality. Paterson's unsparing psychological analysis traces the evil to "innocence" itself:

> The lust for power is most easily disguised under humanitarian or philanthropic motives. . . . An amiable child wishing for a million dollars will usually "intend" to give away half of this illusory wealth. The twist in the motive is shown by the fact that it would be just as easy to wish such a windfall directly to those others without imagin-

ing oneself as the intermediary of their good fortune. . . . Carried into adult years, this naive self-glorification turns to positive hatred of any suggestion of persons helping themselves by their own individual efforts, by the non-political means which imply no power over others, no compulsory apparatus. [153-54]

Paterson suggests that the kind of world that the modern political humanitarian "contemplates as affording him full scope" is "a world filled with breadlines and hospitals" [242].

She distinguishes modern "humanitarianism" from the traditional "benevolence" enjoined by religion. Benevolence acts voluntarily and in regard to the immediate difficulties of individuals; humanitarianism operates by means of massive social planning enforced by the unjustifiable and even unnatural power of one group over another. A modern humanitarian "cannot admit either the divine or the natural order, by which men have the power to help themselves. The humanitarian puts himself in the place of God" [241].

Pity would be no more,
If we did not make somebody poor

—thus William Blake, a poet whom Paterson liked and who, like her, was a humanitarian weary of humanitarianism. In Paterson's version of Blake's sentiment, the professional philanthropist's "ultimate good *requires that others shall be in want*" [241].

IX

This leads us back to Paterson's notion of social "class." In the year of Roosevelt's accession, she proclaimed: "All our sympathy is with the working classes; belonging to that category, we still maintain that we are human, and do not relish having insult added to injury by our self-appointed saviors."[78] But she felt that the fundamental distinctions among groups of people are psychological and moral, not economic in the narrow sense.

"Class" to her was not a matter of the conflict between workers and bourgeoisie. It was a matter of the conflict between the "self-starters" who work with hand and brain and the people who attempt to regulate, govern, or halt their work. To avoid confusion, she prefers not even to use the word "class" in referring to these two types of people. *The God of the Machine* labels them "producers" and "non-producers" and explores the moral and political means by which the latter dominate the former.

In the modern world, the false consciousness of "humanitarianism" is the moral means; coercive "planning" is the political means. The result is, in the most literal terms, the exploitation of the working class (i.e., the people who actually work) by a nonproductive elite. Paterson's outraged sympathy for working people appears in her emphasis, throughout *The God of the Machine*, on the superiority of the "society of contract," in which individuals can advance themselves as they please by trade and voluntary association with others, to the "society of status," in which risks are avoided and stability is achieved by the confining of individuals in economic roles from which they cannot escape. Once more setting Marx on his head, she describes political power as the cause, not the effect, of fixed economic classes; and behind the political power, she sees the controlling force of ideas. She fears that modern collectivist ideas will recreate the "class system" from which only some of the earth's population has emerged, and only rather recently.

The second half of *The God of the Machine*, which is dominated by Paterson's consideration of specific twentieth-century problems, shows her skill at working out the many implications of a few very basic but strongly imagined economic principles. Her ideas about practical questions are close to those that would later be popularized by economists of the Chicago school and other friends of free enterprise. The essential idea is that a prosperous society requires the "dynamic economy" of capitalism. Capitalism permits workers to compete effectively for higher pay and to keep their earnings in the form of private property; it rewards the accumulation and prudent use of investment capital, without which new jobs cannot be created; it allows the large-scale economic growth that raises everyone's standard of living; and it is capable of quick self-correction when the inevitable mistakes are made.

Paterson makes a crucial distinction between the long depression of the 1930s and the deep but brief (and therefore almost forgotten) depressions of previous generations. In those earlier episodes, she argues, economic mistakes were permitted to liquidate themselves quickly. The state did not intervene to "stabilize" bad investments. But in the 1930s, the state tried to do just that, and the first people who "went on the dole" were "the non-productive rich" [231]. The state had, in fact, invited the depression by its inordinate extension of credit. Then it prolonged the depression by trying to save the nonproductive at the expense of everyone else.

The price for the mistakes of the governing classes was paid by working people who wanted jobs and could not find them in an economy "stabilized" at a low level of investment in productive, job-creating enterprises. Paterson issues a warning both to labor and to business not to sell their birthright of liberty for a mess of "security"—not to acquiesce in a system in which production is regulated by law: "When business men ask for government credit, they surrender control of their business. When labor asks for enforced 'collective bargaining' it has yielded its own freedom" [234].

The threat to freedom lies in people's tendency to "enslave themselves" by their mistaken idea of the kind of "engineering" that will promote their welfare [234]. The concluding chapters of *The God of the Machine* discuss several ways in which the desire for progress subverts itself. After all, "most of the harm in the world is done by good people, and not by accident, lapse, or omission. It is the result of their deliberate actions, long persevered in, which they hold to be motivated by high ideals" [235].

Paterson is not worried that America will lose its war with the Axis powers; she is worried only that America will embrace its enemies' collectivist methods and assumptions, mistaking them for moral virtues or political necessities. Many other advocates of individual freedom were willing to compromise their principles for the sake of the war effort. She was not. *The God of the Machine* suggests that conscription and all other features of wartime regimentation merely undermine the free enterprise system on which victory depends.

The real danger to liberty and prosperity is intellectual, not military. If, for better or worse, "ideas precede accomplishment," the most important battle may be the one fought in the classroom. That is why *The God of the Machine* devotes so much attention to problems of public education, which Paterson regards as a system of state compulsion by no means improved by its recent fondness for "progressive" theories. She argues that the "progressive" emphasis on group activities and emotional self-expression harms children's ability to use their reason to arrive at independent positions. It incapacitates them for liberty and deprives them of their ablity to contribute to a civilization that requires for its survival the exercise of free minds.

The final chapters of *The God of the Machine* are shadowed by Paterson's fear that Americans are losing their defining instinct for liberty. The girlhood in which she had observed the twilight of the aboriginal "stone age" and the end of the frontier West had taught her a good deal about the fragility of cultures. The events of the 1930s left her wondering about the capacity of the "air age" to survive ideological threats to its existence. By 1943, she had lost much of importance to her—friends, lovers, youth—but her overwhelming anxiety was for the loss of the "various, rich and strange" America that had become her greatest passion.

She thought that the tide was running strongly against all her ideas—but she reflected that the image of a "tide" was misleading: "There is no 'wave of the future'; humanity shapes its future by moral purpose and the use of reason" [291]. Because a civilization depends on ideas, not on uncontrollable "forces," it can be restored if it is ever damaged:

> From the known record, it does not appear that men have ever wholly lost any important body of knowledge once attained; though it might lie unused for a time, until the moral principles were affirmed by which material science could be applied beneficially. [290-91]

And a civilization can be preserved, if the principles by which it operates are understood:

> The most extreme fallacy is to believe that nothing can be done, that we must drift to disaster and accommodate ourselves to it. . . .

> Everything can be done for a living future, if men take the long view by which the long circuit of energy is created. Not even disaster by temporary negligence need be final. [291]

This is the hopeful theme with which *The God of the Machine* concludes.

X

Paterson's book has an urgency and an eloquence that make its classification as "historical and political theory" seem wholly inadequate. It is not just theory but rhapsody, satire, diatribe, poetic narrative. Its intensity and scope have both costs and benefits.

When *The God of the Machine* was published, some of Paterson's friends found its organization unsatisfactory, and Paterson was sometimes inclined to agree with them. Most of the book's organizational difficulties can be attributed to its intellectual ambitions. It attempts not only to present a general theory of history but also to argue about particular issues in contemporary life—education, economic depression, the money supply, wartime controls on the economy, and so forth. Paterson's steady narrowing of historical focus in the first half of the book helps to prepare for the topical specificity of the second half. Nevertheless, *The God of the Machine* might easily have been divided into two volumes, each of which might have profited from expansion.

In both parts of the book, Paterson is an imaginative writer in a basic sense of that term; she uses bold imagery to organize tremendously complex material. And her images, as I have said, are something more than *mere* images. But the reader who is engaged by Paterson's subject often desires a more detailed account of the facts supporting her positions, and anyone who has read her columns, her letters, or even her annotations to other people's books knows that she could have supplied from memory any amount of detail desired—but only if *The God of the Machine* had been much longer than it is.

Difficulties are created, in a curious way, by Paterson's virtues as a writer. She is a master of the aphorism:

> In human affairs all that endures is what men think. Humanity as such is an intellectual concept. [15]

> An abstraction will move a mountain; nothing can withstand an idea. [18]

> A blind man cannot see by community. [90]

And even when Paterson is not writing aphorisms, she is frequently writing sentences that rejoice in their self-sufficiency. Her sentences are rich in implications, but sometimes in implications developed by distant, not immediate, successors.

The effect is that of a mind too energetic to be tamed by the requirements of a smooth, simple, and universally accessible argument. *The God of the Machine* is the work of an artist, and it needs to be read with something of the artist's sensitivity to a grand pattern created out of a multitude of vigorous local effects, a pattern that challenges rather than lulls the eye. This is one reason for the book's failure to attract a large audience.

The other reason, of course, was Paterson's rejection of virtually all the respectable political wisdom of her age. (She rejected much of the respectable wisdom of our age, too.) *The God of the Machine* failed to attract the audience that she had in mind, the operators of America's "production system."[79] Reviewers treated the book shabbily. Yet it made a significant contribution to a significant group of people, an isolated band of intellectuals, far outside the mainstream, who were seeking alternatives to collectivist ideals.

One of those people, John Chamberlain, has recalled that in the late 1940s and early 1950s, "libertarians were few and far between, and the new conservatism was still an import from England labeled T. S. Eliot."[80] No one could imagine that the anticollectivist intellectual movement that Chamberlain observed in its feeble beginnings, a movement that was doubly unpopular because it included both a "conservative" respect for American traditions and a classically "liberal" respect for the value of free enterprise, would by the 1980s become a major force in the political life of America, and of the world. Neither, of course, could anyone imagine the lively debates that would arise within the anticollectivist movement itself, debates that would divide people who identified themselves primarily as conservatives from people who identified themselves primarily as libertarians, classical liberals, and so forth.

As one might expect, Paterson influenced anticollectivists of every variety, because she believed in conserving what she regarded as the "liberal" ideas of the early American republic, she defended free enterprise, and she insisted that "the American principle of freedom consists wholly in the limitation of government." She said that she was "conservative in [her] convictions and temperament" and observed that "time's revenges are exemplified in the fact that the convictions of a conservative American are now considered startling."[81] But when the

novelist Louis Bromfield half-jokingly called her "a royalist," a
current term of abuse for "conservative," she "could only say,
all right, we're a royalist. As a matter of fact, not that anybody
cares, we are a solitary survivor of the Age of Reason, an
eighteenth century rational liberal bourgeois."[82]

Readers of *The God of the Machine* will understand the degree
to which the solitary survivor of a past age was able to make
herself a prophet of the next. The political upheavals of 1989-
1991 would not have surprised Paterson. Unlike many
mainstream intellectuals of her time, she never thought that the
century's great experiments with collectivism could possibly
succeed. She scoffed at mainstream thinkers who believed that
prosperity and liberty might somehow conflict:

> The most dim-witted attempt at argument ever heard in this mortal
> world is the supposed retort to any advocate of freedom: "Do you
> mean free to starve?"

We mean, do you think you can't starve with your hands tied? [83]

Paterson stated the human costs of collectivist experiments in
plain terms, noting that, just as the Nazis were exterminating the
Jews, so the Russian Communists had murdered "the most
productive members of the population" [91]. Further, she
showed *why* such acts should be the cost of such experiments.

As a theorist, she was an independent discoverer of several of
the most potent ideas of such European foes of collectivism as
Friedrich Hayek, whose *The Road to Serfdom* was published the
year after *The God of the Machine*. Like Hayek and his mentor
Ludwig von Mises, Paterson argued that because values are
objects of individual choice, it is nonsense to expect central
planning to provide an adequate supply of "socially valuable"
goods and services; that such planning is likely to result in a
closed and coercive society, unable to achieve even its narrow
economic goals; and that the leadership of such a society necessarily devolves upon vicious and destructive people.

As early as 1933, in fact, Paterson had warned that use of the state for "genuinely benevolent and humane" purposes of social betterment and security must lead to "economic serfdom, an autocratic, bureaucratic, supreme state. . . . So it is not security, it is dependence, quite another thing."[84] In company with the European anticollectivists, Paterson discovered the roots of twentieth-century totalitarianism in the intellectual confusions of late-nineteenth-century liberalism, which had been seduced by the idea that the benefits of capitalism could be achieved by noncapitalist ends. She maintained, as would Hayek in *The Road to Serfdom*, that the real source of social harmony is the spontaneous actions of individuals in a society governed by contract, not force; she saw the free-enterprise system as the promoter, not the destroyer, of a humane order of life.

And, like the Europeans, she did manage to find an audience. Her ideas had a success that could not be measured by the modest sales of *The God of the Machine*. The self-described refugee from the eighteenth century provided an intellectual link between a frustrated and alienated older generation of anticollectivist Americans and an aggressive and optimistic younger generation.

Albert Jay Nock, 72-year-old doyen of American individualists, declared that *The God of the Machine* and *The Discovery of Freedom* (published in 1943 by Paterson's friend Rose Wilder Lane) were "the only intelligible books on the philosophy of individualism that have been written in America this century." Nock believed that Paterson and Lane had

> shown the male world of this period how to think *fundamentally*. They make all of us male writers look like Confederate money. They don't fumble and fiddle around—every shot goes straight to the centre.

Paterson's "engineering idiom" gave Nock "a jolt," but he considered it "sound enough, and probably effective."[85]

Exemplary of a younger set of intellectuals was John Chamberlain, a journalist who would become a pathbreaker in the pilgrimage of former leftists toward a libertarian conservatism. When *The God of the Machine* came out, Paterson had long been lecturing Chamberlain, in person and in print, against his weakness for collectivism. The two writers had "some caustic interchanges," as Chamberlain says; but "arguing with Isabel had a way of clarifying issues." *The God of the Machine*, he remembers, "hit me like a ton of bricks." The book seemed to transform abstract individualist ideas (such as those of Nock) into "detailed reality"; it offered a welcome relief from the compromising utterances of American businessmen and the pomposity of mainstream social thought.

> Indeed, it was three women—Mrs. Paterson, Rose Wilder Lane, and Ayn Rand—who, with scornful side glances at the male business community, had decided to rekindle a faith in an older American philosophy. There wasn't an economist among them. And none of them was a Ph.D.

Through Paterson, Chamberlain got to know Leonard E. Read, who in 1946 created the Foundation for Economic Education, a pioneering institute devoted to the ideals of a free and responsible society. Read was a businessman, but he actually believed in free enterprise, and he was an admirer of Paterson.[86]

Another part of Paterson's influence would be exerted through her erstwhile friend Ayn Rand, who scorned to call herself either a conservative or a libertarian but who influenced people in both camps. Rand strongly recommended her teacher's book to her own numerous disciples. Although she issued stern warnings against Paterson's religious views and judged Paterson's "philosophical frame-of-reference" as "far from perfect," Rand said that *The God of the Machine* offered "an unforgettable experience"; it was "a sparkling book, with little gems of polemical fire scattered through almost every page, ranging from bright wit to the hard glitter of logic to the quiet radiance of a profound understanding."[87]

Intellectual leaders of the nascent conservative movement found Paterson a woman to contend with, in both senses of the word "contend." Russell Kirk began an exchange of letters with Paterson during World War II, when he was a soldier stationed in the Utah desert. Paterson's correspondence with the future philosopher of conservatism left him with a vivid impression both of her character—"indeed she was thorny"—and of her ideas. "*The God of the Machine* had an immensely strong influence upon me," he has said. "IMP stood out courageously, in defiance of the Lonely Crowd. I thought that everyone must be reading her book and her book-reviews, and could never forget her; but I was mistaken."[88]

Yet Kirk was not the only one who remembered Paterson. When, in 1955, William F. Buckley, Jr., founded *National Review*, which would soon become the strongest institutional influence on American conservatism, Paterson was one of the authors whose assistance he sought most assiduously. She consented to write for him, at the highest rate of pay he could provide, and she gave him a good deal of cantankerous advice for free. The relationship seems to have amused both parties, but it could not last. Paterson was too independent to be edited, or to neglect her talent for sarcastic dissent. After 1959, Paterson and Buckley no longer communicated. When she died, Buckley summarized his view of her: "She was, for all her temperamental shortcomings, a great woman."[89]

Today as always, it is the rare reader of Paterson who does not respond to her in a variety of ways. Conservatives, classical liberals, modern liberals, and almost everybody else can find something in *The God of the Machine* that is daunting and provoking, and something else that is revealing and inspiring. Few will deny that Paterson's ideas express a generosity, an intensity, an originality—in short, a greatness—of intellect.

And few will deny that her work is addressed to issues of enduring importance: the nature of human action, the shape of human history, the proper function, structure, and extent of government, the moral status of the reforming instinct, the causes and effects of tyranny, the prospects for liberty.

The passage of fifty years from the book's publication has provided sufficient evidence of its ability to illuminate the great controversies of this century. Now that *The God of the Machine* has attained its jubilee, one can see more plainly than ever that "arguing with Isabel," as Chamberlain remarked, is "a way of clarifying issues."

Stephen Cox

Notes

1. Birth notice, *Manitoulin Expositor* (13 February 1886): 4; Anon., "Chronicle and Comment," *The Bookman* 43 (May 1916): 242; William Bowerman, "As I Recollect," *Through the Years* [Gore Bay, Ontario] 2 (January 1985): 23; Isabel Paterson, "Turns With a Bookworm," New York *Herald Tribune "Books,"* 24 November 1935. Henceforth, Paterson's weekly column in the *Herald Tribune* will be designated as "Turns," followed by date.
2.. "Turns," 29 December 1929; 18 February 1934; 20 March 1927; 27 November 1927.
3. "Turns," 10 February 1929; 26 July 1936.
4. Paterson to Lillian Fischer, 5 June 1931. Paterson's letters to Fischer are in the collection of the New York Public Library.
5. "Turns," 26 July 1936; 13 November 1938; 16 September 1934; 23 December 1934; 20 March 1927; 19 June 1932.
6. "Turns," 27 October 1929; 7 October 1934.
7. "Turns," 23 September 1928; 11 February 1934; 20 March 1927.
8. "Turns," 20 February 1927; 28 December 1930.
9. Paterson, *Never Ask the End* (New York: William Morrow, 1933): 69.
10. "Turns," 14 February 1932.
11. "Turns," 20 March 1927; Elsie McCormick, "She Had To Be a Writer," New York *Herald Tribune "Books"* (12 February 1933): 23; "Turns," 3 March 1935.
12. "Turns," 17 December 1933.

13. "Turns," 10 August 1930; 14 August 1932; Paterson, "What Do They Do All Day?" (unpublished ms.), Paterson papers.

14. "Turns," 22 February 1931.

15. Marriage certificate, Paterson papers; W. L. Hamm to Paterson, 27 June 1918, Paterson papers; Paterson to Fischer, 26 December 1924.

16. McCormick: 7.

17. "Turns," 6 June 1926; 1 November 1936; 30 May 1937; Anon., "Chronicle and Comment," 242; Paterson to Fischer, 5 June 1931; Anon., "'Books' Covers the World of Books," *Publisher's Weekly* (30 September 1939): 1341.

18. "Turns," 22 February 1931.

19. "Turns," 8 April 1934; Sinclair Lewis to Paterson, 24 December 1914, Paterson papers; Paterson to Fischer, 3 October 1924.

20. Paterson to Fischer, 3 October 1924.

21. "Turns," 6 November 1927; 13 June 1926; 27 February 1927.

22. Burton Rascoe, *We Were Interrupted* (Garden City, N.Y.: Doubleday, 1947): 140-42.

23. "Turns," 10 June 1928

24. Anon., "'Books' Covers the World of Books": 1341.

25. Rascoe: 142-143.

26. "Turns," 6 May 1934.

27. "Turns," 23 February 1930; 13 March 1932.

28. "Turns," 30 January 1927.

29. Paterson, review of *Such Is My Beloved,* by Morley Callaghan, New York *Herald Tribune "Books"* (18 February 1934): 4.

30. "Turns," 8 April 1934.

31. "Turns," 14 October 1934.

32. John O'Hara to Thomas O'Hara, 16 August 1934, *Selected Letters of John O'Hara,* ed. Matthew J. Bruccoli (New York: Random House, 1978): 94.

33. "Turns," 4 November 1934 (on *A Man With a Purpose,* by Donald Richberg).

34. Paterson, review of *Dead Lovers Are Faithful Lovers,* by Frances Newman, New York *Herald Tribune "Books"* (6 May 1928): 3.

35. "Turns," 29 July 1928.

36. "Turns," 24 June 1934.

37. "Turns," 1 October 1933.

38. Paterson, review of *Exile's Return,* by Malcolm Cowley, New York *Herald Tribune "Books"* (27 May 1934): 3.

39. "Turns," 12 February 1939.

40. Mary McCarthy and Margaret Marshall, "Our Critics, Right or Wrong," *The Nation* 141 (23 October and 6 November 1935): 468-72, 542-44. I.M.P. commented on her advance copy of McCarthy's critique as follows: "If Miss McCarthy can find a field in which her peculiar—very peculiar—talents are at home, she would be well advised to work in it. It should be as far removed as possible from literature, and require no care for accuracy" ("Turns," 27 October 1935).

41. On Rand and Paterson, see Barbara Branden, *The Passion of Ayn Rand* (Garden City, N. Y.: Doubleday, 1986): 164-66, 171-72, 177, 181-82, 203-6; "Turns," 23 September 1945.

42. "Turns," 17 October 1937.

43. Paterson, "As the Author Sees It," *Saturday Review* 22 (7 September 1940): 10.

44. "Turns," 2 March 1930. Paterson's adventures with the Meader group are recorded in her correspondence with Fischer.

45. "Turns," 16 July 1933.

46. Burton Rascoe, "Contemporary Reminiscences," *Arts and Decoration* 25 (June 1926): 49, 80; Elinor Wylie, review of *The Fourth Queen*, by Isabel Paterson, New York *Herald Tribune "Books"* (11 April 1926): 1.

47. "Turns," 1 February 1931.

48. McCormick: 7.

49. Paterson to Fischer, 15 February 1930; Wilfred P. Meredith to Paterson, (?) August 1930, Paterson papers.

50. Paterson to Fischer, 26 December 1924; "Turns," 4 January 1931; McCormick: 7.

51. Paterson to Fischer, 8 September 1932; "Turns," 2 April 1933; 5 April 1936; 5 February 1939; 6 October 1940; Wendell Willkie to Paterson, 11 September 1939, Paterson papers.

52. "Turns," 6 July 1941; 16 November 1941.

53. "Turns," 6 July 1941; 22 June 1941.

54. "Turns," 28 January 1934.

55. "Turns," 10 August 1941; Paterson, review of *A Short History of Women*, by John Langdon-Davies, New York *Herald Tribune "Books"* (6 November 1927): 4.

56. Paterson to Garreta Busey, (?) November 1929, Paterson papers.

57. Paterson, *The Shadow Riders* (New York: John Lane, 1916): 85-86, 145, 203.

58. Paterson, *The Singing Season* (New York: Boni and Liveright, 1924): 33.

59. Paterson, review of *The Happy Tree*, by Rosalind Murray, New York *Herald Tribune "Books"* (13 February 1927): 4.

60. "Turns," 27 November 1932.

61. "Turns," 9 November 1941; Thomas T. Read to Paterson, 30 March 1942; Paterson to Robert Selph Henry, 12 November 1942; Helen Ferrigan to Henry, 17 March 1943; letters from these correspondents are in the Paterson papers.

62. Paterson, typescript notes, Paterson papers.

63. A. V. Miller to Paterson, 31 December 1954; Paterson to Miller, 5 January 1955; Paterson papers.

64. Paterson to Henry, 30 May 1959.

65. William F. Buckley, Jr., "RIP, Mrs. Paterson (A Personal Reminiscence)," *National Review* 10 (28 January 1961): 43.

66. Paterson to Gertrude Vogt, late December, 1957; William F. Buckley, Jr., to Paterson, 7 January 1958; correspondence in Buckley papers, Yale University Library.

67. "Turns," 30 April 1939.

68. Paterson, *The God of the Machine:* 90-91. Henceforth, page numbers from *GM* will be cited in the text in brackets.

69. "Turns," 30 April 1939. Paterson comments on the proper nature of theory in "Turns," 8 December 1940.

70. "Turns," 14 June 1931.

71. "Turns," 6 August 1939.

72. "Turns," 2 July 1939.

73. "Turns," 13 March 1932.

74. Paterson's reference to the payment of debts as constituting half the exchange process by which economies operate indicates an influence of Harry Scherman's *The Promises Men Live By: A New Approach to Economics* (New York: Random House, 1938), which Paterson cites on p. 219 of *GM*. Paterson considered Scherman's book "extremely valuable" ("Turns," 18 January 1942; see also 12 February 1939).

75. "Turns," 27 October 1935.

76. " Turns," 23 December 1934.

77. "Turns," 29 April 1934; 19 November 1933.

78. "Turns," 30 April 1933.

79. Paterson to Henry, early April, 1943.

80. John Chamberlain, *A Life with the Printed Word* (Chicago: Regnery Gateway, 1982): 138.

81. "Turns," 1 June 1941; 1 March 1931; 2 August 1936.

82. "Turns," 18 February 1934.

83. "Turns," 16 July 1939.

84. "Turns," 28 May 1933.

85. Albert Jay Nock to Mrs. Edmund C. Evans and Ellen Winsor, August 1943, and to Mrs. Evans, 7 August 1943, *Letters from Albert Jay Nock, 1924-1945* (Caldwell, Idaho: Caxton, 1949): 181, 183; to Paul Palmer, 28 July 1943, *Selected Letters of Albert Jay Nock,* ed. Francis J. Nock (Caldwell, Idaho: Caxton, 1962): 146.

86. Chamberlain: 35, 96, 136-37.

87. Ayn Rand, *"The God of the Machine," The Objectivist Newsletter* 3
    (October 1964): 2-3.
88. Russell Kirk to author, 30 November 1990; 20 January 1991.
89. William F. Buckley, Jr., to Paterson, 16 September 1955, Paterson papers;
    Buckley, "RIP, Mrs. Paterson": 43.

Acknowledgments

The author wishes to thank the Marguerite Eyer Wilbur Foundation for its grant in aid of this work, and to acknowledge the kind assistance of Paul Beroza, R. W. Bradford, Barbara Branden, Eric Brosio, William F. Buckley, Jr., John Chamberlain, Cory Craig, James Greene, Robert Hessen, Mary Jane Hodges, William Holtz, Erika Holzer, Henry Mark Holzer, Russell Kirk, John McQuarrie, Dwight Miller, Tom Sasvari, Gertrude Vogt, the staff of the Tehkummah, Ontario, township office, and (for access to manuscripts cited above) the New York Public Library and the Yale University Library. Special gratitude is owed to Muriel Welles Hall, Paterson's friend and the executrix of her estate, for access to the Paterson papers and to a never-failing source of remembrance and encouragement.

THE GOD OF THE MACHINE

CHAPTER I

The Energy Circuit in the Classical World

Toward the end of the fourth century of the pre-Christian era, a colonial Greek navigator sailed from the port of Massilia (now Marseilles), his native city, through the Straits of Gibraltar, and thence up the coast of Spain and France and the British Isles to Ultima Thule, the designated end of the world. Possibly Thule was Iceland; it remains a matter of conjecture. The name of the enterprising sailor, Pytheas, has come down to us. He appears to the imagination, a solitary figure framed in light, as if a gate had swung open between the Pillars of Hercules toward the western world.

Now what is peculiar about this aspect of the venture of Pytheas is that he was very far from being the first civilized man to pass the fabled portal of the Atlantic. On the contrary, it had been a trade route of Phoenician merchant ships time out of mind. Tin from Cornwall, furs and amber from the Baltic, were staple cargo, delivered to the markets of the East for the profit of Carthage, which drew its riches from its position as an intermediary.

When Pytheas made his voyage, the Punic wars and the Roman empire were still in the future. Not that Carthage was at peace; it had never been so for any extended period. Taken altogether, the series of wars which run through the story of the Phoenicians make a geographical pattern resembling the track of a hurricane, a cyclonic flow of energy continuing for almost a thousand years, and moving irresistibly along the midland waterway between the great continents of classical antiquity, Asia, Africa, and Europe. This unceasing stream of human activity swirled through its tideless channel always in one main direction, a direction which in view of the extant knowledge of geography was senseless, for it drove toward the empty ocean. This is not to deny the value of the traffic from the outer coast of Europe, but the pull from that quarter seems disproportionate to the volume of goods. During the period of traverse, the Phoenicians rode the storm, or composed part of it.

What manner of people these Phoenicians were we learn from Scripture, under another name. It was a Phoenician, Hiram, king of Tyre, who sent his servants to Solomon on the latter's accession to the throne, and obtained a commission to build Solomon's palace and later the Temple. Hiram supplied materials, transport, and skilled labor on a pre-fabricated structure; cedars hewn to measure in Lebanon were brought around by floats, and stone dressed at the quarry, and elaborate metal work wrought to specifications; so that the royal house was raised "without the sound of hammer or axe or any tool of iron." In payment Hiram received annually "twenty thousand measures of wheat for food to his household, and twenty measures of pure oil," and a closing settlement of "twenty cities in the land of Galilee." It is noted that Hiram thought poorly of the "cities," having accepted them sight unseen; it is a fair surmise that he extended a little too much credit. When Solomon sent out ships of his own, they went under Phoenician convoy.

Obviously the Phoenicians were the leading industrial and commercial nation of their considerable day. Mysteriously failing to resolve into the positive frame of an empire, the center of their undefined sphere of authority and influence was determined by the forces in motion, on a line from Syria to Spain. It shifted progressively through Tyre and Sidon to their last capital city, whence they vanished from the roll of nations. Their historic mode of being was implicit in the character of Carthage, their final and supreme achievement, as indicated by its position between sea and desert, a solid nexus of the confluent energy at a given point. Though the city was backed by a grain-growing district, the arable land bore no normal relation to the population, which has been estimated at a maximum of a million persons. Allowing for exaggeration, or for the inclusion of tributaries, the figure remains impressive. Carthage was less a territorial entity than a knot tied in wind and water.

Against the old despotic monarchies of the East the Phoenicians had established and maintained their special place successfully. With the Greeks they held their own fairly well in a running fight. Manifestly the Greeks were their natural rivals, islanders trading in the same waters, and likewise spreading out from port to port where they touched mainland. Neither Phoenicians nor Greeks proved capable of keeping their colonies in strict confederation; the subsidiary cities changed sides under pressure, and made their own treaties whenever they dared. Some element was lacking in their system, to bind them together.

There are as many explanations of the dominance and decline of nations as there are examples. The favor of the gods, or "the stars in their courses," were once thought determinant. The modern view reckons by temporal factors, chiefly raw materials, high economic development, naval strength, and military genius, the latter exhibited in understanding of the grand strategy, and in a brave and ready soldiery utilizing a special discipline or type of armament. The drawback is that each theory will be found applicable only to one age or people, with nothing to account for the actual existence of the given factor. Let comparisons be tried according to the rules laid down.

The conflict of Greece and Carthage may properly be called a trade war. They were in competition for stations, goods, charters, and customers. In this respect Rome was comparatively negligible at the given time. Possibly Rome became a permanent settlement as a local trading center. (Mommsen argued reasonably for this supposition on internal and historic evidence.) The mixed origins of the population, the location on a river and near enough to the sea to be reached by small vessels, the early building of bridges, and the use of money, would indicate commerce; and contractual relations were inextricably woven into Rome's political system. Apparently the flow of energy was sufficient to require habitual accommodation, and consequently to make the Romans realize the equivalent need of strong bases fixed on the land. But they did not get into the main stream of world trade during the formative period, in which they established their civic structure. "For various reasons at various times Rome has never from its foundation until today been an industrial city. . . . For international trade Rome was badly placed. . . . Only by courtesy could the Tiber be called a navigable stream . . . the estuary (was) of little value as a harbor; and the rapidity of the current rendered the journey from Rome to the sea a laborious business even for river barges. . . . The familiar pictures of sea-going merchantmen engaged in general trade sailing regularly up and down the Tiber and using a port beneath the Aventine may safely be dismissed as works of imagination." In their earliest treaty, "Carthage, as might be expected, is insistent on her commercial domination in those regions which she controlled," while Rome "was indifferent to those considerations which must affect every community with a right to be called industrial." *

Compared to Greece, just then Carthage probably was ahead in economic organization and technical knowledge, and had the greatest number of ships under single command, monopolizing the most extensive provinces rich in natural resources. The struggle between Greece and Carthage had been going on for centuries, and was still undecided when Pytheas made his voyage. Within fifty years, Rome thrust between the two, commencing the long, bitter, intermittent effort that broke the Phoenician power, razed the walls of Carthage, and left the site a waste. Nor did the Greeks

* CAMBRIDGE ANCIENT HISTORY: The Early Republic. Hugh Last. Macmillan.

benefit by the ruin of their mighty antagonist; on the contrary, the subjection of Greece was to follow shortly. Economic determinism failed.

The outcome of this particular quarrel was so conclusive that the main issue has grown dim. History is obliged to fall back on geographical terms: Rome and Carthage fought for the mastery of the Mediterranean. Consequently the changing scene of hostilities is taken for granted. Carthage was situated on the north coast of Africa, and lived by its keels. Yet we see the Carthaginian general Hannibal leading an army, with elephants, against Rome by a toilsome march over the Alps.

The most positive proponent of the naval interpretation of world events, Admiral Mahan, told how the idea came to him. Reading Mommsen's "History of Rome," he recalled: "It suddenly struck me . . . how different things might have been could Hannibal have invaded Italy by sea, as the Romans often had Africa, instead of by the long land route." From that reflection, Mahan wrote "The Influence of Sea-Power Upon History." He might as well have called his book the influence of history upon sea-power. Undoubtedly things would be different if they were different. Especially if sea-power, a superior navy commanding main trade routes from impregnable bases, were necessarily decisive, Hannibal would never have been compelled to his Alpine detour, and Carthage must have won. Rather, by that criterion, Carthage should have won a generation earlier. Instead, "with the strongest fleet on the seas, and with a naval experience gained through centuries, the Carthaginian admirals lost six out of seven of the naval battles, despite the fact that the Romans had never possessed a quinquireme before this time (the first Punic war), and very few Romans had ever set foot on shipboard." *

Briefly sketched, the method by which Rome swept the

* CAMBRIDGE ANCIENT HISTORY: The First Punic War. Tenney Frank. Macmillan.

seas verges on burlesque. "While Carthage kept a fleet of 120 quinquiremes," (the standard biggest battleship), Rome had neither ships nor shipwrights nor sailors. To make up the deficiency, the Romans salvaged a stranded Punic vessel for a model, laid down a fleet, and meanwhile trained the necessary crews on land, using stationary benches fitted with oars. All their ships were "built, manned and officered by Romans." When they put to sea, their green pilots were "helpless whenever a storm arose." It is difficult to repress the spirit of levity which suggests they may have been seasick. Ignorant of naval maneuvers, and with no chance to learn, the Romans simply transformed an encounter at sea into something as like a land battle as possible, and fought it their own way. Having equipped their own craft with cranes and grappling irons, they drove straight alongside the Carthaginian galleys, made fast, and swarmed aboard. Thus in their first important engagement they captured or put to flight a Carthaginian fleet which outnumbered the Roman squadron by thirty ships. Again, at Drepana, the Romans were in harbor when the Carthaginian fleet approached. An inshore gale was blowing, which gave the Carthaginians the weather gauge. Indifferent to this handicap, the Romans drew into line across the enemy's course, took seventy Carthaginian ships, and sank fifty more. Between victories, the Romans generally wrecked their own fleets by inexpert seamanship.* After each loss they set to work and launched replacements. The expense bore heavily on Rome; Carthage had a vast advantage financially. Nor did Rome resort to state absolutism on the plea of emergency; there was no seizure of private means. When the Roman public treasury was exhausted, and "taxes could not be raised to a higher rate," the wealthier citizens subscribed to provide a new navy, with the under-

* In 255 B.C., a newly built Roman fleet defeated the Punic main fleet "with ease," but on the homeward voyage ran into a storm off Sicily. Out of 364 ships only 80 were saved. It is reckoned that over 90,000 persons perished, mostly free men, a greater disaster than the loss of the Armada to Spain. It was the most terrible calamity at sea known until then, and remains so to this day.

standing that if they won they should be reimbursed. They won.

The Carthaginians were so baffled by this inexplicable performance that at one time they considered founding a land empire in imitation of Rome. The materials were at hand. But they did not know how.

It should be noted also that though Roman military discipline was strict, and esteem was proportionate to conduct in the field, a Roman general, or his troops, stood in less fear of penalties from their own government than the Punic commanders. For losing a campaign, the Carthaginians crucified one of their admirals.

As for naval bases, Rome began with none. Carthage was the first great nation to occupy Gibraltar, which was certainly the key to the future as of that time. Obviously it would be easy to acquire from the primitive inhabitants. But Gibraltar has since belonged to one empire after another. Being the fortress ready set to guard the Iberian peninsula, it reverted to Spain in her brief period of glory. The riddle is that it fell to England eventually, and only after England had reduced Spain to secondary rank by operations at sea. The defeat of the Great Armada is usually explained as the result of inadequate management, poor equipment, and above all, bad weather. But it is hardly to be believed that Spain was wanting in seamen, of the race that laid claim to the whole western ocean and almost maintained it. The English fleet was improvised, largely of privateers; it was ill-found in provisions and short of powder. Finally, when the Armada was dispersed and shattered, the English ships were not in drydock; they had to endure the same tempest. Spain surely had sea-power, while it lasted. Unless the absurdity be conceded that sea-power does not consist in ships, sailors, ports, and commercial opportunity, all its tangible attributes, sea-power failed.

On the other hand, if the secret of the development and longevity of the Roman empire inhered in military aptitude, the conquering regime of Napoleon should have struck root and flourished for an equal duration. By a series of actions which rank among the classics of the art of war, Napoleon brought the whole continent of Europe under his sway. His invading armies were tacitly welcomed by an influential part of the conquered peoples, who were already disaffected toward the old regime and imagining a new order. Kings went down like ninepins; barracks organization was praised as the instrument of unity which should usher in a millennium of efficiency; America received an incongruous assortment of exiles. Napoleon rode the crest of the wave of the future. Nevertheless, the glittering semblance of empire reared on bayonets crumbled to nothing after one major defeat in far-off Russia. Rome lost more than one great battle, and revived with increased vigor. Napoleon's disaster at Moscow, with its consequences, is laid to the cold and the snow. The Russians did not spend the winter on the Riviera. Military means failed.

Again, if the Roman empire derived from its antecedent social order, the citizens of Rome, whether aristocrat or plebeian, prided themselves on being simple farmers, alternating sword and spade. Home from the wars, Cincinnatus asked no more than to resume his unfinished furrow. The most honorable reward that could be imagined for Horatius, who held the bridge, was of the same kind:

> They gave him of the corn-land,
>   That was of public right,
> As much as two strong oxen
>   Could plough from morn till night.

No doubt these are romantic versions, if not pure myth. What they do signify is the tradition, with a substantial origin back of it. The description, glossing also a harsh groundsill of slavery, fits equally the agrarian culture claimed by the Southern Confederacy.* Unfortunately, these are the

---

* In cold fact, the Roman landed gentry seem to have been loan sharks as well, or enough of them were to create endless trouble, lending on mort-

very reasons adduced to indicate why the South had no chance, in our Civil War, against the mechanical and mercantile North reinforced by its shipping interest.

Carthage is supposed to have weakened in martial virtue by the use of foreign troops. Subsequently Rome ruled for centuries while the famous legions were recruited in part from similar sources.

In the grand strategy, Carthage had an acute perception of vital points. Losing Sicily, Carthage was put on the defensive in the eastern Mediterranean, pinched between Greek sea power and Roman land power. Hannibal's move through Spain was a boldly logical flank attack rather than a desperate expedient. He drew on the interior for troops and supplies, including silver, which was sound currency. Beyond the mountains he expected another compensating circumstance, but was disappointed. Many of the tribes or cities of northern Italy were in alliance with Rome, to whom they were more or less subordinate. Hannibal assumed that they would join the invader to throw off the Roman yoke. Instead, they stood by Rome, at least tacitly. Yet when Scipio carried the war into Africa, the most useful local auxiliaries of Carthage, the Numidians, went over to the Romans, and victory with them. Whatever is involved in the making of empire, the behavior of tributary peoples and the dependability of allies must be a part of it; the crucial point is whatever induces them to choose a side. Proximity is not enough. The conventional explanations are merely superficial statements of what happened.

As an event, what happened when Carthage was destroyed was of immense and permanent importance. Though the consequence could not be apprehended at once, it portended the

gages and enslaving creditors who could not pay. So too the Southern planters were cash-croppers rather than true cultivators of the soil. Neither a financier nor a money-grubber is regarded as the makings of an ideal soldier; but it cannot be denied that these were excellent fighting men. These details are doubly confusing since they did not work out to identical ends; Rome triumphed, the South was defeated.

future rise of Europe, and the subsidence, in the balance of world power, of the eastern hemisphere. Rational inquiry should investigate the nature of the process which had been brought so far by the Phoenicians and could be further effected only through Rome; and the apparently accidental appearance of Pytheas, a Greek, as the opener of the door.

The facile answer, why Pytheas is remembered and his predecessors anonymous, is that he wrote a narrative of his voyage. As the Phoenicians were literate, this must arouse wonder that they had not done so long before, from much wider experience.

They did not because they sought to preserve a complete monopoly of the Atlantic. It was not a matter of high tariffs or favored nations or blockade in time of war. With the straits in their grip, no vessel might pass but their own, in peace or war, on any conditions. Carthage staked its existence on this policy of exclusion. Occasionally no doubt some reckless privateer ran the blockade, but if he did he might never return. Wherever he put in on the forbidden seaboard, he risked encountering the Phoenicians, in which case the unauthorized ship was liable to seizure and the crew to death. No word would come back. Rumors filled those remote regions with vague terrors for a purpose. It is surmised that Pytheas was able to make his exploration safely and write his report while Carthage was under attack from Syracuse, leaving the straits insufficiently guarded. If so, the watch was shortly resumed, and kept to the end. In the main current, the flow of energy at last jammed the Phoenicians up to the narrow sluice which they had reserved for their sole benefit. It was too strong, and smashed them to driftwood.

In the sense that engineers speak of a head of water, the Romans represented a head of the channeled forces. Neither their location nor their material progress, no economic clue, accounts for their function. And if it is now true that even our most recent history is devoid of instruction because we live in a changing world and have to deal with entirely new conditions, then it was always true. It is not true, nor ever was. What the past shows, by overwhelming evidence, is that the imponderables outweigh every material article in the scales of human endeavor. Nations are not powerful because they possess wide lands, safe ports, large navies, huge armies, fortifications, stores, money, and credit. They acquire those advantages because they are powerful, having devised on correct principles the political structure which allows the flow of energy to take its proper course. The question is, how; for the generator and the possible transmission lines and available outlets to either benefit or destruction are always the same. The only difference between past and present in respect of energy is quantitative, a higher potential available at a higher flow, which makes a wrong hook-up more appalling in its effect by the given ratio, becoming apparent literally in a world explosion. The principles of the conversion of energy and of its appropriate mechanism for human use cannot change; these are universals.

If Rome in due time forced the locks of the Atlantic, there was a reason. Still, it was a Greek who went through alone. Moreover, the personal character of Pytheas is so relevant that fiction could scarcely invent him. He was a scientist as well as a merchant adventurer. His book is lost; a few excerpts and references are preserved in the works of later geographers. They quote him in disparagement; he was not believed, for his observations contradicted orthodox theory regarding climate and general conditions in northern latitudes. Vilhjalmur Stefansson * has lately rehabilitated the reputation of Pytheas on the score of accuracy. Though Pytheas was admitted to have made valuable contributions to the exact mathematical science of astronomy, applied in navigation, he was accused of lying about what he saw with his own eyes, by men who had never been there at all. What should be marked is the form of opposition he was obliged to encounter, a political ban while he was alive, and academic

* ULTIMA THULE. By Vilhjalmur Stefansson. Macmillan.

censure after his death. Theories, when they have gained credence, become vested interests. The prestige and livelihood of schools and teachers are bound up in them; they tend toward enclosed doctrine, not open to fresh information.

Pytheas opened the way, where the Phoenicians, for all their shrewdness and hardihood and their factual priority, did not; because he was endowed with the rare combination of disinterested curiosity, speculative intellect, and active enterprise, qualities which impelled him to slip through an official barrier of the utmost rigor to try the chances of the unknown. Pytheas ranks among the notable discoverers, an exemplar of the free mind. He could not know that he was looking toward America.

CHAPTER II

The Power of Ideas

In historical perspective, the Phoenicians are unique; for though they had a tremendous and active part in the events of their time, it was that of antagonist. On the instant of their disappearance, they faded into unreality, leaving no residue. We do not feel that they bequeathed us anything substantial, to become incorporate with our bones, woven into the texture of our lives. This is the more paradoxical, since our inheritance from Greece and Rome consists of abstractions; while the Phoenicians were practical, and did succeed with a kind of international organization. Above all, they touched the points where our vital ideas originated. Their activity stimulated Greece to inquiry and forced Rome to expand; they erected the Temple at Jerusalem and took in pledge the humble villages of Galilee. They were carriers and catalysts. Yet we seem to start *de novo* with Greece and Rome. In reason, this cannot be true; but the illusion must have a reason. It is that the Phoenicians were intrinsically a physical phenomenon. They effected a hook-up of an energy circuit which their political mechanism could not accommodate. In human affairs all that endures is what men think. Humanity as such is an intellectual concept. As a nation, the Phoenicians disintegrated from the impact of a new idea. But three new ideas were already nascent, which were to form the structure of Europe; and later, in re-combination, to create the New World. These complementary ideas need to be recalled.

The fame of Greece is usually identified with art and letters; but the lasting influence of Greece derives from neither. Greek architecture is of the simplest design, inorganic as a crystal, distinguished by exquisite proportion and refined ornament but indicating no further development. Greek sculpture fixed in immutable perfection a chosen type. The art of Greece was self-contained and static. It escapes limitation by the timeless quality of a moment of beauty saved and set apart in defiance of the eternal flux. In their social system the Greeks were likewise at a dead end. Their divinities enjoined no moral order, representing rather the indifferent caprice of nature toward man. Moreover, the gods had grown remote; for educated men faith was thinned to poetic fancy. As a consequence, the Greeks tended to regard the universe as pure phenomena. Greek domestic manners did not make the home a center of strong emotional attachment. Mental companionship was sought elsewhere; normal restraints were loosened to an unprecedented degree. The Greek political method was of a correspondent type, as might be expected when logic has superseded tradition and yet found no principle. Democracy is pure process, consisting of a series of pragmatical expedients, arrived at by majority vote, the verdict of numbers. It has only chance sequence, and no continuity except in the persons concerned. It actually works on the strength of custom, and is therefore inoperable except with a small community of a fairly homogeneous culture. Yet by the Greek habit of thought, free inquiry, custom was already discredited. Democracy inevitably lapses into tyranny; but while in flux it may temporarily leave a wide margin of conduct and thought unregulated. This is not presumed to be of right; it occurs because the power of the whole (the people) is theoretically a plenary power undifferentiated in its parts or agencies. What is everybody's business is nobody's business. The full power can be exercised only in a closed economy, such as obtained in Sparta, where indeed it left no margin whatever. The Athenians, being open to commerce, for a time took license to think. Trade and travel enabled them to make comparative observations; they were eager to hear new

things. The idea they evolved, taken by itself, was a solvent
of such institutions as they possessed; it aggravated the peril
in which they stood by further attenuating the social fabric.
Yet they formulated it courageously; and it was their contribution to the future. Pytheas embodied it. The Greeks had
the idea of science.

Savages acquire information without making categories by
the attributes or qualities of things. More advanced societies
still established on tradition cherish separate branches of
knowledge which are largely regarded as given; hence further investigation is apt to be forbidden as impious. The
Greeks had their premonitory fables of Prometheus and
Icarus. Nevertheless, they perceived that all knowledge
might be interconnected and capable of indefinite enlargement by rational inquiry. They examined the processes of the
intellect, sharpened and tested their minds, to concentrate
upon generalizations and search for axioms. Inconsistently,
they expressed contempt for practical application. Science,
they said, should be pursued for the intellectual pleasure
of knowing the truth. This singular attitude arose from political conditions. The application of science to production
requires assured possession of private property, free labor,
and time enough to return benefits for the effort and capital
expended. With the Greeks, the hopeless instability of democracy allowed no security of the individual against the
mass nor of the nation against external attack. But as long as
a man's ideas remain purely speculative, and the usufruct
confined to intellectual pleasure, he cannot be deprived of
them while he lives, and he will leave it at that. A man can
think and work effectively only for himself.

Yet this extraordinary denial may have had some use in
the circumstances, by stressing intrinsic value in thought. And
it is true that when men have become engrossed in practical
devices they are apt to narrow their field of vision and lose
sight of the interconnection of the various branches of knowledge. More than that, as is now the case, they will even

forget the larger principles they have applied, and on which their well-being depends.

But the implication which the Greeks put aside was ultimately inescapable. Science is the rule of reason. Instead of being resigned to inexorable destiny or blind chance, it might be possible, by discerning the causation of events, to order them at will, and bring about what men desire. An abstraction will move a mountain; nothing can withstand an idea. The Greeks had found the lever.

Apparently events mocked them. While they philosophized, the mountain moved of itself in an avalanche; Rome overpowered them. On the face of it, this would seem a victory of gross substance, a refutation of the concealed premise of the superiority of mind over matter. It was not; on the contrary, even in its immediate incidence it was a vindication of the intellect. Rome had evolved an abstraction, a political concept, which was likewise among the universals. Rome had the idea of law.

All nations have had laws; the most primitive savages were bound by custom, and a binding custom is a law. A taboo is a petrified law. Primitive peoples believe that their laws are permanent even though arbitrary, like "the law of the Medes and Persians, which altereth not." The effective meaning is that custom may alter only by imperceptible degrees, if it is to remain valid. Custom cannot be new. The attendant drawback is that if a ruling custom is broken abruptly, no substitute is at once available. What may happen, by war, pestilence, or migration, or even by innovations otherwise beneficial, is a period of confusion, in which habit is interrupted and expedients tried; but the resultant institutions cannot endure unless they are imbued with traditional sentiments. Of course the fabric of tradition is never wholly destroyed. However, since custom cannot meet change quickly, and above an elementary level of culture there will be occasional necessity for deciding a course of action which must affect the group, an informal council and a leader comprise the obvious development. These seem to suffice for a nomad band of hunters. The next stage, either the pastoral nomad, or primitive agriculture, calls for more definite organization of a permanent character; to secure continuity, the chief's position was allowed to become more or less hereditary, with the patriarchal clan system. The clan was a permanent family; many languages still testify to this concept. If a distinction is to be drawn between a chief and a king, by modern usage it would consist in the degree of formal organization, marked by the appointment or recognition of officials with fixed rank and specified duties. The simultaneous evolution, alongside of secular government, of a priesthood with moral authority, is to be observed. It had its own significance. "Division of powers," or opposed agencies of moral authority and physical power, is a natural feature of society; hence it is also necessary in the form of government to secure stability.

But all of these forms of association were effective only in appropriate conditions, and had their innate defects. Custom could not deal with the unexpected. Leadership will not serve with organized institutions. Monarchy becomes despotic. *Each type of association is suitable to a certain mode of conversion of energy,* and will either break down or become fused into rigidity when it is made to receive a higher potential than it can accommodate.

When a nation has experienced the conditions in which custom is proved perishable, leadership disastrous, and monarchy oppressive, reason must define the prime source of authority, to invest it with viable form.

By such a sequence, probably foreshortened, Rome became a political laboratory. What went into the crucible must be deduced from the myths, legends, traditions, and institutions which took shape in the obscure centuries of the city's early history. It does not appear that Rome was ever primitively barbaric, if the city had its inception in trade, using money,* and holding land as private property; these are elements of an advanced civilization. And the fables are frequently inconsistent, as would be the case if they were partly imported and intermingled. Such tales as those of Romulus and Remus and the rape of the Sabine women cannot be accepted literally; nor need they be of local origin. Bride stealing belongs to a barbaric culture, in which it is no dishonor. The belief that the she-wolf suckled Rome must be still older, and might be derived from a savage totem; but not necessarily, for when Europe was barbarian, an outlaw was a "wolf's-head," a very ancient figure of speech. The suggestion in all three stories is that Rome was always more or less an open city, admitting refugees, exiles, or immigrants. They would bring in varied customs which must be reconciled under general rules.

In any event, the feature of asylum certainly became incorporated in the Roman social and legal system; and ultimately created the special character of Roman citizenship. Distinctively, one had to be born a Greek, but one could become a Roman.

Again, a memorial of past trouble in finding the workable mode of association of a high type may be suspected in one institution peculiar to Rome, and most extraordinary in a civilized people, because it lay entirely outside the social order. Nobody knew any more what it was for, in the sense that everyone knew what the Vestal Virgins signified. The office had served its purpose so completely that the purpose had been forgotten. Though famed for their military courage, the Romans did not practice dueling, nor countenance informal private vengeance. Yet there was one man, who

---

* Familiarity with the function of money enabled Rome to govern an empire in due course. It is said that the Spartans, being unaccustomed to money, were quickly demoralized when they abandoned their bare subsistence economy. They could not maintain the minimum of honesty in contractual relations, having been bred to communism. At the lowest level, they didn't even understand the limits of graft.

must be a criminal, dedicated to a position which had to be gained and held by murder. The man was the Priest of Nemi, "beneath Aricia's trees."

> Those trees in whose dim shadow
> The ghastly priest doth reign,
> The priest who slew the slayer,
> And shall himself be slain.

The incumbent of this sanguinary office obtained it by killing the previous occupant. He might never leave the shelter of the sacred grove, and he was always liable to attack by any other outlaw who could reach that sanctuary of death. The Priest of the Golden Bough has been explained by scholarly references to rites of sacrifice, the scapegoat who bears the sins of the people, or the king-god who died and was restored, like the sun, to ensure fertility of fields and folk. These magic rituals may have sanctioned the priesthood of Nemi. But the Romans were solidly matter-of-fact even in their superstitions. Their deities were mostly useful, assigned to definite duties of a practical kind. Now there was one fitting use for the priesthood of Nemi at its origin. That was to deter attempts at leadership. No more ironically effective measure could be imagined to discourage such ambitions than the assignment of a spot on which aspirants must meet contenders, and where the winner must abide ever after under the same challenge. Let him have what he asked for, and welcome—a resort to force. Obviously only men already under ban would seek the terrible shrine. The meaning of this particular embodied legend is not confined to its immediate use. It reveals an abstract principle. Such are the terms on which man must exist without law.

Being already far advanced beyond custom and leadership, and aware of the incompetence of democracy, the Romans were obliged to solve the problem of government in rational terms, working with what they had. They had the family as the social unit, offset by contract law in respect of property, which made the individual the political unit. Thus the family could not resolve into the true feudal form. They had clans (gentes), of ancient local stock, which could be recognized as an aristocracy, though not in feudal hierarchic order. They had a large miscellaneous population, the plebeians, which just means plenty, the masses; but not necessarily all poor people. The most important element was the tribes, that is, divisions of the city in specific areas, supposed to have remained from the previous union of three different communities. These divisions were strictly territorial and political, with fixed boundaries; persons were comprised in them by residence, not by descent. These tribes had equal representation by franchise resting on landed property, households; and they were required to supply equal contributions for military defense. *The representation attached to the area.* Subsequent changes, additional areas or redivisions or subdivisions for political purposes, retained this form; they had regional boundaries and representation.

Rome was never an undifferentiated "whole," a simple aggregation of particles, as the theory of democracy postulates. From the beginning, the city of Rome was a federation, with the federal form, which comprises permanent bases and structure, the elements of architecture.

Both elements and form called for an elective system; and the Romans first tried life tenure for an elected executive. It was thoroughly unsatisfactory, because there can be no dependable control or limitation of executive powers in such case.* Having got rid of their life presidents (kings), the Romans took rigorous precautions against a return by usurpation. They would have no single chief executive; and even in lesser positions, they inclined to duality in office, which worked very well on the whole. Political offices were

* Hereditary constitutional monarchy is possible only as developing out of true feudalism. The necessary check is found in the survival of a landed aristocracy with entail. When that vanishes, the monarchy must founder shortly.

also restricted to fixed and short tenure, with rotation in office and intervals in which an office-seeker was not eligible for re-election. The latter provision is sound, for the sole object of setting a term to office is to get the incumbent *out*. The main object of voting in any case is to vote against persons or measures. The Romans also watched their generals with unrelaxing jealousy, forbidding even a victorious commander to re-enter the city without formal permission. They were determined to prevent military seizure of civil authority. And they succeeded amazingly, considering their position, which necessitated a good deal of fighting in defense, and constant military readiness. No other ancient nation maintained the same civil control of the army for hundreds of years.

Political offices were mainly vested in the aristocracy, and were partly elective, partly appointive or filled by co-optation; the different methods, with life tenure only for Senators, prevented excessive rigidity while preserving continuity. It was also possible for men of exceptional talent to rise from the lower ranks. Nothing was absolutely petrified into status. The equality of Senators (as distinguished from a hierarchical aristocracy), and the election of other officials, not only permitted but required public debate in the governing body and free expression of opinion by the citizens. As both voters and officeholders in the Republic were propertyholders, they had a solid interest in keeping the nation a going concern, with a concomitant obligation in defense.

But the unique stroke of political genius was that the Roman state made provision not only for delay but for positive deadlock. The power of the plebs, through their tribunes, was flat obstruction. The tribunes of the plebeians could not initiate any measure, but they could stop the works; and their persons were sacred. Nothing is more essential to the welfare of a nation than the countercheck on government, by legitimate means. A mechanism without a brake, a motor without a cut-off, is built for self-destruction.

The Roman system was durable because it was so framed that stresses became strength, and control was ensured by separating the function of the executive agency and the cut-off.

This achievement became possible by defining the source of authority. "The Romans possessed from very early times the conception of *jus*, which is wider than that of positive law laid down by authority, and denotes an order morally binding on the members of the community, both human and divine." *

This idea of law, as an abstract concept, is not predicated by custom, leadership, council or king; nor is it compatible with democracy. With all these authority is arbitrary, being either given in the particular custom, or lodged in persons by precedence (parenthood or seniority), or assigned to number. The Romans affirmed a moral order in the universe.

* CAMBRIDGE ANCIENT HISTORY: The Primitive Institutions of Rome. H. Stuart Jackson. Macmillan.

CHAPTER III

Rome Discovers
Political Structure

Needless to say, the actuality fell far short of the ideal. Penalties in Roman law were excessive and cruel. Slavery and class privilege were legal institutions; they cannot obtain otherwise. Equality before the law was limited to citizens, which meant only freemen; and a debtor risked slavery. This brutal and irrational view of debt, a false equation, sometimes caused alarming social disturbances; under political pressure, cancellation was resorted to by ex-post-facto legislation, a remedy which in particular instances was almost as unfair as the grievance, and only in lesser degree dangerous. To sentimentalize Roman law and gloss over its harsh and faulty aspects is to miss the point. Its solid virtue was its mere existence, since at worst it proved preferable to the unpredictable will of either king or people. In their ordinary conduct the Athenians were probably more humane, or easygoing, than the Romans; but the quality of Roman law was that it was dependable. Though the anecdote may have been invented as a joke which related that an Athenian voted for the banishment of Aristides because he was tired of hearing Aristides called The Just, the thing was not impossible by the democratic system. In Roman law a man must be charged with a specified act having known penalties, and convicted on something more positive than opinion, to incur sentence. He could not be guilty for no cause. A single instance, expressed by the most famous secular conversation in all history, shows how Roman law created an empire, held it together, made it workable, and made it work.

On the occasion of a riot, the Apostle Paul was taken into

custody by the Roman guards. When he was about to be beaten, "Paul said unto the centurion that stood by, Is it lawful for you to scourge a man that is a Roman, and uncondemned?" (Slaves were scourged when they gave evidence merely as witnesses; and apparently this procedure was likewise permissible with aliens.) The centurion at once informed his superior officer of Paul's protest. "Then the chief captain said unto him, Tell me, art thou a Roman? He said, Yea. And the chief captain answered, With a great sum obtained I this freedom. And Paul said, But I was freeborn. . . . And the chief captain also was afraid." Since Paul was in danger from fanatical opponents, he was given protection, and later brought before the governor, Porcius Festus. His opponents then sought by influence either to obtain a summary sentence, or to have Paul handed over to them. Festus said: "It is not the manner of the Romans to deliver any man to die, before that he which is accused have the accusers face to face, and have license to answer for himself concerning the crime laid against him." The charge of sedition was offered, but nothing could be adduced which the Roman law defined under that head. The case was precisely the kind which any Roman official in a provincial post most disliked hearing; but the very reasons which made it distasteful to the governor made it impossible to avoid or dispose of arbitrarily. Seemingly Festus endeavored to persuade Paul to submit to local jurisdiction under Jewish law, as a Jew. Of course the Jewish court could not have tried Paul for sedition; but some other accusation might have been made, within their legal competence, which need not have been the concern of the Roman governor. Presumably, finding no valid accusation, Festus could simply have discharged the prisoner, but then if Paul had been arrested by the local authorities under another charge, Paul might have demanded trial by Roman law none the less; and Festus would have had the affair back on his hands, doubtless with fresh complications. Or if Paul had been put out of the way surreptitiously, Festus might have been suspected of connivance in a local political broil at the expense of a Roman citizen.

Paul stood his ground. "I appeal unto Caesar."

"Then Festus, when he had conferred with the council, answered, Hast thou appealed unto Caesar? unto Caesar shalt thou go."

The crux of the affair is that a poor street preacher, of the working class, under arrest, and with enemies in high places, had only to claim his civil rights and none could deny him. Here the whole historic process becomes apparent in its imperial fulfillment.

The value of the idea of law in its primary use of framing legislation is clear. It sets moral sanctions above force, while recognizing human fallibility. Men made the statutes; and it was understood that a statute might be inequitable or ill-advised, but a bad law reflected on the legislators; statutes were open to change, without impairing the majesty of the law in principle. The means of repeal or alteration were provided, without recourse to violence. Thus the idea of law answered to reason though it was superior to expediency. Finally, the idea of law posited that a man had rights which must be respected, and which he could forfeit only by his own act. Though not all men were free, the condition of a free man had been defined. And since freedom was found to be inherent in the order of the universe, logic must ask in time why all men were not free.

The practical use of the concept of law in founding the empire began with international relations. Their habit of mind made the Romans more reliable in keeping treaties and more steadfast against reverses, and therefore made their alliance desired. Legal clarity likewise served to specify bearable terms. Citizenship being formulated as a legal condition rather than an accident of birth, Rome could bestow it on the people of another nation. A general grant took effect on individuals; the orbital attraction first exerted on the mass thus acted on the particles separately. The result was a true fusion or welding, a chemical compound rather than a simple mixture or binding together. The former local governments could be left with subsidiary authority; no change of custom was forced upon the people; and the risk of revolt was minimized. Under stress, the citizens as individuals would cling to Rome for protection against local tyranny, as Paul did; for Roman law was super-territorial, like canon law in the Middle Ages.

The particles having formed a homogeneous substance, it was firm enough for an enduring structure. In analyzing or describing the successive stages and forms of association men have devised, it is accurate and consistent to refer to the representational order as architecture, and to the political agency in action as mechanism. The structure must accommodate the mechanism; and each must correspond respectively to the type of culture and the mode of the conversion of energy. These forms and mechanisms do not occur and assemble fortuitously by material determinism. They are created by conscious intelligence in the light of experience. Naturally progress tends to be uneven; prolonged failure to make the various developments approximately is the cause of the decline and desuetude of nations. But the production methods will catch up with advanced political ideas; whereas if an advanced physical economy develops within a political framework that cannot accommodate it, production must either be choked down again or it will destroy the political entity, being subverted to the wrong ends. The Greeks actually invented a crude steam engine, but were unable to perfect it and put it to use, for lack of a political organization which would allow such a high potential. Nor could the Roman system admit it. The required organization was not to be devised for almost two thousand years. But Rome alone, in the ancient world, had found the political principle which would accommodate the potential of energy already released.

As architecture, the form of the Roman republic utilized the great principles of building in stone: the arch, by which the thrust of opposing parts makes for cohesion under super-imposed weight; with ashlar masonry, units overlapping in the courses; and the flying buttress, for stability. The civic tribes, the patrician families, and the members of the Senate, were the arches and keystones. The individual citizen's double fealty, to family and state, gave the overlap. The composi-tion of the republican army, a militia with quotas raised by the tribes, and officers of the highest rank belonging as a rule to Senatorial families, was identical in its vertical structure with the state and society; thus when the army was called into service it stood as a flying buttress in relation to the whole.

The political organization of republican Rome worked on the mechanical sequence of a block and tackle, the power line going up a vertical structure from a fixed base, to oper-ate an extensor arm. With the accession to empire, this be-came inadequate to the field of action. The empire used a gravity flow system with the effective apparatus to divert a moiety of the energy for upkeep of the channel.

Time and distance are the two factors which necessitate formal government. Why and how they do so must be con-sidered later. Each type of government is suited to certain time-space relations of individuals to one another and to their environment. The appropriate scope or dimension be-comes evident in territorial size estimated with the co-efficient of the speed of transport and communication.

While confined to its appropriate area, the political struc-ture of the Roman republic was the strongest that has yet been put together. In respect of this proportion of form and space it was most nearly adjusted shortly before and during the Punic wars. It was further capable of gradual extension over immediately adjacent areas, not too far, by judicious admissions to citizenship and auxiliary alliances; but time was a factor in assimilation, and there must still have been a territorial limit beyond which the system would have become ineffective. The military strength of Rome derived from the complete subordination of the army to civil authority; but this does not occur merely by saying it shall be so. An army is a diversion of energy from the productive life of a nation. Modern mass armies are supplied through a single power outlet but with a complicated and lengthy transmission arrangement for the pick-up and again for the spread, by which a great deal of energy is used in transit, and if there is a break or an overload or an inadequate current on the trunk line, nothing else will hold. In the Roman republic, control of the army was ensured by the multiple direct hook-up, in local control of conscription. The soldiers' reward for winning a campaign was to go home. Their loyalty to the commander was restricted to military orders given under the Senate's commission. The commander on active service was subject to direct instructions from the Senate, which were enforceable because the army was likewise dependent on the Senate for supplies. If a commander was superseded, his soldiers would obey the Senate; they were a citizen army. A commander had very little chance of sitting tight and establishing an independent regime in a foreign region.

The permanent acquisition of conquered provinces changed the whole set-up. The armies were enormously increased by mercenaries and dubious allies. Expenses had to be met from tribute. Vast wealth was at the disposal of a victorious general in a distant province; and if their pay was in arrears the soldiers looked immediately to their commander. There were also chances for big deals by civilians with political connections and no scruples. It was a tempting gamble for a Roman financier to back a general with personal loans to be recouped by favor. Caesar owed millions before he gained preferment. The Senate was divided by factional interest.

As has been seen, the army of the Republic operated spatially as a lateral instrument of the civil authority, an extensor swung from a universal joint. The extensor weakened as it lengthened, while the load it clutched was much greater. When the several armies occupied the provinces, the weights at the outer ends, which could neither be dropped nor managed, dragged them from the socket, and then impelled them against the center like gigantic battering rams. The "arm of the law" was unequal to the reach and retractive action demanded by such an unprecedented spread of its field.

Hence the sudden accession to world power literally tore Rome apart, in the civil wars of the Triumvirate. The state could not have survived if the cohesive principle had not continued to act upon the particles.

The republic did perish. What had happened was that the primary direction of the current of energy was reversed, and with it the incidence of physical power. The republic was formed by a community that produced its own livelihood, including the personnel and maintenance of the army; the energy originated within the state. It could meet extraordinary demands in war because the normal expenses of the state were moderate; and the agencies of direct authority were so arranged as to provide the most economical pick-up. When a state relies upon a citizen army for defense, the intrinsic difficulty is to find a way to connect and disconnect the individual for intermittent military duty at minimum expense and with the least dislocation of the civil economy. That problem was fairly well solved by the republic, with a centrifugal mechanism as the source of energy required. It could not operate in reverse.

With the world in fee, an incalculable flow of energy poured into Rome from external sources, a centripetal force, conveyed by the money from the provinces. Money is indispensable to a long-circuit heavy load energy system. It must be used when a sufficient surplus is being produced to allow a margin for exchange, and cost of transport, over a considerable distance. Money represents a storage battery when idle, and a generalized mode of the conversion of energy when it is in motion, with a function of equating time and space.

To adapt the disrupted mechanism of Rome to the new potential of energy from outside, the parts had to be interlocked or offset again by an indivisible nexus and semi-automatic distributor. The best that could be contrived by a desperate resort to expediency was a kind of jury rig.* One man was used as if he were a separate, and breakable, but replaceable object. His new position had no reference to his previous place in the social organism. He was something like a crude fuse plug, which may blow out; but it should be borne in mind that the blowing-out of a fuse plug is a measure of safety in certain contingencies. Practically any man who would do for the job would do; and if one failed, another must be thrown into the gap by the turn of events. He was the emperor, as long as he lasted. He had to take the incoming current and re-distribute it outward. So he must not have any other social function in particular. The first man who made it stick did so mainly by that negative qualification, being neither a great soldier, an eloquent orator, nor a popular figure. The various men who had those gifts—Julius Caesar, Cicero, Mark Antony—died by violence, which was their natural end, since they represented the instruments in collision: the army, the Senate, and the Roman populace. They had to take the impact, which Augustus nullified by representing no separate part. He did not have a visible party; but he did use, or was used by, the new moneyed men. Augustus broke the patricians by proscription, thus reducing the Senate to impotence (though keeping the shell of it); he put the army on a professional basis; he paid off the plebs with the dole, and organized a bureaucracy which furnished places and perquisites for the upper and middle class.

For two thousand years the example of Rome has been

* The Romans of the Empire for centuries retained a vague hope of restoring the Republic.

cited erroneously, to the confusion of nations, as a military empire. It was not. There has never been a military empire, nor ever can be. It is impossible, in the nature of things. When Augustus became emperor, his first move toward consolidating the Roman dominion was to reduce the size of the army. Subsequently, when Rome included within its boundaries most of Europe, the near East, and North Africa, the task was performed with less than four hundred thousand soldiers, of whom half were auxiliaries, that is, regiments supplied by subject nations and officered by Romans. Comparison with the numbers under arms in Europe during recent world wars is proof enough that the Roman armies would have been pitifully inadequate to hold such a wide territory for six months by pure force. In its strictly military capacity the army defended the borders. Its internal duty was mainly that of quashing factional quarrels, police work. There were few genuine popular uprisings. The ordinary man wished to live under Roman law. The victorious Legions were a result and not a cause.

The test of a military society lies in the question whether the civil or military authority is recognized as superior. The Roman civil authority was supreme, as with Paul, when the man of the sword was "afraid" before his prisoner. An empire can exist only if it offers to the world some negotiable benefit in exchange for tribute. Roman law was Rome's export commodity. "With a great sum," the nations obtained the law, but weighed against arbitrary rule it was thought to be worth what it cost. This was what the Carthaginians did not have to offer, and did not understand when they saw it; they never knew what hit them.

The manifest corruption of imperial Rome, and the apparently despotic prerogative of the emperor, seem to deny the basic premise of moral authority residing in the concept of law. Since the power of the emperor had no express restrictions, it must be called absolute; but it is not hairsplitting to inquire whether it was so in theory or in the absence of theory. The republic had provided for the appointment of a temporary dictator; but that office is misunderstood unless the whole civil system is kept in view. The dictator was appointed by the consulate, which was self-perpetuating. The office of the dictator expired automatically after a fixed and short term. He had no patronage to bestow on Senators. His orders therefore had to be carried out by an organization already in being, of a complex and vital character, which owed nothing to him and expected nothing from him. He must exact services and privations of everybody, which would not win him favor. Finally, what is singular about the dictatorship is that it was simply the position of military commander-in-chief; and it shows the republic as having no such functionary as a regular thing. And the dictator had no direct access to the public treasury.

The emperor of course had full command of the army, control of the treasury, and incalculable patronage at his disposal. Further, he was the Supreme Court in person. Such an aggregation of powers under one head is certainly as nearly absolute as can be imagined. How then can it be said that Rome was not a military empire? or how could the law still be respected? The behavior of Festus indicates the answer. The emperor himself was precariously situated between the forces which nominally he commanded. If the army got out of hand, it might and sometimes did depose or assassinate an emperor and appoint a new one by acclamation. Further, the army had to be paid by taxes drawn from the provinces; while the provinces presented a continual threat of separatist insurrections. But the latter contingency made the position of the provincial governors perilous. Festus dared not deal arbitrarily with a humble citizen involved in a riot because he might have been reported to the emperor as fomenting a plot. His job and perhaps his life were at stake; he must keep his province quiet. Likewise the emperor had to keep a standing army subordinate. The provinces and the army were "raw" forces acting by check and balance, which the emperor must gauge accurately enough to let them counterpoise. The necessity of the emperor being replaceable if he proved defective as a bit of the mechanism is evident, since the lapse of centuries did not establish the principle of hereditary succession. As Festus the governor would have had less chance of a fair trial than Paul the tent-maker, so the emperor was less safe than the least of his subjects. Whenever an emperor lacked intelligence to comprehend the reality of his situation, the raw forces broke loose and crushed him; in plain words, he was killed. Domestic and political murder were the imperial tutors, instructing the emperor exactly where his power had its limits.

The horrible abuses inherent in such a compromise—political graft, the demoralization of the dole, and the degradation of personal standards incident to the money intake of Rome, and the increase of slave labor from punitive border wars, which also deprived the citizen of political responsibility—indicate that the ordinary man must have had a compensating reason to persuade him to tolerate such evils. In fact, every other known system on the same economic level bred the same abuses, or worse, with less hope of remedy in any particular instance. But the positive reason why the world accepted Rome was that under Roman rule the productive energy already tapped could flow continuously.

Rome excelled in the construction of roads, bridges, and aqueducts. These are the visible features of a system adapted to the mode of conversion of energy which combines animal traction, the waterwheel, handicrafts advanced to the stage of the forge and foundry, and skilled agriculture. The flow is commerce, the exchange of surplus products, especially trade of finished goods for raw materials. Rome raised no exclusive barriers, and refrained from granting formal monopolies. Roman law affirmed private property, and in the circumstances was bound to be most careful of the citizen; this tended toward individualism.

The great stream of commerce was unceasing. The administrative system took steady toll from it, to run the machine, but left the channel open. The law was the insulating medium of the live current. If the line was down anywhere, the nearest officials were in trouble; while the man at the center, the emperor, had to face a net percentage of risk from every quarter. The toll was abstracted in taxes.

Of course the producer paid the taxes and felt the burden. With a common grievance, the subject nations might have been expected to repudiate the central authority, had there been a better alternative. But there was not. On the whole, life and property were secure under Roman law; and citizenship was a solid asset even to a poor man.

It is doubtful if allegiance can be gained and held solely by material advantages; probably the decisive factor was imponderable. The sense of expansion and elevation of personality indicated by Paul in describing his conversion, his conviction of being re-born into freedom, are expressed in phrases which were intelligible by the secular analogy of his rights of citizenship. Paul's exposition of the law and the new dispensation, his view of custom as a matter of local observance, his apostleship to the Gentiles, are saturated with the Roman civic concept of man as an entity. Paul devoted his life to affirming the third new idea, and the most important of the three: the idea of the individual and immortal soul. Faith as the evidence of things not seen might well be apprehended when one could say, "I am a Roman," though he had never seen Rome. But Paul proclaimed a greater thing, the City of God.

CHAPTER IV

Rome as an Exhibit
of the Nature of Government

Rome governed the world. Neither before nor since has any other nation occupied a wholly equivalent position, exercising one function exclusively in the comity of nations. The isolation of a function is the only means by which its nature can be determined. Rome was the political power crystallized out of the social solution for the first time, and thus fixed as a historical exhibit of the nature of government. What it reveals is a peculiar negative; during her regime, Rome contributed nothing to the actual productive processes.

This is not to say there were no productive persons among the Romans. In the republic, they had been capable craftsmen and good farmers, disposed to thrift, else they would never have developed their keen sense of property; but from the beginning of empire, the ratio of production to population diminished in Rome, while unemployment increased and became chronic. And in the imperial set-up, Rome was strictly a consumer of material goods.

The whole energy which sustained the empire as a going concern came from outside the imperial city. Further, it arose from private effort and intelligence, from the enterprise and labor of individuals, who asked in return—simply to be let alone. What Rome did for them, as compared to any other known form of government, was to do nothing; the margin of benefit consisted in the limitation of government. The political power being withheld from economic activity, production was thus left to private management. The government of Rome was better than that of its predecessors because Rome governed less. This was the first demonstration of the axiom that the country which is least governed is best governed.

The stream of energy welled from innumerable tiny springs to flow into the great trade routes. It had been rising little by little for centuries, washing away innumerable obstacles, carrying down the wreck of kingdoms. Before Rome found her formula, no clear distinction had been made between the public and private domain. Egypt was fossilized by government ownership of the land; the absolute power of government made the country a helpless prey of invaders. Private property was the norm with the Athenians; but they tried to impose monopolies on commerce with their colonies. Carthage was a corporative state. When the enterprisers of any nation tapped a source of trade, forthwith they sought to use the political power to impound the resultant flow completely. It cannot be done; once energy has been released, it must obey its own laws. Greece and Carthage were continually rocked and fissured by the energy which backed up and pressed for an outlet; they could never achieve equilibrium. The Phoenicians were dragged along the track of the energy from Tyre to Carthage. Precisely because Carthage did contrive to clamp a monopoly on the main channel of trade with Europe, Carthage was swept away. But because the Romans were not primarily traders, having been engaged with their great problem of finding the political principle, they were predisposed to allow the stream to follow its natural course.

The structure of the republic was vertical and its source of energy internal. It collapsed from the horizontal drive of an overwhelming current of energy from without. The mechanism of the empire operated horizontally, by a centripetal intake of energy. Given the existent factors, it was capable of wide extension; but its continuance called for positive resistance to the agencies of government from the peripheral parts. It was really maintained by the residual separatist tendency of the component nations. While the sentiment or aspiration toward independence remained in the provinces, the bureaucracy was restrained from taking a heavier toll than the traffic would bear. As receiver of taxes, the provincial governor was in immediate danger if he took too much. Then if Rome made excessive requisitions generally, the next person endangered was the emperor. The mechanism was thus constructed to utilize the pressure of latent revolt in its action, to kick back, recoil. When finally the provincials regarded themselves as Romans, and could not imagine themselves reverting to a separate nationality, the empire was done for. In effect, it blew the cylinder head.

The latent opposition became negligible. The exactions of the bureaucracy increased, and the number of officials multiplied. More and more of the flow was diverted from production into the political mechanism. Whatever elements in motion compose a stream of energy, enough must go through to complete the circuit and renew production. Water running in an aqueduct to turn a millwheel is a stream of energy; or electricity going through insulated wires; or goods in process from raw materials to finished product and conveyed by a system of transport. If the water channel is pierced with many small openings en route; or electricity taken off by more and more outlets; or the goods expropriated piecemeal at each stage of the process, finally not enough will go through for maintenance of the system. In the energy system comprised in an exchange of goods, the producers and processors have to get back enough to enable them to keep on producing and working up the raw materials and to provide transport. In the later Roman empire, the bureaucrats took such a large cut, at length scarcely anything went through the complete circuit.

Meantime the producers, receiving less and less in exchange for their products, were impoverished and discouraged. Naturally they tended to produce less, since they would get no fair return; in fact, effort from which there is no net return automatically must cease. They consumed their own products instead of putting them into exchange. With that the taxes began to dry up. Taxes must come from surplus. The bureaucrats inevitably came down on the producers, with the object of sequestrating the energy directly at the source, by a planned economy. Farmers were bound to the soil; craftsmen to their workbenches; tradesmen were ordered to continue in business although the taxes and regulations did not permit them to make a living. No one could change his residence or occupation without permission. The currency was debased. Prices and wages were fixed until there was nothing to sell and no work to be had.

"The reforms of Diocletian, A.D. 260-268, made still heavier the already unendurable load of citizenship." *

Men who had formerly been productive escaped to the woods and mountains as outlaws, because they must starve if they went on working. Sealed at the source, the level of energy sank until it was no longer sufficient to operate the mechanism. The Roman Wall in Britain marked high tide. When the Legions were withdrawn from the Wall, they had not been defeated by the barbarians; they were pulled back by the ebb of energy, the impossibility of maintaining supplies and reinforcements. The barbarians were not a rising force; they floated in on the ebb. They had no objective, and no ability to take over or set up any system; they came in as wild animals will graze across once-cultivated fields when the cultivator cannot muster sufficient strength to keep his fences in repair. The tax-eaters had absorbed the energy. A map of the Roman empire in the fourth and fifth centuries traced with the routes of the barbarian migrations is a network of wandering lines showing where the East Goths and the West Goths, the Huns and the Vandals, simply followed the main trade routes. There was nothing to stop them. The producers were already beaten by the bureaucracy.

* ROME AND THE ROMANS. By Grant Showerman.

CHAPTER V

The Society of Status and the Society of Contract

The sense of the past, which is a composite of memories, is not evenly continuous. Thinking back, there is a break where first-hand knowledge pieces onto the secondary stuff of hearsay, and at a third remove belief is spun from written record. The latter falls into two main divisions, concerned severally with people much like ourselves; and with people who might almost be of another species, their motives having become either undecipherable or incomprehensible. Of these alien folk, certain nations from widely separated ages and places appear to be of one type; the stiff hieratic figures of the Egyptians, of the Byzantine period, and of the Incas, bear a resemblance. The Dark Ages are puzzling, not in being obscure, since immense tracts of human history have receded from view, but because they occur between lighted intervals, as if they had passed while we were asleep. These gulfs of time cannot be measured by the square of the distance. They lie between two antithetic concepts of humanity, of the relation of the individual to the group, two methods of association. The distinction was drawn clearly by Sir Henry Maine, with the designation of the Society of Contract and the Society of Status.

The axiom of the Declaration of Independence that all men are endowed by their Creator with the inalienable right to life is now probably read by many Americans as a truism which never could have been denied. On the contrary, in that statement it was laid down for the first time as the political principle of a nation. It is the primary postulate of the Society of Contract.

In the Society of Contract man is born free, and comes into his inheritance with maturity.

By this concept all rights belong to the individual. Society consists of individuals in voluntary association. The rights of any person are limited only by the equal rights of another person.

In the Society of Status nobody has any rights. The individual is not recognized; a man is defined by his relation to the group, and is presumed to exist only by permission. The system of status is privilege and subjection. By the ultimate logic of the Society of Status, a member of the group who has not committed even a minor offense might be put to death for "the good of society." * Japan is a Society of Status; until the middle of the nineteenth century it offered a complete and unique exhibit of this social order, down to the least detail.

In the Society of Status everyone is under obedience from the cradle to the grave; except, by the same logic, a ruler whose will may be supreme, and who is therefore exempt from all obligations. He can do no wrong.

The logic of status ignores physical fact. The vital functions of a living creature do not wait upon permission; and unless a person is already able to act of his own motion, he cannot obey a command. The Society of Status claims the power of life and death; but in fact only persons have the gift of life. The claim of the Society of Status is actually based on the group power to inflict death. Hence the extreme and characteristic expressions of two notable examples of the Society of Status were mortuary: human sacrifice as the ritual of the Aztecs; and the pyramids of Egypt, which were tombs.

However, in formally organized societies, there may be a mixture of status and contract. (The reason why it was possible to imagine that the power of death should or might

---

* With this belief, the Carthaginians threw young children into the brazen furnace of Moloch.

determine the principle of association is important, and will be discussed later.) The Roman republic was remarkable for an almost even apportionment of contract and status, about half and half. Politically, it included more of the contract basis than any previous or contemporary state; much more than the Greek democracies, since it limited the scope of the political power. In the empire, the administration of law by a central authority, and the prerogative ceded to the emperor, tended toward status. The citizen ceased to participate actively in political thought. Men do not quite understand what they have no part in making or doing. When savages acquired rifles, they used them, but without comprehension of the mechanical principles and industrial background which the most ignorant white man at least took for granted. If the supply of rifles from the white men had stopped, the savages could not have manufactured any; and meantime their skill in making bows deteriorated. With the law handed down, the subject nations were unlikely to learn self-government.

As the Roman empire slowly collapsed, since there was no successor nation able to take over by solving the time-space equation, political responsibility devolved on the disjoined communities. Makeshift combinations and variations occurred. The empire split in two. The empire of the East reverted to the ancient regional habit of despotism tempered by anarchy, but still with the shadow of Roman law. Europe, the empire of the West, meantime evolved a general pattern of status with partial exceptions, but with the most civilized and humane structure possible in status, for it was built on the monogamous family under the moral aegis of Christianity. The Society of Status is geared to a lower potential of energy than the Society of Contract, and therefore tends to smaller political divisions; but the family unit has great endurance and stability when the formal political framework is shaken or decayed. It can survive repeated disasters, such as sporadic invasion, because the family tie persistently resumes in the order of nature. In terms of energy, not as a figure of speech but literally, the family is a small dynamo completely equipped with its own appropriate circuit, generating and using energy, including maintenance. Since this book is a study of the flow of energy and the nature of government as mechanism, the relevant aspect of Christianity here is the temporal organization of the church.

The Dark Ages are almost a blank to us because any potential of energy in use has a time-space equation translatable into terms of our physical senses. With a high potential, we can "see" or "hear" through distance and time, by speedy communication and permanent notation. The low potential which is all that the Society of Status will accommodate restricts the view to a short radius; and since the Society of Status resists change, its records are apt to be scanty, with a curious effect of being undated. It uses a different chronology from that of the Society of Contract, a local chronology dating by generations or by the year of a reign, instead of from a point in sidereal time, marked by a unique event. Hence even the highest cultures of status, such as that of Egypt, give an impression of arrested time.

But the church used sidereal time. Because of its historic context, the church is now regarded as having been identical with medieval society in its organization. It was not. Rather it was the non-status element in the Dark and Middle Ages, being essentially a system of contract. Perhaps it is not readily recognized as such because its form of contract was generally indissoluble; an agreement made voluntarily was binding for life. Nevertheless, it was contract, and it determined the temporal function of the church as the channel of surplus energy for the secular society of status known as feudalism.

Production under feudalism was comparable to dipping water from a well in a courtyard. Nearly everything produced was consumed on the spot and nearly everything consumed had to be produced on the spot. Yet it is difficult to keep the springs of human energy so sealed that there will be no overflow, no surplus. Nothing can do that except the absolute state, a slab of stone.

Energy flowed into and through the church because the church afforded the only means of emancipation from status, and therefore a release of individual talent. In secular society, the son was held to his father's calling, regardless of ability. In the church, the son of a peasant could become a scholar, a soldier in the militant orders, or even a prince of the church; he might manage an abbey if he had an executive bent, or become a diplomatic legate, or merely work at a craft he liked. The son of a noble could, if he wished, choose the contemplative life, or be a gardener or a builder, without derogation. But above all, in the church a man might move and act beyond the narrow domain on which he was born. In secular life, a peasant walking on the public road, if out of bounds, was liable to arrest for being away from home without leave; the charge against him was going about as "a masterless man." (Arrest for "vagrancy" in modern times is a grossly unjust anachronism, a survival of feudalism; vagrancy means nothing but traveling.) Certainly in the church a man was also under obedience, besides being debarred from marriage; but he was not fixed in one place or task by his birth; he had an initial choice; and the affairs of the church were world-wide, calling for travel and allowing promotion. The form of secular society is visible in one use to which the church put surplus energy; the upward direction of the great cathedrals. But the size and magnificence of the cathedrals resulted from the lateral mechanism of the church, by which it could accumulate liquid capital for large undertakings; and its continuity in time as a corporate body, to carry them to completion. It was the only long-circuit heavy-road system for the transmission of energy. For this reason also the great wars of Christian Europe were fought under the banner of the church, in the Crusades.

As an extra-territorial organization wielding centralized authority, the church operated by precisely the same mechanism as the secular empire. The attraction of the particles was effected by affiliating the family units in "the household of the faith." With this, the church was able to find the resistance for the necessary reciprocating action. The separatist outward pull was now exerted by the rising monarchies, in place of the former provinces. The church recreated a counter-check by withdrawing the clergy from secular jurisdiction, and allowing the laity an appeal to canon law in various cases which might arise between the secular authority and individuals, even serfs. (Holidays, for example, were declared by the church.) The church, centered in Rome, was thus able to hold Europe together by keeping the feudal lords in line, just as the empire had done, by enabling the individual (in his character of Christian or citizen) to stand against his secular government. To secure him a base, the church recognized private property as a God-given right, making it an article of faith in Christian doctrine. If a duke or king became recalcitrant, the church could excommunicate him, thus exempting his subjects from their duty to him; and if this was not enough to bring him to reason, in the last resort the church could lay an interdict on his realm. What it amounted to was that the church could cause a negative revolt, passive disobedience to the secular authority, which had precisely the same effect in ensuring the reciprocating action of the administrative mechanism as the possibility of spontaneous rebellion of the provinces had in the imperial set-up.

Now it may not be perceived on the surface that this was the same principle that had been worked out by the republic in a definite political agency. As a proposition in physics, it consists in the relation of energy to mass. The property of mass is inertia. In politics, inertia is the veto. A function or factor can only be found where it is. No plan or edict can establish it where it is not. The limited size and direct hook-up of the mechanism of the republic made it possible for the tribunes of the people to be invested with the formal veto power. When it was the only specific political instrument the plebs had, the tribunes of the people successfully maintained it against the Senate. At one time, the tribunes of the people "stopped the whole machine of government" for a number of years, refusing to approve and thus permit any act of government whatever, even the appointment of curule magistrates or the regular military muster, until their grievances were redressed. They were able to do so because the power they exercised did inhere in the body they represented. It was there. If the people will not move the government cannot. Though laws are passed and orders given, if mass inertia is found opposed, the laws and orders will not be carried out. In the empire, it was impossible, because of the enlarged time-space conditions, to continue direct representation of the people's veto power; but it was utilized no less, as indicated. So it was in Christian Europe by the church. And the three successive phases of Rome in government spanned two thousand years, an unparalleled record of stability. It was possible because the function of mass, which is taken for granted by mechanical engineers, and usually ignored by political theorists, was understood by the Romans. They used it where it belongs for stability, by attaching to it directly that part of the mechanism proper to the factor of inertia, the device to "cut" the motor when necessary.

The same function has been rightly expressed in modern government by placing with the representatives elected by the people on short tenure the power of the purse, public finances, the grant of supplies. The effective veto was thus exercised, as it should be, by negation, withholding supplies. When unlimited supplies are voted automatically in unapportioned lump sums, it is obvious that the function of mass, the stabilizing element, is no longer included in government; the connection has broken somewhere. The citizens as such, the people, *have no representatives at all*. Their presumed delegates actually represent the spenders of supplies, as must be the case when the elections are carried by such expenditure. Then the inherent veto power can register its weight only by informal devices, indicating imminent danger that the overcharged motor, being out of control, will tear loose from the base and be smashed. It is interesting to observe this true veto power reasserting itself spontaneously today by "polls of public opinion." This is the first warning, but gravely ominous; for the final expression of the intrinsic mass-inertia veto when it is deprived of legitimate represen-tation consists of men quitting their tools and throwing down their arms. The crowning folly of governments is to sup-press the signal.

Because Rome mastered the problem of the function of mass, it endured through successive phases until the trans-mission part of the mechanism failed. In the third phase, the church enabled feudalism to survive, with gradual modi-fications, for centuries, not by unqualified approval, but by drawing off the surplus energy from local production, which must otherwise have burst bounds, and using it in lateral channels. The defense of the borders was continued by the church, with an expansive tendency, by missions to Chris-tianize the barbarians.

In both culture and organization, the striking feature of the Roman civilization throughout its course is that the "unity of Europe" consisted of dualism, opposition, and diversity.

The Society of Status is obliged to restrict production to the energy potential it can accommodate. It does so by collectivism. Group ownership as the norm of property re-quires the denial of liberty to persons. Collective land tenure makes for inferior agriculture; and prevents the improve-ment of tools.* Medieval farming gave a miserably low

* Group ownership experiments tried out by communities within a contract nation, as in the United States, have no bearing on the conditions of a genuine collective or status society. Such communities hold their land by private title, with what is called an undivided interest which is nevertheless individually divisible and open to suit for division. Further, members enter voluntarily and can leave unhindered; while the group admits only selected candidates and may

yield. The resultant poor standard of living ensues famine and plague, thus reducing the vigor and numbers of the population and making it amenable to control. Only the most meager economy—coarse diet, manual labor, the minimum of comfort, convenience, and pleasure—can be adjusted to a planned economy; for a planned economy cannot even be imagined except under political subjection. A complex economy necessitates the political simplicity of free contract. The imposition of political power over production instantly begins to reduce the economy to primitive methods, and correspondingly to lower the optimum population. On the other hand, a high production society emerges from the regulated Society of Status by proclaiming liberty, which requires the abolition of political control over economic activities.

As the level of energy in Europe rose again, its first product being the church edifices, sometimes several in one small town, the overflow once more sought the outlet of trade.

This is usually described as the emergence of the middle class. The term is grossly inaccurate. The three estates of feudalism were the nobles, the clergy, and the people; two secular classes and another class co-extensive with them, or if it must be ranked, rather above them, which would make the nobles the middle class. What is now called the middle class was not and is not a class; it is a different form of society, a classless society, the free society, the Society of Contract. The merchants and independent craftsmen had none of the characteristics of class. They did not render feudal service, having paid a quit-claim. They supported the body politic with money in the way of taxes, and with their own militia. They established civic sovereignty so unequivocally that if a serf could escape to a town and reside

---

expel members; whereas in an authentic collective society the members are born into it, are not free to quit it, and must be either assigned and forced to accept a place or exterminated.

there for a year he gained freedom by virtue of standing on free soil. Every reference made by the members of this resurgent Society of Contract to their own condition stressed the fact that they were free men. And they had their own judiciary. In England the queer name of the Court of Pie Powder is a memorial of the real, physical difference between the two types of society; for it was the Court of Pied Poudré, of the Dusty Feet, which adjudicated the Law Merchant. The men of the dusty feet were the men who traveled, the traders, as distinguished from the members of a static society who were fixed in one spot. The traders necessarily formed a Society of Contract, and lived by contract law. Whenever and wherever it is made a crime to move about or to buy and sell, the type of society there has defined itself; it is a static society.

But the concept of the free man, though imperfectly glimpsed, had never been quite effaced in Europe. An English magistrate, Justice Herle, in 1309 laid down this rule: "In the beginning every man in the world was free, and the law is so favorable to liberty that he who is once found free and of free estate in a court of record, shall be free forever, unless it be that some later act of his own shall make him villein." It was the voice of Roman law that spoke; and the verdict in its full implication set aside a thousand years of status.

Trade and money, which go together in the stream of energy, inevitably wash away the enclosing walls of a society of status. They seep below the foundations and penetrate every crevice. In Europe the infiltration, being gradual, had many fantastic and apparently contradictory effects, which can be discerned in long perspective. At first it seemed to fortify the regime of status; and the phrase may be read literally, as when Richard Coeur de Lion erected the massive bulk of Castle Gaillard with borrowed money for which he pawned his kingdom. Gaillard was designed to be impregnable according to the technique of medieval warfare; and it was an anachronism from its inception, serving no purpose except to complete the bankruptcy of Richard, piled on the debt he had already incurred for his share in the Crusades. From the tenth to the fourteenth centuries the external changes in the social aspect of Europe were curiously comparable to the effect of a great flood that lifts buildings from their foundations to deposit them on distant and unpredictable sites. The Norman-style fortresses set down by reflux along the Mediterranean route, in Malta and Cyprus and as far as Palestine, were so conveyed, with the outpour of energy from Europe in the Crusades. So the rising tide was welcomed and facilitated by those in authority who had no prevision that it must undermine their order.

Trade would commend itself to a noble by bringing him luxuries or paying him rent in cash instead of in kind when a village grew to a market town. Money would buy a serf his blood. Trade could furnish ships to embark a seigneur for the Holy War; money was available for a lien on his domain to equip him for fighting. Money was to empower kings to subdue the nobles; and kings could not have been convinced that trade must presently enable parliaments to execute kings.

The stream of energy flowed again from continent to continent. The Arab empire came into being, occupying much the same terrain as Carthage and with many other points of resemblance, especially in lacking stability and a fixed center. It recaptured Spain and thrust into Europe beyond the borders of France, to meet repulse. But the impact loosened the European status system instead of consolidating it. Nothing but money could furnish, pay, transport, and subsist a sufficient defense; nothing but trade could supply the money. Trade went on in the midst of war. Politically, the Arab empire had no structure, and constantly tended to fall apart with success. The Roman heritage of Europe was reasserted, and under adversity it tended to cohesion. The advent of the Turks was a peculiar phenomenon; for the Turks as conquerors absorbed into military use the energy of the East and hurled it against Europe. Apparently they were irresistible; in fact, they were a declining power from the moment they blocked the great trade routes, both overland and by water, and thus cut the line of the energy which supplied their armies. They imposed a static society, of a singular kind, on the East, just as Europe was emerging from status. Asia sank into desuetude once more. And with the trade routes to the East barred, Europe at last caught up with Pytheas and looked across the Atlantic.

CHAPTER VI

Liberty, Christianity, and the New World

Ideas precede accomplishment. Race, to the extent that it exists, is a fact. Nations and cultures are ideas. The racial stock which appears to preserve its identity does so only by means of an idea. If an idea contains a universal principle, it will merge races; if it cuts across an idea previously accepted, it will divide nations in fatal strife. Every achievement is foreshadowed in fancy; every major disaster is the result of inadequacy, error, or perversion of intelligence. An idea may be previsioned in myth. Europe was a myth before it grew into a rich and complex civilization; and it is called a continent in defiance of geography, for the division between Europe and Asia was drawn in the minds of men.

America was a myth centuries before its physical reality was certified. Whether Plato invented Lost Atlantis or elaborated it from a scrap of folk lore, it is equally inexplicable. Later European legends of the Blessed Isles to westward, where there was no death, St. Brendan's Isle and Avalon and Hy-Brasil and Tir-n'an-Og, are susceptible of a slight factual hypothesis in the Canaries or a glimpse of the Azores; their felicity may have resided in being unattainable. As recently as the end of the eighteenth century, it could be said (by Baboeuf) that happiness in Europe was a new idea.

As the prerequisite of happiness, the hope of liberty was from the first placed in America. Appropriately, the preliminary discovery was made in quest of freedom. During the tenth century of our era, a few intractable men of Viking blood exiled themselves from their homeland rather than submit to the imposition of a feudal monarchy. The Scandi-

53

navian sea-rovers telescoped the history of Europe in their national development. They were practically the last of the barbarian raiders; but they became literate before they ceased to live by looting, and they had the Roman clarity and matter-of-fact type of mind. They were widely acquainted with the civilized world, and supplied a mercenary regiment to the Eastern Empire. They turned from piracy to trade at the same time that they adopted the graded status society which commerce tends to dissolve. In their semi-barbaric condition, the equality among their fighting men obliged them to work out a measure of contract law and local deliberative government; but when they conquered Normandy and later England they set up a detailed feudal system. In this form again their earlier tradition of independent equality at the top impelled them to resist royal pretensions to absolutism by well-organized rebellion; and they went back to contract law to embody the capitulation in a written charter in which the concept of the free man was again implicit, for the future to unfold. They traced a full intellectual circle. Toward its close, the small irreconcilable group who held out for their original condition retreated to the world's end, Ultima Thule, and occupied Iceland, whence the boldest presently pushed on to Greenland. Sailing direct from Norway to the Greenland settlement in the year 1000 A.D., Leif Ericsson was swept south of his course in storm and fog, to a strange landfall, the Wonder Strand of the new world. It is remarkable that the prospect of Vineland the Good should have been abandoned after the briefest attempt at colonization. This was not due to discouragement. The Norsemen were drawn back toward Europe by their belated acceptance of Christianity. Leif Ericsson himself became converted shortly after his voyage of discovery. It was as if the equipment for America had been incomplete without that faith; which was true if they sought liberty as a general condition, not a privilege of class asserted by the strong arm; for they had slaves. The objection occurs that Christian

Europe wore the iron collar of serfdom, and countenanced outright chattel slavery. Nevertheless, the axiom of liberty cannot be postulated except on the basis affirmed by Christian philosophy. For its realization, the secular principles educed by Greece and Rome are no less indispensable. Yet America was regarded as its native soil.

About 1560 or 1570, Etienne de la Boetie, the friend of Montaigne, filled with despair by the Wars of Religion, wrote:

"What think you of the dire fate that has brought us to birth in these times? and what are you resolved to do? For my own part, I see no other course than to emigrate, forsake my home and go wherever fortune bears me. Long now the wrath of the gods has warned me to flee—showing me those vast and open lands beyond the ocean. When, on the threshold of our century, a new world rose from the waves, the gods—we may well believe—destined it as a refuge where men shall till free fields under a fairer sky, while the cruel sword and shameful plague doom the ruin of Europe. Over there are fertile plains awaiting the plough, a land without bourne or master—it is there I will go." *

Life, liberty, and the pursuit of happiness—what men found in America was the wish they had sent in anticipation. They brought with them the effective knowledge to make it come true. Hence the association persisted in spite of the prompt and atrocious contradiction offered by the treatment of the Indians and the early importation of African slaves. Montaigne himself, whose subtle candor disestablished authority as the weather brings down a stone wall, commented: "If anything could have tempted my youth, it would have been the ambition to share the dangers of this new enterprise." Yet Montaigne, like his friend, was no serf, but a seigneur, enjoying the privileges of rank and a good estate. It was his mind that was tempted to range abroad. He was the epitome of his age, furnishing his medieval tower as a

* THE AUTOBIOGRAPHY OF MONTAIGNE. By Marvin Lowenthal.

study in which he pondered tranquilly the ideas which must undercut the whole structure.

The effectual discovery of America was made by enterprise capitalism. Columbus was a promoter with a scheme. The ships were of private ownership, one under charter. Skilled management (captains) were employed. Some cash capital was subscribed. The crew worked for wages. Such an organization today could attempt any legitimate business. But most of the money was advanced by the Queen of Spain; two of the ships had been requisitioned by the government as a fine; and the expedition sailed under an official commission. Contingent on the success of his voyage, Columbus was promised the hereditary title of Admiral of the (Atlantic) Ocean, and a percentage on all trade to be opened by his route, to him and his heirs. His objective was Japan and China; but even if he had landed there, the stipulation could never have been fulfilled. An ocean does not tolerate monopoly. The venture thus carried within itself the two conflicting systems of status and contract which were at odds in Europe. The continent had first been civilized and organized by the energy flowing through contract; with the breakdown of the mechanism it had lapsed into status; contract was again emerging into recognition with the increase of trade. But Spain was moving in reverse, caught by a kind of tide-rip at the Straits, toward absolutism, precisely when the geographical location as the jumping-off place gave the Iberian peninsula the first connection with the new world. Of course the shortest line between Africa and South America is scarcely half the distance Columbus covered from Spain to the West Indies; but there was no surplus energy in either Africa or South America. Europe was generating energy; it had been cut off from the land route to the Orient. The voyage of Columbus was like the leap of an electric spark across an arc.

The subjugation of the native American races was a foregone conclusion, because Europe used a much higher potential of energy. The people of the most advanced American culture did not even employ animal traction, and had not invented the wheel, much less the water-wheel, nor come to the iron age. They traveled afoot, and were their own beasts of burden. Their mode of the conversion of energy was the human body and manual appliances. Their terror of the European invaders with horses and fire-arms is usually attributed to stupefaction at the mere strangeness of the phenomena. It was rather the intelligent apprehension of a stepped-up power they could not match. Primitive ignorance is not alarmed by novelty. The savage tribes were less submissive than the most civilized, because they had no conception of the mastery of energy, although they were equally doomed by the superior potential.

It may be set down as an axiom that in a clash between two nations or cultures, if one uses a higher potential of energy than the other, that one must win. The differential is in the time-space equation, which offsets primitive manpower. A hundred men can move as fast as fifty men, and are therefore twice as effective; but no multiple of men can move as fast as a bullet, and numbers are nullified by inverse ratio to speed and range.

As between two nations using the same mode of conversion of energy, it might seem that man-power and raw materials should determine the issue. But this does not work out; as has been shown, the results are so variable that no answer hitherto offered will fit even two given examples as a post hoc guess.

If ever a nation and dynasty had the physical components of empire thrown in its lap by sheer chance and all at once, it so happened to Spain. The peaceful method of territorial enlargement under feudalism was by marriages which combined inheritances. In Europe the Hapsburg dynasty, by a run of luck, became the residuary legatee of this system. After the union of Castile and Aragon, Spain was joined to the Austrian conglomerate of nations, including the Netherlands and large chunks of Italy. Concurrently, the whole Iberian peninsula was brought in piecemeal, later including Portugal for a time. The ruler of these wide dominions was formally acknowledged to be pre-eminent in Europe, by his elective office as head of the Holy Roman empire. Presumably this aggrandizement would have come about if America had not been discovered. How long it might have held together is a matter of conjecture; but at least its tenure was as secure as that of any contemporary political set-up. Thus Spain controlled the richest part of Europe, what with the Spanish and Austrian mines, the industrial towns of the Netherlands, and the diversity of other resources embraced in such extensive territory. The dominant position in respect of the Mediterranean also meant something. And then the wealth of America poured into Spain.

By comparison, the man-power and material at the disposal of England were ridiculously small; and English territory comprised only half of a foggy little island and a slippery foothold in Ireland. England had the port of Calais but lost it before entering the struggle with Spain.

Finally, it should be observed that within its national borders Spain did attain perfect unity. Never has any people been so unanimous in sentiment, in thought, in manners and morals and religion and political loyalty, as Spain became subsequent to the expulsion of the Moors and the Jews. It was solid as an iron bar.

That was what was the matter with it. In a living organism, such a condition is most akin to the rigor of epilepsy; if it becomes permanent, it is death. In mechanism, which must operate by the opposition of parts, it is equivalent to stalling. Though a nation may appear to act when it is thus solidified, the movement is that of dislocated mass, a falling body. It has no intelligent direction or definable objective.

Spain was electrocuted, burned out, by receiving a high voltage of energy into a political structure and mechanism without proper transmission lines, outlets, and insulation.

Making contact with America, Spain picked up a vast stored charge of energy in the form of the precious metals which were convertible into European currency. Thereafter the country presented an almost incredible spectacle, with treasure ships unloading bullion year by year in unprecedented quantities, and the people increasingly impoverished by inverse ratio until they were reduced to hunger and rags. Every ordinance now recommended and applied in the name of a planned economy was tried out in Spain during that period on the same pretext of public necessity, with the inevitable consequences of stopping production. Business could be done only by license; manufactures and trade were restricted; mines in Spain were shut down by order; real money was seized from private owners, who were forced to accept government paper in exchange, and imprisoned or executed if they attempted to refuse. Taxes and tariffs multiplied. Everything went into government; and the government was always bankrupt. Yet the functions of government, alleged as the pretext for such measures, were carried on with grotesque inefficiency. The greatest military exertions incurred the most disastrous defeats, and when victorious Spain could not obtain peace. The Netherlands revolted and would not be pacified. England fought a good deal off and on during the same period, and was not invariably victorious either; if reckoned in proportion to population and available wealth, the effort of England was greater. Yet English losses were quickly repaired and her power augmented, while Spain lapsed into the unhappy position of being the battleground of Europe. The condition of Spain while still in possession of her New World empire (circa 1700) was thus described: "A country without an army, justice or police, and absolutely without liberty.... The grandees are contemptuous and contemptible. They have nothing except pride, poverty, laziness and the pox. They have no education and no sort of knowledge." Commerce and industry were at a standstill, agriculture in decay; and though there was still a considerable revenue from America, there was no money in circulation.

During the seventeenth century, the decline of Spain allowed France to make a bid for primacy. Louis XIV contrived to make his monarchy absolute, and thus threw the whole energy of the nation into war. He obtained unity by expelling the Huguenots. To avoid being bothered with figures, "the silly dollar mark," he bestowed on one man, Chamillart, the ministries of war and finance. A first-hand observer of the result said despairingly: "No treasure will suffice for an unbridled government." When Louis had taxed his subjects into famine, anticipated several years' revenue, depreciated the currency, and found himself penniless just the same, he felt a twinge of conscience, wondering if he had a moral right to gouge deeper. He called in a selected group of professors from the great University, the Sorbonne; and they obligingly informed him that as king he owned all the property in the realm; his subjects were merely tenants; and if he permitted them to retain any portion of their possessions or the product of their labor, he was doing them a favor. So he extorted new taxes. With unity and total control, in his old age he was compelled to beg for peace on any terms; and before his death intelligent Frenchmen, such as Cattinat, foresaw the French Revolution with dread. They knew that the political and economic structure was fatally unbalanced. The organic unit of the family as the pattern of society withstood the strain for a hundred years, but it could not hold forever. Meantime England survived a civil war, and with no particular ambition for empire, acceded to the dominant position for which Spain and France had spent themselves in vain. Energy in human affairs tends to flow with wind and water by natural law, following the line of least resistance, but as between points fixed by raw materials in quantity. Of the voyages of discovery from 1492 to 1611, only four went from England, and none of them struck it rich. Nevertheless, the world map shows that subsequently another positive factor intervened, directing the flow between Europe and America somewhat north of its natural course, that is, from England to the comparatively undowered North American coast of New England and down to Virginia. These again became radial.

The train of events corresponded point by point to the internal political development of England, Spain, and France. The scope and pretensions of government in Spain and France increased continuously. The claims of government in England were no less persistently refuted, diminished, and qualified. *Empires are made by private enterprise.*

This is the rule which determines victory between rival nations using the same technical mode of the conversion of energy: that one in which government is most limited will win. A greater territorial extent and concomitant resources may actually prove a disadvantage to a nation under absolute government, because they will make the government recklessly exorbitant toward its own citizens, and will also yield an occasional windfall to the enemy free nation, which is able to put such pickings to effective use. Though much of the energy which Spain drew from the new world served only to fuse Spain into agonized rigidity, some had to go on through, and was thus returned to productive channels elsewhere in Europe. The money circulated, and stimulated rival nations and rebellious provinces to break the Spanish monopoly by trading on their own account. The energy had a dual effect on Europe as a whole, disrupting the feudal compromise along ancient lines of cleavage and at the same time merging small principalities and free cities into national forms.

The balance of power fell to England because England allowed the energy to flow most freely, which is to say that England conceded the most liberty to the individual by respecting private property and abandoning by degrees the practice of political trade monopolies. Of course England did not desist from the granting of monopolies all at once, and it was the remains of monopoly which precipitated the American Revolution; but free enterprise had enough leeway to beat Spain and France hands down.

The crucial test of private property is the attitude of government toward money. Devaluation of currency is outright expropriation. The British empire was founded when the debased coinage was restored to standard during the opening years of the reign of Elizabeth, on the advice of Gresham. At the time, English trade was in distress, the national treasury was empty, the national credit was gone and mercantile credit shaky, war was threatening and rebellion a possibility. In such circumstances, governments usually resort to repudiation, confiscation, and fiat currency. Instead, England took the opposite course. The world came under her sway. The British empire ended three hundred and fifty years later, when England again debased her coinage, defaulted on her debts, confiscated private property, and abrogated personal liberty.

These are not sentimental considerations; they constitute the mechanism of production and therefore of power. Personal liberty is the pre-condition of the release of energy. Private property is the inductor which initiates the flow. Real money is the transmission line; and the payment of debts comprises half the circuit. An empire is merely a long circuit energy-system. The possibility of a short circuit, ensuing leakage and breakdown or explosion, occurs in the hook-up of political organization to the productive processes. This is not a figure of speech or analogy, but a specific physical description of what happens.

CHAPTER VII

The Noble Savage

The first abstract generalization made by Europeans in regard to the American aborigines was that the less civilized tribes had no government.* Europe was far enough from that condition to be struck with astonishment. The fact gave rise to the myth of the Noble Savage, which now seems like a gratuitous fabrication because it was translated into poetic and pictorial form. The Noble Savage was a syllogism, a logical construction from the premises of the European theory of government. Secular authority resided in society, which was an entity; and men were born in subjection to it. It was assumed that without government every man's hand must be against his neighbor, and every kind of crime would be committed by everyone. Possibly the memory of the barbarian invasions entered into this conviction; while the doctrine of original sin, if taken by itself, could be construed to support it. And since plenty of crimes certainly were committed, it was arguable that more would be if individuals were allowed leeway. How or why a society composed of individuals eager to do murder should restrain its members by force may appear incomprehensible, especially when the church exercised an authority superior to that of the secular organization by appealing to the conscience of the individual, intervening in armed disputes with moral injunctions. But the discrepancy was accounted for by the divine mission entrusted to the church. The order of secular society made it necessary to tie men to a given locality and class, and

* The word government, as here used, signifies a formal political organization of denominated persons having definite functions, with authority for enforcement.

therefore to prescribe what they must and must not do, say, write, or think. Both exile and "preventive arrest," imprisonment without trial (as by *lettre de cachet*) are the ultimate extension of this theory.

Thus it was a profound shock to discover that crime was rather less prevalent among savages with no government than in a society with authoritarian government minutely applied. The savages practiced most of the lay virtues: courage, hospitality, truthfulness, loyalty, perhaps even chastity. True that they made war and were sometimes cruel, but Europeans made war and legalized torture.

Still, men do not readily abandon an opinion by which they have justified their institutions; therefore it could only be supposed that savages were peculiarly noble by nature; or anyhow, American savages were so.* The Noble Savage was not an entirely new creation; Tacitus had idealized the barbarian in like manner, while the barbarian remained at a safe distance. Only the rationalization was new. But the Noble Savage passed into European mythology without gaining credence in America. The early white settlers, to whom the savage was a present and sanguinary enemy, were apt to overlook his virtues. Precisely at this point the schism or cleavage between American and European political ideas began.

The impact of a high energy system on a lower one has an internal effect upon the latter which is much more disintegrating and conclusive than the direct consequences of war. For example, if the North American Indians had been supplied with fire-arms and ammunition for their own use, while otherwise left as they were, their way of life would have been seriously deranged. The optimum population which a hunting economy will sustain is scanty. There are recurrent years when game is scarce anyhow; in such seasons the

* The theorists ignored the Caribs, whose cannibalistic practices were unspeakable. And the Apaches were then unknown. People were simply sick of too much government.

weaker members of the savage tribes perished; and at all times the ordeal of survival was severe. With guns, it would have been possible for the hunters to kill more game, so that the population would have tended to increase over a certain period of time, at the expense of the future food supply as the game was thinned out, until an exceptionally bad season brought wholesale starvation. As it was, much the same thing happened by degrees. No large numbers of North American Indians were slain by the white men in war. Instead, their economy was superseded; and those in contact with the white men were demoralized long before the continent was fully occupied by whites.

The lapse of the Noble Savage from his pristine virtue could not escape observation. The myth remained, in European thinking, but had to be modified to a tentative hypothesis that perhaps all men were equally noble until corrupted by—what? By "society," at least as it was then organized, especially its political form. Approximating to the law of physics that action and reaction are equal and opposite, European minds began to swing to this extreme from their previous theory of status.

Emigrants to America had already made the physical move, so that their thinking tended to seek a balance. In the opinion of the frontiersman, the only good Indian was a dead Indian. But the frontiersman had no excessive attachment to government either. Informed and thoughtful Americans remained aware that the savage in his original condition did obey a moral code although he had no government. Being acquainted at first hand with the limitations of a primitive culture, such men of intellect had no desire to revert to savagery in quest of a sentimental illusion; what interested them was the reasonable question: if government did not prevent crime and enforce virtue, what did it do? If in certain conditions government could be dispensed with altogether, why and to what extent was it actually necessary in any condition?

The American colonies furnished a further object lesson and proving ground. Nominally they were under the same kind of authority as the European nations from which they were drawn; but the English settlements especially, for historic reasons, tended strongly to self-government, in which the strictly traditional element was diluted or eliminated, and the liberty of the individual was taken for granted. Yet they prospered; people got along with one another, and with much less government than in Europe there was no more crime. The existence of slavery at the same time can be understood only if the two theories of society are understood. Slavery occurs in what has lately been called a "mixed economy." Contract had become the prevailing relation, but the theory of status had not been explicitly repudiated by limitation of the scope of government. The presumed moral value of status is that it gives everyone "security," a place in society from which he cannot be ousted, and which, conversely, he may not leave. If there is any benefit in status, the serf enjoyed it as much as his lord.* By the complete and absolute theory of status the land could not be sold at all, but only inherited; and should be held in perpetual tenancy; it could not be transferred away from the hereditary cultivator. This sounds so admirable that of late attempts have been made to reinstate unbreakable tenure, by piecemeal devices such as seniority in jobs (beginning with civil service), and government-endowed "subsistence colonies." These are accepted without recognition of the inevitable corollary; it is the return of serfdom. If employment cannot be terminated by the employer according to contract, or tenancy by the owner on the expiration of a stated lease, presently the worker or tenant must lose the right to quit his employment or his allotment. Nor will he have, under the

---

* The serf was not free to starve. He had to starve under arrest, and he did starve pretty often. Famine was recurrent even in fertile regions. The United States is the only country on record that has never had a famine since it became a nation.

"state," the human character which pertained to the serf under feudalism, onerous as it was. He can be nothing but a cog in the machine.

But chattel slavery was a monstrous combination of status and contract, the epitome of the "mixed economy." The unequal condition of the slave is status, but he is bought and sold by contract. In theory, the serf was still a man, while the chattel slave was an object.

This anomaly was bound to trouble the conscience of slave-owners for the very reason that they were free men. It left freedom at the mercy of accident. The facile proposition that the Negro was a slave by the curse of Ham did not cover the fact that white men also were condemned and shipped to America to be sold as slaves for political offenses. So the whole course of history was repeated, run off again, before the eyes of Americans. One man in his lifetime could see it all, if he cared to contemplate what lay in view; theories and arguments were put to the test by demonstration. Looking back to Europe, he could see the system of status still in force or yielding to various modifications. He could observe the portent of a new and terrible tyranny, "the state," emerging in its ancient guise of absolute monarchy. He could discern the ultimate position of men as subjects of that absolute state; they were slaves. He could study the reality of savage life at its best and worst, contrasted with the difficulties, the pains and the rewards of civilization. He could see men who had rejected civilization to embrace savagery, sinking to the worst instead of achieving the best. He could see others who had taken to the wilderness with the innocence of a deer or a hawk, but their recourse availed only for one generation.

He could also see free men in free association making and building, working for no master yet industrious, and meeting approximately as equals without disorder. Amazingly, most of the social problems brought from Europe were never solved nor settled; they just evaporated. The wars of re-

ligion dwindled to a little local persecution. The barriers of
class dissolved; and where persons of various nationalities
mixed in one community, they dwelt amicably. Yet as individuals they did not undergo any notable transformation;
they remained human beings.

Clearly then their behavior and mode of association was
practicable, and must have deducible principles, intrinsically
different from those of Europe. The presence of slaves gave
the answer; other distinctions were so nearly obliterated that
the two possible conditions became starkly evident. A man
was either free or not free. And where it had formerly been
assumed that men were not fit for freedom, it was now think-
able that nothing but freedom was fit for men.

During centuries past, in Europe, various "liberties" had
been wrested or bought from authority, but such concessions
had always been phrased as grants from above, not right but
privilege. When the sum became considerable, the Society of
Contract could at least be imagined. It had been imagined,
and projected to the New World. In the New World it had
become a fact. At length the time was ripe to affirm it as a
political concept, without reservations.

The terms were found: all men are endowed by their
Creator with an inalienable right to life, liberty, and the
pursuit of happiness.

Freedom was indivisible, a pre-condition. To talk of several "freedoms" is to use the language of Europe, not of
America; it is an abandonment of the basic principle on which
the United States was founded.

But for the concept of freedom, the appropriate form of
government remained to be devised. The fallacy of anarchism
was not entertained. Though it was not exactly clear why a
measure of government was unavoidable, the necessity was
felt. The puzzle of the savages—why they had no government although they were subject to human weakness—had
to be left unsolved, though it was not forgotten and it had
much influence in sustaining the theory of freedom. The

change from the European basis of government was made by positing that men are born free, that since they begin with no government, they must therefore institute government by voluntary agreement, and thus government must be their agent, not their superior. Since volition is a function of the individual, the individual has the precedent right. Then even if it was presumed that government did equate roughly with the moral shortcomings of humanity, it should still be limited and subsidiary. If everyone were invariably honest, able, wise, and kind, there should be no occasion for government. Everyone would readily understand what is desirable and what is possible in given circumstances, all would concur upon the best means toward their purpose and for equitable participation in the ensuing benefits, and would act without compulsion or default. The maximum production was certainly obtained from such voluntary action arising from personal initiative. But since human beings will sometimes lie, shirk, break promises, fail to improve their faculties, act imprudently, seize by violence the goods of others, and even kill one another in anger or greed, government might be defined as the police organization. In that case, it must be described as a necessary evil. It would have no existence as a separate entity, and no intrinsic authority; it could not be justly empowered to act excepting as individuals infringed one another's rights, when it should enforce prescribed penalties. Generally, it would stand in the relation of a witness to contract, holding a forfeit for the parties. As such, the least practicable measure of government must be the best. Anything beyond the minimum must be oppression.

By this view, men are neither wholly "noble" nor incorrigibly bad, but rather imperfect creatures gifted with the divine spark and so capable of improvement, perhaps in the long run of "perfectibility." This is essentially a secular application of the Christian doctrine of the individual soul, born to immortality, with the faculty of free-will, which includes the possibility of sin or error, yet equally enabled to strive toward salvation, its heritage. Let anyone who does not recognize the connection of these principles try to re-write the Declaration of Independence without reference to a divine source of human rights. It cannot be done; the axiom is missing. A philosophy of materialism can admit no rights whatever; hence the most grinding despotism ever known resulted at once from the "experiment" of Marxist communism, which could posit nothing but a mechanistic process for its validation.

The Christian idea was necessary to the concept of free-dom. The Roman idea was indispensable for the form—a government of laws and not of men.

The question posed by the absence of government in savage society had to be dropped for the time being, because nobody recognized it as a matter of engineering; and it cannot be expressed otherwise. It is of course a moral prob-lem, since it concerns the relation of human beings; but the specific relations involved are *those which include time and space*. The organization of actions over time and space con-stitutes the science of engineering.

Anyhow, the immediate task was to determine the mode of minimum government, by examination and comparison of historic examples, checking intentions and devices against performance. The source of secular authority having been postulated as residing in the individual, the object then was to prevent that authority being usurped by its agent. How-ever, one engineering factor was certainly understood—the function of private property as the sole basis of liberty. It is no accident that the original draft of the Declaration of Independence nominated private property as an inalienable right of the individual.

CHAPTER VIII

The Fallacy of Anarchism

To call anarchism a fallacy after having stated that savages have no government, which is certainly a condition of anarchy, must sound like flat inconsistency, unless it is borne in mind that the mode of the conversion of energy must correspond to the mode of association. Anarchy is practicable only to savagery. It has been attempted with an agricultural economy, which is more advanced, and the result is highly instructive. The religious sect of Dukhobors have made the trial, exhaustively. Within its limits, their reasoning was completely consistent. They were resolved to have no government whatever, not even self-government as the term is understood in describing a formal organization. A reporter *** making a factual study of a Dukhobor colony in Canada asked a Dukhobor if he would promise not to burn some manuscript notes if they were left about. This would have been the easiest kind of promise to fulfill, being mere abstention from an act which no conceivable circumstances subsequently arising could make necessary in the given instance. The Dukhobor answered that he "would not want to burn those notes." The reporter conceded that undoubtedly the Dukhobor at the moment thought he would not, but supposing he felt otherwise later? In that case, the Dukhobor said, "if the Spirit truly moved me to do it, then I would have to burn them."

The essence of self-government consists in keeping promises; the formal organization is instituted by agreement, and its power is delegated for the purpose of maintaining contract

* SLAVA BOHU: The story of the Dukhobors. J. F. C. Wright.

freely entered into—the contract embodied in the constitution, and private contracts between individuals. The Dukhobors were quite logical in avoiding the first step toward self-government, since they did not wish to have any. But the sect throughout its existence has alternated between disputes which stopped production and autocratic leadership which disposed of a large share of the product arbitrarily. Such is the inevitable outcome of the most conscientious attempt to remain in a condition of anarchy after the moral relationship of the members of the community has been extended in space and time to permit a higher economy than that of savagery. Labor is wasted; and the members of the community are held down to poverty, distress, and ignorance.

The stage of development in which government becomes necessary is easily discovered; and its correspondence to the mode of the conversion of energy, or failure when the synchronization is not right, can be discerned. What has not hitherto been elucidated is the specific connection of the mechanism of government and the productive order. This has led to various conflicting guesses as to the origin and nature of government. One theory of history asserts that government arises from war, and therefore is force *per se*. This is doubly false since it is a reversal of the true relation. It has been adopted by philosophers committed to the doctrine of the Absolute State, because it is the sole argument they can muster which seems to afford them a factual base; but it rests only upon the error of *post hoc, ergo propter hoc*.

Government by force is a contradiction in terms and an impossibility in physics. *Force is what is governed*. Government originates in the moral faculty.

The subsidiary relation of force to the moral faculty is self-evident from the location of the source of the energy applied in human affairs; and this relationship is demonstrable by the mechanism of every known or imaginable mode of human association. The earliest form of society, subsisting by the direct bounty of nature and held together by the instinct of species, is that of the savage. The Eskimos are believed to exhibit a survival of the Stone Age culture, scarcely modified until recent times. Their habitat does not permit accumulation of possessions beyond portable objects and small caches of food; neither may they hope for improvement in their lot beyond an obvious narrow margin. Old age is brief; incompetence, sickness, or severe disability mean death. Marriage is a working partnership easily dissolved; and sex behavior is accordingly lax. The process of conversion of energy has the smallest possible circuit, with the man as hunter bringing in raw materials and the woman forthwith turning them into consumption goods; these go into maintenance, and the children are replacement. The group cannot become very large; it must disperse and wander, and cannot establish a regular place of assembly. Hence it has no secular head. No Eskimo has authority over another; but Stefansson notes that without seeking it the abler men have influence without privilege. Under acute necessity, which is the mold of pure custom, the Eskimos really have no government, no political structure or agency whatever.

Eskimos do not make war. Their energy is absorbed in the immediate struggle for existence; and their environment, the white Arctic waste, eliminates the possible aspect of war as sport, which consists in surprise, escape, and pursuit.

In temperate regions, savages do make war; and still have no formal government. But war and leadership, with an informal council, seem to be synchronous developments. This is what lends plausibility to the theory that government originates in war and therefore that government *per se* is force. The error can be maintained only by rejecting both the facts of savage behavior and the specific testimony of intelligent savages as to the meaning and purpose of what has been called the council of war. The significant point is that in their beginnings *neither chief nor council had any power*. They exercised only accredited influence. The chief had no permanence of tenure and no positive authority. Council and chief debated when war was in prospect; but the manifest occasion for their exhortations was to instill prudence, that is, to speak for peace. This was put on record by a famous chief, old Seattle, who had been instrumental in uniting a number of Pacific Coast tribes. When the white men came, he saw that his people were done for. In a valedictory oration, acceding to a treaty, he explained, recapitulating the function of the chief simply as matter of fact:

* "Youth is impulsive. When our young men grow angry at some real or imaginary wrong, and disfigure their faces with black paint, it denotes that their hearts are black, and then they are often cruel and relentless, and our old men and women are unable to restrain them. Thus it has ever been. Revenge by young men is considered gain, even at the cost of their own lives, but old men who stay at home in times of war, and mothers who have sons to lose, know better."

Chief Seattle described an indisputable physical phenomenon, a diversion of surplus energy. Obviously primitive war can be begun and carried on by impulse on the part of the fighting men. In the conditions, it could not be conducted by any other means. If the young men were in militant mood, nothing could conceivably restrain them except persuasion. They *are* the force. Thus the council might either prevent war by moral influence, or sanction it, or admit their inability to forbid it, while ready to make peace afterward. In no case could the council, the old men, apply force, either for prevention or to compel war. They simply had none. Likewise in such primitive warfare no authoritative command is possible; every man must fight on his own. The chief could offer advice on crude strategy, and give an example of bravery and expertness. That was about all. Consequently he was chosen for wisdom as much as for valor.

Hence his position did not, because it could not, rest upon force, with his own people. Personal prowess is no more

* GATEWAY OF THE NORTH. By Archie Binns.

than the strength of one man, while the tribe is many. Where free movement is necessary to get a living, one strong man can scarcely dominate a single inferior by intimidation; he certainly cannot hold numbers in subjugation. The chief and council did not give positive orders because they had no means to compel obedience. Offenses against persons were open to personal retaliation; serious infractions of custom might be punished by a committee of the whole making the offender run the gantlet, or expelling him from the tribe.

It may be suggested that at least a minority comprising the strongest might command by force the weaker members of the tribe; but even to essay this, a basis of accord must be adopted by the junta. The expectation of loot or tribute requires agreement on division of the spoils. "Honor among thieves" reveals that a moral basis remains indispensable.

For analysis, the successive cultural stages utilizing different modes of the conversion of energy must be distinguished. It is convenient to designate the next step above savagery as barbarism. The barbarian culture, though still nomadic, owns flocks and herds. It is at this stage that the necessity for a measure of government arises, with the extension of human relations over time and space. When the problem is so stated, it may be thought that the roving habit of savages brings in a space relation. On the contrary, it obviates the need, for nothing is left behind. Moral relations between adult individuals, and the group relationship predicated by the economy, are resolved immediately. Two men who are inclined to quarrel may fight it out on the spot; space enters into the matter only as a chance of escape. Husbands and wives who cannot agree may separate and take up with new mates. There is no way of preserving food, so it must be eaten at once, and therefore will be shared. The kind of agreement which must be executed at a distance is unknown. The moral relation of savages does extend in time, as regards parents and children; but instinct takes care of that, except in extremity. Where the burden of the aged becomes impossible to manage on the natural basis, the old are abandoned to die. Hence the idea of tenure, in savage life, is vague and pragmatic. Personal articles are in possession. Territorial usage is elastic. Otherwise, first come, first served, and finders are keepers, serve as working rules. In hunting, whoever sees game has a right to kill it. The absent can have no claim.

But animal husbandry, even if it be nothing but herding the beasts on wild pastures, involves a time-space relation of human beings. All property, which is ownership, is a claim through time. The beasts must be watched; they may not be killed nor the product consumed except by the owners. The time-space factor is likewise introduced by primitive agriculture, between sowing and harvest, imposing a claim on plots of ground and seed to be preserved. Hence the barbarians conceded positive power to their chief; his word would be enforced, not only immediately but at a distance, as long as it was in accord with custom and property rights.

To avoid a break in authority, that is, in the time relation, the hereditary principle came in. Its odd variations, such as matrilineal succession and in some places inheritance by the youngest instead of the elder child ("borough English"), are what might be called engineering devices to gear the system over the shortest space and distance by the physical connection obviously existent. The relation of a child to its mother is indisputable; and the youngest child would still be at home when the elder children might have gone out and become independent. In either case, the force obeys the moral sanction.

However, the hereditary system cannot be invariable; nature again forbids that finality.* The succession may fail, or if it falls to an infant, it becomes temporarily ineffectual and liable to be disputed. For these emergencies some re-

* When it was urged that the good of the realm required Henry VIII to put away his queen and re-marry in order to beget a son as heir to the throne, an objector asked: "Who hath promised him a son?"

course resembling elective choice must be posited. Even with the "divine" dynasty of medieval Japan, though the throne was reserved to one line of descent, the principle was blurred because monogamy did not obtain; and by custom the emperor abdicated after a short and nominal reign, when a new incumbent was selected by the great nobles from a number of candidates of royal blood. In the Ottoman empire, the death of the Sultan meant a sudden grab for power by whichever of his offspring or kin had enough backing; then the new Sultan promptly exterminated all other pretenders, murdering his brothers, nephews, and uncles out of hand. There is nothing novel in the "blood purges" of rivals by modern dictators. Wherever a legitimate means of political succession is not provided, it must occur. And the form of voting is not enough; if the energy of the nation has been subverted, so that elections are controlled from above, bought by the use of tax money, this resort to violence will soon be made.

Since the elective principle exists in the nature of things, underlying monarchy, whenever monarchy becomes too oppressive, the elective principle is called in. Whatever makes kings can unmake them. In Europe, though feudal monarchy was the prevailing usage for a thousand years, and had the triple support of embodied custom, military command, and the family pattern of society, yet the pretension of kings to rule by divine right and exercise absolute power was never for a moment conceded in theory by any nation, nor long tolerated in fact without overt rebellion. Resistance was constant; and in the last resort, assassination was the answer. And it is a genuine refutation of the royal encroachment in its own terms, no less logical than regicide by legal deliberation which indicts the king for treason. In theory, the noble (as head of family) was noble by status, being born to his position; the king was king only by contract, "first among his peers." The oath of allegiance, renewed to each king, is a contract. The gravamen of the charge of treason against a king is that he has exceeded his office or proper authority, by usurped force. And in terms of force, one man is about as strong as another. Thus the initial truth is again brought to light whenever a citizen or subject is sufficiently determined; *force cannot compel obedience in the social order*. What it can effect is death, whether of subject or king.

When the assassin is otherwise sane, and acting from a strictly political grievance, assassination is a symptom of a grave imperfection in the mechanism, a relatively weak connection, or a point of disproportionate stress, where a break occurs. In terms of mechanism, it stops the machine until the broken part has been replaced; but it does not and cannot institute a better type of mechanism. At the given moment, government is nonexistent, and has to be resumed by a moral act, the acceptance of a new incumbent. Such recurrent breakdowns naturally weaken the moral sanction. But in this also they reveal the relation of government to force. A dead subject is no longer subject; and a dead king is no longer king. Where force is the arbiter, government ceases.

This is so because of the intrinsic nature of the political mechanism, which is and must be the same whatever the form. *It is an instrument of negation,* and nothing more. When government begins to rely upon force or intimidation, if the various factors involved could be discovered exactly, and expressed in a mathematical equation with the ratio of the increase of force, the sum would give the length of time remaining before either the government or the nation, or both, must collapse. The event must depend upon the volume of energy in use for production, and the type of government imposed, as regards structure, mechanism, and dead load. If the energy is sufficient to shatter the structure and mechanism, it must do so (by war, civil war, revolution). Unless liberty is regained, the mode of conversion of energy will revert to a lower level, and the population will be reduced by war and famine to the lower optimum which can be subsisted at that level. This process is now going on in Europe. The prime cause was the introduction of a high energy potential—industrial development—in Germany, when the political form could not accommodate it. While industry got up steam, during the nineteenth century, political changes were in reverse, more and more power accruing to government under "socializing" measures. The present explosion is the result.

An attempt to revert to a type of association suited to a lower potential of energy will bring this about. The informal advisory method suits a nomadic savage society. In such conditions, the lack of tenure of the chief is salutary. An unfortunate choice has a quick remedy. Leadership is obliged to justify itself daily. In a settled and productive society, leadership is completely impracticable, because continuity is necessary, with the time-space factor in economics. The two cannot exist together, because the essential characteristic of leadership, the bloodless deposition of the leader by the dropping away of his following, has been lost. With permanent institutions, the form of government must include fixed tenure; this does not mean irremovable persons, but the contrary; it means legitimate change of persons in an office of defined powers. When "leadership" is attempted instead, what can occur is a degenerate and temporary manifestation, the rule of popularity, by which the permanent institutions are subverted to make the leader irremovable. The characteristics of both are thus negated, cancelling out the moral element, as evidenced by the leader denying his own credentials by an immediate resort to force and intimidation.

In terms of mechanism, the control is disconnected, the motor is still running. The consequence is external collision and internal disruption, more or less simultaneously. A regime of popularity is effective for starting a war; and indeed must do so. If the energy and mechanism engaged are those of a productive society with a considerable surplus capacity, the regime is likely to begin with an appearance of enormous success in aggression, the march of an Alexander or a Napoleon, to end by disintegrating in civil war and possibly subjection to a foreign power. The two things are different aspects of the same physical phenomenon, of dislocated mass crashing by momentum, shattering whatever is in its way and likewise breaking apart of its own weight and impact. The Napoleonic empire was such a swathe of destruction.* A century earlier, Louis XIV laid the train for it. His minister Colbert fostered industry under monopoly, which enabled Louis to reduce the aristocratic order to impotence and transfer the mechanism of government to a bureaucracy. Thus the ancient structure of France was rendered obsolete, but it still remained as dead-load, and so held the nation more or less stationary, frustrating the effort of Louis to get the mass in motion through his wars. Subsequently, when the dead load (which unfortunately served no other purpose) was thrown off—that is, the aristocracy was formally disestablished—the accumulated energy was released and augmented by the proclamation of liberty and equality. But this torrential energy was thrown into a society which did not understand the relation of the mechanism to the base. Napoleon himself was little more than a figurehead hurled about in front of the moving mass. The energy tore the nation apart, flung fragments of it to every corner of Europe in the form of armies, and only subsided by disintegration and inertia. Napoleon was the first of the modern "leaders." What a really high potential can do in that line is painfully evident.

When the word leader, or leadership, returns to current use, it connotes a relapse into barbarism. For a civilized people, it is the most ominous word in any language.

---

* As part of the destruction was of obsolete obstructive institutions, it is not recognized as random destruction, though it certainly was. Millions of men also were destroyed, in mangled heaps.

CHAPTER IX

The Function of Government

Since government and power have always been more or less synonymous, and "machine politics" is a popular phrase, it is remarkable that the political agency has never been examined rigorously in that light, as a specific problem of engineering. When energy is used in a mechanism the result must be in accord with the type of machine. The source of the energy can be known; the nature of the mechanism is easily discovered in action; and it is absurd to expect any other action than that of which the parts in combination are capable. Even though a contrivance fails to work at all, or effects only destruction, the laws of energy and mechanism have not altered nor varied; the fault is in the appliance. But this has not been fully understood in relation to human affairs, for various reasons implicit in the development of human intelligence.

First, energy is a natural phenomenon, calling for no abstract definition at that stage of human association in which energy operates only through the units and modes of conversion found in nature.

Second, in mechanical engineering, dealing with inanimate objects, the prime consideration is so obvious that it does not need to be postulated or given a separate value in conscious calculation. This is the factor of the underlying base. The physical earth is the base of all mechanism. The engineer need only choose a spot and level or solidify it to permit the engine to rest upon it, and of course he must balance, weight, or clamp down his machine so that it will not turn turtle. But he knows the earth is there; all his calculations have that factor included as a distributed component; mass, weight, extension, stresses, volume, are measures established *from* the base.

Third, in mechanical engineering, which is confined to material terms, the source of energy is designated; a unit can be determined, and the transmission and load proportioned to the flow. Every factor is capable of measurement.

Finally, and most important in that it obscures the nature of government, *physics has no name for the exact function which is delegated to government.* It is something which *does not exist* in any manifestation of energy through inanimate material. It is peculiar to living creatures. Energy is pre-existent in the universe, and cannot be created out of nothing; but in a specific energy circuit, it is possible to designate an approximate point at which a moiety of the universal energy is introduced to the circuit; this is the dynamo, generator, converter, or motor. In the social organization, man is the dynamo, in his productive capacity. Government is an end-appliance, and a dead end in respect of the energy it uses. Now in principle a mechanism composed of inanimate material, utilizing energy, is wholly calculable. A motor of a certain power will propel a certain load on a certain gradient; if the power is cut off, mass and momentum will determine its stopping point on the level, or an obstacle of a certain resistance will stop it. No similar prediction can be made of the actions of a human being functioning as such. True, his muscular strength can be measured; but while he is moving about under his own power it is not possible to measure and predict what will cause him to start, stop, turn, or accelerate. That depends on what he thinks, a non-measurable factor.

He has a faculty for which no equivalent is found in the processes of inanimate nature. He is self-starting, and *he can inhibit himself.*

Energy is the medium of life. An infant is able to move its limbs and absorb nourishment (fuel) when it is born; it grows up in instinctive spontaneous activity and gains the requisite control simultaneously. Thus "in nature" the energy, the mechanism, and the control appear as one, and the individual can function without defining them separately or abstractly. Neither do the social and economic relations of savages necessitate any such distinction. External contacts call the several factors into operation as one. Necessity is immediate; there are practically no deferred consequences, so far as the savage is aware. Since he cannot lay up provision for the future, it is prudent for him to gorge when food is plenty, and thus store up some energy in his body. If he meets a grizzly bear, or quarrels with one of his fellows, he must make the instant decision to fight or run away. He executes his own justice, if there be any, either individually or by a committee of the whole. If he has any form of shelter, he carries it with him. In these matters he is dealing with cause and effect, which are the factors of engineering; but they do not include transactions over time and space. On the other hand, in personal relations, even the savage will recognize intentions as qualifying to some degree the appropriate response or retaliation. An intention is an imponderable; it belongs to a non-mathematical order of abstractions. Thus, though it is a proper consideration in human relations, it must delay formulation of the principles of physics, or engineering. The absence of this distinction is the main difference between primitive and scientific thought; and is a sufficient explanation of the origin of the belief in magic. Since it is possible for one person to propitiate another, or persuade him to action, by means of words, it is not altogether irrational, though mistaken, to imagine that beasts, or objects, or disease, or the weather, might be influenced by a similar approach. This unfortunate assumption is almost inextricably embedded in the mental habits of mankind. Science begins by barring it from the field where it is irrelevant. Science is aware that inanimate objects do not heed what is said to them, nor care about intentions. Yet the name of science has been used to carry the error one step further, into a sequence where it is even more subtly false and difficult to eradicate, with the proposition that man is no more than a physical mechanism; and that since he *may* be induced to release his energy by words or compulsion, he must needs respond infallibly by formula if previously "conditioned," as the machine must answer to controls. What is forgotten is the fact that even if regarded as mechanism, man is a genuinely automatic machine, self-starting and self-acting, in the sense that no inanimate mechanism can be automatic.

He is so by virtue of initiative and the inhibitory faculty. Initiative is life itself. Complete inhibition is death. Yet a living creature incapable of inhibiting itself would speedily destroy itself.

As has been seen, the inhibitions required by savage life are directly operative, just as the result of initiative returns directly to the individual. The hunter makes a weapon for himself, keeps it in possession, eats the game he kills; and his woman makes the hide into clothing. In civilization, the processes of getting food and shelter are protracted. It takes at least a year's foresight to cultivate the soil and reap the fruits; grain has to go to the mill, hides to the tanner, textiles to the weaver, before they are ready for use. When a civilized man builds a house, the plans must be laid out and materials assembled over a considerable period, and paid for by savings involving exchange of labor with many other persons. He must therefore impose restraints on himself for objectives distant in time and needing to be directed through space. He lives in the past and future as well as the present. His initiative will be wasted unless he also inhibits himself; and further, he must be able to count upon others who participate in the exchange to observe like long-term inhibitions. At an early stage in trade it becomes inconvenient to depend upon barter of goods from the hand of one owner to another. With objects of unequal worth, or in a series of exchanges, or in case of deferred deliveries, a medium of value is wanted; this is money. And throughout the series, a succession of inhibitions must be maintained; otherwise at some point the goods will be consumed and no return made. The energy circuit is broken.

This is why savages have no occasion for formal government, while it is necessary to civilization. For a civilized economy, which consists of production and exchanges in a sequence extending through time and space, there must be an agency to witness long-term contracts and see that they are fulfilled in the absence of either of the parties, or to enforce an agreed penalty in case of default. The appropriate authority for this purpose is therefore delegated to government.

As the word indicates, the inhibitory faculty is a function of the individual; strictly speaking, it cannot be delegated. No faculty can be delegated. One man may bestow the product of his labor and talent upon another voluntarily; one man may deprive another of his product by force or fraud; or men may trade their labor or product. But a man cannot transfer his strength or intelligence to another man's physical frame. What can be done, in case an individual fails to inhibit himself as he has agreed to do, or if he infringes the liberty or takes the property of another, is to exact a forfeit or impose external restraints; and officials can be empowered by delegated authority to execute the seizure. By the same means, such officials can take a cut from production, in taxes, to support themselves and pay the expenses of their organization. That is what government does, and all it can do. It is a prohibitory and expropriative agency. Its type of mechanism necessarily corresponds to its function.

Exception will be taken to the above statement if the whole process is not kept in view. The following quotation is a clear and concise exposition of the point at which misunderstanding occurs. "The governor of a steam engine is not merely a prohibitory mechanism, but turns on more steam when needed; and various electric controls work the same way; why cannot political government so function? The Lewis and Clark and other government exploring expeditions in the West were not prohibitory actions. The role the government played in the development of the Western public lands was not merely prohibitory."

When the governor of a steam engine turns on more steam, obviously the steam (energy) must be there to turn on; and it must have been previously confined. The governor has no part in getting up steam, producing energy; and as mechanism it is a release instrument, which implies previous restraint. A prohibitory mechanism can be so made that it will subsequently let go; a brake can be lifted after it has been applied, or take effect only when some force rises against it, so that the pressure lessens if the force subsides. Contract law is a self-adjusting brake of this type. But the function of the brake is nevertheless prohibitory. In such a single mechanism no "function" can be attributed to the cessation of the function. The governor of the steam engine, or the electric control, as described, are different; the confusion arises from the term "governor." If it must be used, the exact statement of their function is that they govern the government; they place a limitation on government. In a political organization, this function is performed by a constitution, which establishes a limit beyond which government has no legitimate power.

To ascertain what was the action of government, its peculiar function, in such a sequence of actions as that of the Lewis and Clark expedition, let all the factors and conditions be noted. The wilderness was there, in the order of nature. Many private persons had explored a great deal of it. The knowledge and skill of the two named explorers had been developed by themselves. Why did they go to the government before making their expedition? To obtain funds and an official commission. What did the government do that Lewis and Clark could not do? Expropriate funds from other private persons, by taxes. The supplies for the expedition came from private production. The *action of government* was merely expropriative. The official commission was the preliminary notice of a prohibitory claim on the territory traversed. Later private individuals went out at their own expense and did the work of bringing the land under cultivation. The government exercised its prohibitory function to record and enforce the terms on which individuals could establish title to any part of the land. It was for that purpose the prohibitory function was delegated to government in the first place, to establish titles of record; but it is a prohibitory power and nothing else. Its "grant" is a stamped release. Whenever and wherever the government intervenes in a sequence of actions, it does so with an authorized act of prohibition or expropriation. Whatever else it may "do" is merely an act of release, a cessation of function. That is its nature and function and type of mechanism. This is no less true if it is said that "the government builds a dam," or any other construction. The government expropriates funds and hires persons to do the work. The peculiar action of government is the act of expropriation.* Private persons can and do build dams, but they cannot expropriate funds. Despotic governments, such as that of Egypt when the pyramids were built, expropriate energy at the source by compulsion of persons, forced labor.

Where several factors operate in a sequence of actions, the

* The post office is usually pointed out as the prize example of government undertaking; but postal service depends entirely on the means of conveyance invented and operated by private enterprise. It is the simplest form of business imaginable, pure routine; yet, even as a government monopoly, it always runs at a deficit; and the lucrative appointments go by party favor, the biggest job being awarded to a man whose time is mainly occupied with collecting votes. Good roads exist only by reason of private enterprise progress in materials and machinery. City water supplies were first provided by private enterprise, and expropriated by government. For centuries government fostered disease, discomfort, and gloom by window taxes, hearth taxes, salt taxes. Private enterprise dug the Suez Canal and provided the machinery, knowledge, and skill to dig the Panama Canal. Always and everywhere, progress has been made solely by private invention, enterprise, labor, and savings, and in inverse ratio to the extent of government.

function of each can be defined only by elimination. That which invariably occurs when a given factor is present, and does not occur in its absence, must be its function.

Let any sequence of actions in which government is involved be examined. The first thing government does and must do is to issue an edict or pass a law. No edict or law can impart to an individual a faculty denied him by nature. A government order cannot mend a broken leg, but it can command the mutilation of a sound body. It cannot bestow intelligence, but it can forbid the use of intelligence. What is the prime provision to put a law in effect? There must be an "enabling clause," and an enabling clause is one which appropriates money or materials from taxes laid upon private resources, in cash or kind or labor. A private person who seizes the goods of another is a criminal; this action is reserved to government. Likewise, government by its judiciary branch may try persons accused of capital crimes and put them to death. It is in the physical power of individuals to kill one another; but it is never held to be their right to do so unless in self-defense (of which vengeance is felt to be an extension). That a man may not be the judge of his own cause, it is thought proper to depute authority for vengeance, and so far as possible to supply aid in self-defense. That is the power of death. The power of life cannot be deputed or delegated. Government then is solely an instrument or mechanism of appropriation, prohibition, compulsion, and extinction; in the nature of things it can be nothing else, and can operate to no other end.

Its exact definition in action shows how accurate was the phrase "a necessary evil." Seen in this light, it is so horrific—and its actual operations in the past have been so horrible at times—that there is some excuse for failure to realize the necessity. But that also must be acknowledged, to discover its extent. Government is certainly necessary for economic relations over time and space; the necessity derives from the necessity of the inhibitory faculty in the individual. But the basic error of the authoritarian or statist premise consists of making these public and private necessities co-extensive. Government is a marginal requirement, necessary only in so far as the individual inhibitory faculty is not exercised according to agreement and natural right (equal liberty). Beyond that differential, government is an enthronement of paralysis and death. Hence the perversion of logic which affirms that the citizen exists only "for the state" and has no individual right to live. In fact, life can exist only in its own right; i.e., it is ridiculously futile for the state (or anyone) to order a man to live, if his faculties fail him; nor can a life be created by order. The creative processes do not function to order. But death can be ordered. Thus government is secondary, instituted by agreement; life, which pertains to the individual, is primary. Government is an agent, not an entity.

This has to be re-stated, for the simple meaning of the statement that the right to life and liberty are inalienable has been forgotten or deliberately obscured. Persons unaccustomed to attach exact meanings to words will say that the fact that a man may be unjustly executed or imprisoned negates this proposition. It does not. The right is with the victim none the less; and very literally it cannot be alienated, for alienated means passing into the possession of another. One man cannot enjoy either the life or liberty of another. If he kills ten men he will not thereby live ten lives or ten times as long; nor is he more free if he puts another man in prison. Rights are by definition inalienable; only privileges can be transferred. Even the *right* to own property cannot be alienated or transferred; though a given item of property can be. If one man's rights are infringed, no other man obtains them; on the contrary, all men are thereby threatened with a similar injury.

There is no collective good. Strictly speaking, there is not even any common good. There are in the natural order conditions and materials through which the individual, by virtue of his receptive and creative faculties and volition, is capable of experiencing good. Let it be asked, is not sunlight a common good? No; persons do not enjoy the benefit by community, but singly. A blind man cannot see by community. The same degree of sunshine may induce sunstroke in one person while another derives benefit from it; although incidentally, it will not even be the same ray of sunlight which falls on both. Alexander the Great, with the power of empire at his command, asked Diogenes: "Is there anything I can do for you?" Diogenes replied: "You can stand aside from between me and the sunlight." Man as an individual is capable of experiencing and inflicting both good and evil, having choice, and also incidental liability to error in judgment. Allowing for error, good is obtained by reception and mastery of the forces of nature, and through voluntary association of individuals in equal free choice. But even in such voluntary relations of individuals, it is possible for one person to receive pleasure while another experiences pain; there is no collective sum or equation of good. "The greatest good of the greatest number" is a vicious phrase; for there is no unit of good which by addition or multiplication can make up a sum of good to be divided by the number of persons. Jeremy Bentham, having adopted the phrase, spent the rest of his life trying to extract some meaning from his own words. He meandered into almost incredible imbecilities, without ever perceiving why they couldn't mean anything. If ten men enjoy playing checkers and only one enjoys a symphony, which is the greatest good in sum? and if a choice must be made which shall be provided, and the symphony could be proved to be eleven times as "good" as the checkers, what then? the allotment must be either the greatest good to the lesser number or the lesser good to the greatest number. In any case, it is impossible to disguise the fact that good accrues only to individuals (the "number" gives that away, for it must be the number of persons); but if the good of one person is supposed to equate with the suffering of another, it is monstrous. It would justify abominable tortures of a minority if the majority claimed to benefit thereby; for if "good" is quantitative and makes up a sum by majority, there can be no judge of what is good except the majority. This rule is, in fact, the justification alleged by the Nazis for the extermination of the Jews, as of the Russian Communists for the beastly murder of the most productive members of the population. Both have acted on the same theory.

The fact that there is no collective good does not controvert the fact that man has natural and social relations, which are also of the spiritual order. And it is this spiritual possibility which the collectivist society forbids expression. The Christian society differs fundamentally from previous forms, being organized for the full development of personality. The cleavage is most clearly evident in the institution of marriage. Under the Christian dispensation, a valid marriage can be made by consent of the two parties, and not otherwise; nor can it be nullified by parents, guardians, or the community, against the will of the married couple, because every person is born with a right to a life of his own. And the parental authority, in the Christian society, cannot extend to the power of death or real injury to the child; it is only co-extensive with the necessity of care and nurture, arising from the natural relationship and the moral obligation voluntarily undertaken in marriage. Natural rights and natural obligations, personal rights and personal responsibilities, volition, and the moral sense, are inseparable.

In primitive collectivist societies, parents had the power of death over their children. In modern reversions to this unnatural rule, the same power is allotted to the state. In Japan, the absolutely collective society, the family had the power to force young people into marriage; and indeed there was no way, no legal recognition, of marriage otherwise. Further, divorces could be ordered and enforced by the family; and this might be done for no other reason than that the young couple grew fond of each other. Their personal affection was considered detrimental to the collective interest of the clan-family. Significantly, this feature of collectivism reappeared spontaneously from the same principle, in the Oneida Community, in the United States. To prevent "selfishness," promiscuity was practiced; and if two young people had a strong mutual affection, which was called "special love," it was denounced as anti-social; the young couple were separated and persuaded to change partners frequently. The idea is so revolting that it seems hardly credible, but the thing was done. Always collectivism denounces natural affections and relations and suggests shifting personal obligations onto "society." It promises easy divorce, state support of children, the pleasures of promiscuity; it ends in slavery and violation of personality.

Then as man has the capacity to do or inflict evil deliberately a device is called for which shall cause the action to recoil upon himself, so far as possible. It must be either a static barrier or a reactive mechanism, or both—prohibition and penalty. This power is found in the collective, and authorized in government, to act by law.

The confusion in respect of collective action arises from the initial power of man to do evil, and the consequent nature of law. In proposing any law, the proponent will not realize what he is undertaking unless he asks himself: "Is it my intention to impose restraint or inflict loss or pain on some person in the contingency specified?" Because that is what the law must do. The question follows: "Does the contingency arise from the initial action of that person inflicting injury or loss upon another by intent or negligence?" It is a fundamental error to suppose that a law may do some good and cannot hurt anyone. Whether it does any good or not, a law enforced must hurt someone. The right question is whether or not that person has set the machinery in motion *by first injuring another.*

"The law in its majesty forbids the rich as well as the poor to sleep under bridges," Anatole France wrote. But that is all the law can do, unless it decrees that both rich and poor may not sleep anywhere else, or must sleep in jail. Poverty can be brought about by law; it cannot be forbidden by law. What is called moral legislation must inevitably increase the alleged evil. The only way to prevent prostitution altogether would be to imprison one half of the human race; aside from this, the law can take a share of the prostitute's earnings, with a fine, and thus induce her to earn more and to pay for "protection." The drug traffic is made profitable by prohibition, and thus increased. The acts forbidden are those by which persons injure only themselves; hence the law can only injure them further.

On the other hand, laws which are designed to act in case one person injures another willfully do not necessarily afford any inducement to the perpetrator to continue in his course. If the law forbids murder, it may not be able to prevent murder altogether, but the reasonable presumption is that it must be deterrent. The law can also exact restitution of stolen property—though it must also perform a like action of expropriation by taking a tax on property to enable it to punish thieves. Its limitation is that it must be set or intended to recoil upon an action with like action, evil for evil. Such is the power of the collective, and its use.

Yet it must be borne in mind that the *constituent* element of government is not force; it is the moral faculty which decides and devises the check by which force must recoil on itself. And the moral faculty is in the individual.

CHAPTER X

The Economics of the Free Society

History within nations consists of the struggle of the individual against government; and between nations, of the free economy against the closed economy. These are two aspects of the same process. The primitive life of humanity is a unique phase of natural history, being occupied with the effort of man to master his environment instead of merely adapting himself to it. The use of fire, of hunting weapons, and the taming of animals, come under this head. When he has succeeded in such direct contacts, the next step is to begin changing his environment, by cultivation of the soil, by building permanent shelter and storage, and finally by contriving mechanism for the conversion of energy; these call for time-space organization by delegating authority. But since such authority can only be prohibitive, the problem is to keep this repressive agency subordinate to the creative faculty. The difficulty is enormous; an advanced understanding of engineering principles is required for its solution. In default, the class system developed, an order which places the whole community under arrest,* estops energy at the source, and restricts it to a local circuit. Original thought therefore becomes a crime, because it would release energy. Even in a high culture with a class system, the repressive principle exhibits its character by imposing the death penalty for unauthorized opinion, as heresy or treason.

* As lately as the reign of Louis XIV in France it was advisable for a noble about the court to ask leave even to go to his own estate, because he could be imprisoned at the king's pleasure indeterminately without charge or trial by *lettre de cachet*. Or he might instead be forbidden to quit his estate, or to return to Paris.

We see this system returning now, first by degrees and then by blanket orders preventing movement or herding people into concentration camps. Before the world war of 1914, this medieval condition of general arrest had been largely thrown off and half forgotten almost everywhere except in Czarist Russia, which remained a muddle of barbarism, absolutism, and anarchy. The more civilized nations did not require passports, but issued them on request of their citizens merely because they might be called for in such backward regions. The reactionary drift toward status government is also signalized by the persistent discrediting of reason, and the deliberate corruption of language, to prevent communication.

Misuse of language is the means by which the Marxist cult of Communism has done the most serious injury to intelligence. There is a natural obstacle to progress in abstract thought which has often delayed rational inquiry; an erroneous concept or theory may be expressed in terms which embody the error, so that thinking is blocked until the misleading words are discarded from the given context. The ancient classification of earth, air, fire, and water as "elements" was such an error, which had to be abandoned before the elements could be distinguished and denominated as such. The theory of elements was a correct and penetrating guess; but the phenomena assigned were wrong. On the other hand, the notion of the four "humors" of the body was an erroneous theory, which seriously hindered the science of medicine. Likewise the Cartesian theory of "vortices," and the assumption of the existence of a kind of essence of fire or heat, called "phlogiston," were verbal obstacles to extension of knowledge of physics. These are unfortunate fixations of language which the keenest intellects may establish on the borders of the unknown. As they cannot be refuted until something further really is known, while they tend to prevent the advance, they are a more serious handicap than statements which are simply and demonstrably false; yet they occur in the nature of things, and are not immune to reason in the long run.

But the Marxist terminology reduces verbal expression to literal nonsense on the basis of fact and usage; this is not obvious gibberish, nor the humorous nonsense which will sometimes elucidate an intrinsic difficulty of expression or indicate a gap in knowledge, but arrangements of words according to the rules of grammar, in which each word taken separately has a customary meaning, but which in the given sequence, the sentence, mean nothing at all. For example, let it be said that: "An isosceles triangle is green." The several words are in common use, and as parts of speech they are placed in proper order; but the whole statement is absurd. That is bad enough, but it would be rather worse if one spoke of the "roundness of a triangle." The phrase "dictatorship of the proletariat" is like the "roundness of a triangle," a contradiction in terms. It has no meaning. The theory of "dialectical materialism" is a misuse of terms of the same type as the statement that an isosceles triangle is green. It posits an inevitable succession of a thesis producing its opposite or antithesis and the fissiparous abstraction reuniting into a synthesis. As nothing in nature does go through any such transmogrification, endless and senseless debate may be carried on by which social relations are said to exhibit in various phases a thesis, antithesis, and synthesis, each credited with "producing" its "opposite" and merging again into something else, like the Squidgicum Squee that swallers itself. Fools might argue solemnly that an isosceles triangle is not green but blue, or that a green isosceles triangle will produce a blue circle and the two will then synthesize into a purple cow or rhomboid; still these statements are empty. This is specifically the language of fools; for the deficiency which is indicated by the word fool is the incapacity to understand categories and the relation of things and qualities.

Marx was a fool with a large vocabulary of long words. Yet he did have an unacknowledged need to adopt the nonsensical "dialectic" of Hegel. A parasitical pedant, shiftless and dishonest, he wanted to put in a claim on "society" solely as a consumer. He embraced Communism because no other theory can be stretched even on paper into promising "to each according to his needs." Only a presumed "common stock" into which all production is expropriated can be imagined as available for the non-producer to grab what he wants from it, although this is pure imagination, the dream of the incompetent and vicious or of the child mind unschooled in production. On the other hand, Marx was confronted by the historic fact that in Communism as a general order production never rises above a bare subsistence level. How was he then to even imagine abundant production into Communism? He could only assume that the "means of production" brought to a high standard with private property and free individual enterprise, which is capitalism, could be expropriated and kept going by a successor regime of Communism. True, no such thing had ever happened; the nearest approach to Communism as the social norm was always very primitive; but if he first imagined "dialectical materialism," and then arbitrarily called capitalism the thesis; and then designated the unpropertied as the proletarian antithesis, he might further assert that the two would "merge" by conflict and produce a "synthesis" which would have to be Communism if he said so. Since it had never happened, he could say that it was inevitably going to happen. He could also, quite as easily, while he was about it, call the capitalist society of contract the class system although it positively was not.

Marx's theory of class war is utter nonsense by its own definition; it has no reference to either class or war, if it relates to "capital" and "labor." It is physically impossible for "labor" and "capital" to engage in war on each other. Capital is property; labor is men. All that can occur is sporadic rioting and possibly destruction of property, for the very weapons of war in an industrial society can be produced and maintained only by "capital" and "labor" in combination.

In a true class society, classes are the several layers of a stratified order; class is nothing but horizontal *relative position*. Therefore one class cannot *displace* another, nor abolish it by action as a class. When and if classes exist, the persons occupying a given relative position belong to the denominated class. Conceivably the particles might be transposed, but the classes would remain as before—whatever is at the top is at the top, and whatever is below is below. Though invaders might depose the members of an indigenous upper class and occupy the position, neither would this alter the system; and such invasion is not a class war.

But since the class system is imposed on the creative energy to check its flow, it is inevitably liable to internal disturbance. The energy may cause a cleavage between the upper and lower strata, by which they break into violent opposition; this is a genuine class war, and frequently occurred.

Nevertheless, *as such*, a class war can effect no change, and has never done so. Even the transposition of persons as particles from one class to another rarely occurred by violent means. The repeated revolts or jacqueries in feudal society were abortive by their nature—being true class conflicts.

It has been implied—by the statement that gunpowder abolished the Middle Ages—that the peasant was defenseless against the knight. On the contrary, the knight was hopelessly vulnerable to the peasant. A man in armor relying for mobility on a horse in armor could be put out of action, the horse hamstrung, the rider brought down, by one or two quick-footed men with scythes and pitchforks. The knight could scarcely mount unaided; on the ground he was clumsy; if he fell, he could not spring up nimbly. A human tortoise, the knight was equipped only to encounter another knight. He was no less dependent economically. His armor had to be forged by the smith, his food and clothes supplied and his horse maintained by the labor of the peasant. The knight knew no useful art, and was wholly an end-product of a rigid system. If the system were interrupted for more than a very short time, the knight must perish anyhow.*

And in many instances the jacqueries gained an immediate victory by violence. Over considerable localities the peasants slaughtered their lords and took their castles, which they looted and wrecked. Yet they could get no further, and were presently subdued again; nothing could come of it except more severe repression. The majority of the peasants would have no inducement to raise a few of their number to the rank of seigneurs, while all could not attain to it because the order of chivalry necessitated peasants to support it. Acting as a class, the peasants could have no other than the class principle upon which to re-institute society. Hence the jacqueries were bound to be crushed, by the very class principle which united them in their rebellion.

When the society of contract began to emerge again and dissolve the class system, members of all classes and groups fought on both sides, individuals taking part for or against the order. In the French Revolution, the most stubborn defense of the old regime was made in rural Brittany, by the peasants of the Vendée, under a peasant commander. Their stand was unavailing because the weapons of a class society belong to a lower mode of conversion of energy than the weapons of a society of contract. This was the significance of gunpowder; it is the product of a free economy, which does not debar inquiry and invention. It is an instrument or effect, not a cause.

The invention of productive machinery and its continued use is possible only in a free economy, being consonant with

* In recent years, it has been asserted that revolution becomes impossible when a government has machine technology at its disposal, because the unarmed populace is helpless against high-power weapons. On the contrary, the technically equipped army depends absolutely on the uninterrupted free functioning of the civil order for its weapons and supplies. Airplanes and tanks are even more immediately dependent on factory production than the knight was on the blacksmith. And machine production cannot be maintained efficiently by forced labor.

its axioms in relation to energy. The equivalent of the feudal order in the set-up of a machine would be to load the motor with dead-weight so that it could not operate until some of the weight were removed; and to set the brake so that it should be applied whenever the motor started, or rather, immediately before the start. Probably the popular notion today of the medieval economy is that under it the common people were compelled to work very hard. They were certainly subject to forced labor, and their work was performed by slow, exhausting, and unproductive methods; but the real hardship was that they *were not allowed to work otherwise.* Working could be punished as a crime. For example, it was illegal to make, own, or use a handmill at home. (Essentially the same type of penalty has lately been re-introduced with the farm quota tax and the processing tax.) Even the medieval ox-yoke was so ill-designed that when the animal pulled it was somewhat choked. So it was with men; competence and thrift were penalized. The one who tilled the land could never hope to own it; improvements reverted to the seigneur and would be more than likely to ensue additional dues. Further, on the death of a serf, the seigneur seized part of the goods and chattels, as heriot, always taking the best, no matter how little remained for the widow and children. (The re-introduction of death duties, estate taxes, is a reversion to the medieval heriot. At first falling only on large estates, it is rapidly reaching down to the least scrap of inheritance. Heriot was recognized as the mark of the serf.)

In feudal society, when men spoke of rights or liberties, they claimed them as by charter or usage, in either case referring back to a permissive grant in the past, which they must show they had not forfeited by failure to render dues or service. The principle was that a man must pay for license to work or leave to walk about. Finally, restriction of trade limited available materials; people hadn't much to work with.

When the productive element at length regained a measure of natural freedom, they indulged in something like an orgy of work, satisfying a theretofore thwarted craving. Free men drove themselves harder than any seigneur had ever managed to drive his serfs, and produced three times as much even with manual labor, simultaneously devising productive machinery. This unparalleled outburst of energy was beneficial by the increase of goods and of knowledge. But it got under way in Europe while part of the aristocratic structure remained in land tenure. Goods and labor were in the free market, the society of contract; a great deal of the land was not, being entailed and under long lease for ground rents. The landless laborer had nothing to stand on, and was caught, so to speak, between a motor car and a stone wall, or thrown against a rock by a rushing stream. The wage-laborer has never gained a solid footing in Europe. The "mixed economy" invariably includes the onerous features of both status and contract, worsened by combination. In the field of industry, during the early industrial era, the exceptionally shrewd, tough, and capable individuals set the pace for the less able and weaker ones. An employer who got his start by driving himself expected the utmost exertions from the wage-workers he hired. (The margin of compensation was presumed to lie in the chances of the future—but the work was done in the present, and the employer could give no guarantees for the future.) Moreover, the hours of employment were a holdover from the medieval and rural economy, in which men worked from dawn till dark; but the medieval pace was comparatively slow, with slack seasons and as many holidays as the tenants and serfs could win through the church. The free economy quickened the pace, cut down holidays, and kept the long working day, even extending it by artificial light. Yet both the speed-up and low wages were still partly exacted by pressure from the aristocracy, the remains of status. In the full feudal society the seigneurs had to raise and subsist the fighting forces and meet other political costs locally; and the king was supposed to live at his own expense, from his landed property. In the transition period the army and civil list became a national charge, supported by general taxation, while the nobility not only took lucrative offices but drew on industry for ground rents without releasing land to the market for improvement by competitive building. Lord Shaftesbury, the celebrated reformer, admitted privately that he accused the manufacturers though he knew the blame rested equally on the land-owners, because he needed a party to pass his laws. What he did not realize was that he also was acting as an aristocrat, for the "reform" laws he framed, however well-meant, were status law in a new guise.

The gentry also abused their position by grabbing and enclosing the common lands, which had given villagers a modicum of independence, a physical base. In general, while sneering at the profit motive of industry, the gentry never let a penny get by them, whether it came from a slum tenement or a shepherd's hut or even a soldier's food allowance.

Thus the upper class absorbed most of the material benefit of the emerging contract society, and was at the same time relieved of its main duties. The only good which accrued at first to the average workingman was that the door was open; and America existed. (If America had not existed, it is impossible to know whether or not the door would have been forced open.) The free workingman could change his employment, his residence, even his country, if he had courage for the venture.

Yet this possibility was enough, a sufficient number of persons availing themselves of it, in the course of a century, to raise the level of wages and opportunity, of cleanliness and comfort and convenience, to a standard which would have seemed fabulous to the medieval seigneur. Working hours were likewise shortened; the drive was transferred to machinery; freedom yielded its fruits. Now, with the contemporary decrease of liberty, hours are already lengthening even in America; production is lessening; and the speed-up is being re-imposed on men instead of machines.

The deadlock of class can be broken either by reverting through barbarism (leadership) to savagery, or by advancing to the political organization appropriate to the society of contract. But the advance could not be made until a structure had been erected to accommodate the mechanism, including the type of control which is used in motor mechanics by the various applications known as safety devices, whether brakes, governors, or stabilizers. The essential feature of such appliances is that they do not and cannot take effect until the actual need arises. They are set to operate only if the motor and transmission goes wrong. A railway airbrake locks the wheels if the coupling gives way; a safety valve opens at the danger point of steam pressure; a fuse blows out with an overload of current, saving the wires; a gyroscope is neutral while the plane is in balance. What must be borne in mind is that these are not *preventive* controls, but corrective; they are not primary but secondary.

Contract law is the same type of mechanism in the political organization. The legal restriction does not occur until after individuals have made a voluntary contract and one of the parties fails to carry out its terms. Contract law has no primary authority, no jurisdiction unless invoked by the individual; and then it can take cognizance only of the point at issue, which is determined by the previous agreement of individuals. It is indisputably nothing but an agency, initiative being vested in the individual.

It is the only method of organization which leaves the creative faculty and corollary productive processes their inherent and necessary freedom. The political instrument must be of a secondary character.

But any type of organization predicates a permanent base. It must have fixed locality for its structure. This is true even of mechanisms expressly designed for mobility; an airplane requires a base no less than an old-fashioned grist-mill. The landing-field is the base of the plane; but in a larger view, the plane is part of the transmission line of a very long-circuit energy system which rests on the base of private property as an institution. It has to be individual private property; neither group property nor state communism can generate such a high potential of energy. The collectivist nations of today (Russia, Italy, Germany, Japan) are operating airplanes on energy taken off at the *end* of a long-circuit of energy generated in free economies in the recent past.

The problem of structure for a political organization delayed the founding of a full Society of Contract for thousands of years. The first political structure men were able to find or devise was that of an aristocracy. Though it must have begun as an extension of the family (unwarranted in nature), it was later supposed to be validated by a concept or theory which had even less relation to fact. The noble came to be regarded, or regarded himself, as of a superior species, elevated to his position by a semi-mystical, semi-physical difference from the peasant or commoner, a difference of "blood" confirmed by divine ordinance. Biology can discover no evidence to bear out this theory; for though a noble family may have been founded by some person of exceptional talent, it does not breed true; the descendants revert to the average. Furthermore, the line was frequently broken, and the blood mixed with that of recruits from the presumedly inferior lower ranks. Finally, aristocracies have been disestablished, and no mystical divinity intervened in their favor. It is impossible to define in rational terms just what the aristocratic quality was thought to be. That epitome of the order, the Duke de Saint-Simon, who "believed" in it fanatically, described many of his fellow nobles as scoundrels, imbeciles, lunatics, cowards, liars, toadies, pimps, wastrels, and profligates, deformed, diseased, ugly, feeble, disloyal, and otherwise useless or detrimental; yet his faith remained unshaken.

And there was a fact beneath the fantasy. Though it was obsolete in France when observed by Saint-Simon, and so doubly corrupted, aristocracy in its time had a practical use. It delimited the fixed bases for a political structure, by local sovereignty of territorial subdivisions. The original titles, privileges, and offices of the great nobles were attached to particular areas of land and inseparable from them.

It was not the class solidarity of an aristocracy which enabled it to serve as structure, but the separateness of the units, a system of decentralization. The bitter indictments of aristocracies were true enough; the order is oppressive not merely by abuse but in principle. However romancers may prettify the picture in retrospect, the seigneur was not above extorting cash to permit a girl to get married or a boy to learn to read, or taking the bereaved widow's one cow and best bed; a regular perquisite of the lord of the manor was the manure from the livestock of the tenantry. The aristocracy blocked out light and air. It was bound to evoke hatred, the emotional expression of frustrated energy. The mechanism of government it used, status law, is that of the preventive clutch. Its social atmosphere is tinged with despair; during the Dark Ages, when aristocracy prevailed, men had visions of death and hell and the end of the world, misery here and hereafter. But men tolerated it sullenly because they did not know what to put in its place. If they pulled down the pillars of the structure, the roof fell on them. They had to have some local form to resist both the barbarians and the centralized bureaucracy which had delivered them to the barbarians. Complete stagnation was obviated by the flow of energy channeled through the modified contract society of the church, with some concurrent trade; and it is no accident that commerce was carried on in the shelter of the cathedral. The church also preserved learning, since the written word is indispensable to a long-circuit energy system.

So the forces of static and of kinetic energy effected an uneasy accommodation, though in constant peril from within and without.

CHAPTER XI

The Meaning of Magna Carta

In the long run, England was to make the most successful adjustment in the Old World, but not without a continuous struggle and recurrrent crises of violence, over five centuries. The first crucial effort of the English to set the foundations of an enduring structure is marked by Magna Carta, exacted from King John by his rebel subjects. The provisions of this great document are seldom mentioned today, excepting the sentence: "To none will we sell, to none will we deny, to none will we delay right or justice." Certainly this is admirable, defining abstractly the essential purpose for which government is instituted; but given merely as a promise from the chief executive, the king, it was unlikely to be observed unless the whole organization was designed to work that way against the king's will. Now even without the contemporary context, the practical features of the Charter still reveal what were the existing bases and the forces in motion. The static political structure was feudal. The larger towns, having obtained their "liberties," contributed to the national treasury through various money taxes, direct or indirect, and levied somewhat irregularly, therefore liable to dispute. The church was in a dangerous intermediate position, being interlocked with feudalism by the system of land tenure on its immense properties, while in doctrine it asserted and protected the primary principle of contract by which trade was carried on. Necessarily also the long energy circuit of the church, its connection with Rome, was maintained in money, funds remitted to Rome; this could not have been done any other way.

The original authority of the English monarchy derived wholly from the feudal order, which contains its own checks and balances, automatically regulated by the limited energy circuit; the surplus could only be delivered to the king in men-at-arms and their supplies. But in King John's time a considerable share of the customary feudal service dues had been commuted into cash fees. These, added to the crown revenues from trade, gave the king a money income, over which the producers had no control. They could neither stop supplies at the source except by forcible resistance, nor exercise any legal check on the king's expenditures after the money had been paid into his hands. Thus the king could raise and subsist an army composed of men detached from regional bases, fragments of dislocated mass, into which the kinetic energy of the nation was diverted to put them in motion. Here is the formula for wars apparently initiated by the will of a king, executive, or dictator; the hook-up ensues the result, and can operate to no other end. King John had such a mercenary army, partly recruited abroad, as indicated by the clause of the Charter requiring him to "remove out of the kingdom all foreign knights, crossbowmen and stipendiary soldiers, who have come with horses and arms to the molestation of the kingdom."

In historical references, the gaining of the Charter is usually credited to "the Barons"; but in fact the document was written or drafted by the Archbishop of Canterbury, Stephen Langton; and the names which lead all the rest in the preamble are those of the dignitaries of the Church, being the Archbishops of Canterbury and Dublin, seven bishops, the Master of the Templars, and the papal legate; while the first clause exacts that "the English Church shall be free," including "freedom of elections" to clerical offices. This was to prevent the king from making appointments to abbeys and benefices, through which he could siphon off the revenues of the church. Obviously he had been doing so.

Next the interest of the feudal aristocracy was to be

guarded against the royal or central power, by fixing the dues on military fiefs at the traditional rate; and leaving the assessment of cash fees and extraordinary "aids" to "the common council of the kingdom." Similar dues or aids taken by the lords from "their own free men" were also limited. The general purpose was to prevent the gradual expropriation of small holders by the lords of the manors, and of the lords by the king; that is, to maintain the regional bases against the central authority, and the individual bases against the regional authorities. Since these constituted the static frame of the political organization, the problem had at least been correctly apprehended, although it would not have been expressed in our terms.

But taxation is not the only means by which kinetic energy may break down static structure. As no method of maintaining regional bases was thought possible other than by hereditary succession to land, one clause of the Charter exempted land from passing by title through foreclosure of mortgage. Land could be pledged as security for a loan; but in default, only the revenues might be sequestrated toward payment of the debt. Further, if the debtor died and the heir was a minor, interest on the mortgage ceased during his minority. Feudal dues, dower rights, and provision for children of the deceased debtor, also took precedence of payment on a money debt, which could be liquidated only "out of the residue." Probably this limitation of debt had a double effect, partly contrary to its intent, especially with the short life expectancy of those days; it would tend to keep down the principal of loans, and equally to raise the interest rate. The high usury of the period should be understood in this context.

Then a curious clause indicates the centripetal effect of kinetic energy thrown into the political channel; for the Charter contains a promise from the king that if any man died in debt "to the jews," or money lenders, "and if that debt shall fall into our hands, we will not take anything except the chattel contained in the bond." It is obvious that property owners were apt to borrow more than they could conveniently pay; and that the money lenders, finding collections difficult, especially against the estates of minors, had been discounting their notes with the king, who could then use the royal prerogative to foreclose. The persecution and expulsion of the Jews from various European nations, and the lingering resentment in anti-Semitism, traces mainly to this unhappy combination of the power of the executive and the action of kinetic energy (money) undermining the static structure. As it was easy to focus popular anger on "the jews" as non-citizens, the king invariably and promptly turned against them when it was convenient to exculpate himself and loot their fortunes. But the process had no relation whatever to the nationality or race of the persons involved; it occurred at other times in other countries when the financiers were of native stock, and the public fury was just as easily aroused against finance, or financiers as a group, for the same intrinsic reason. The true remedy for such an injurious condition is to strengthen the regional bases and limit the control and absorption of the national finances by the central executive. That is what the Charter was intended to do; with a wisdom in advance of the age, it did not propose either penalization or expulsion of "the jews" or financiers, but restriction of the authority of the crown. Here it may be said that at any time when finance is under attack through the political authority, it is an infallible sign that the political authority is already exercising too much power over the economic life of the nation through manipulation of finance, whether by exorbitant taxation, uncontrolled expenditure, unlimited borrowing, or currency depreciation.

The final and not least vital restriction of the executive authority (the king) is of peculiar significance, as showing that the industrial-commercial group must have been strongly influential in the framing of Magna Carta, though not named as parties to the formal act. For there was a third method by which the king could find a pretext for expropriation of his subjects of every degree; that is, by exorbitant fines on trumped-up charges. To prevent this, it was stipulated that fines might be "amerced" only in proportion to the offense; with the still more vital exception of "saving" to the free man his "contenement" (landholding); to a merchant his merchandise; and to the villein his wainage (farm carts and other equipment). That is to say, no man could be stripped of his capital, and thus of his livelihood, by a fine, for an alleged political offense. As a solid precaution, it was stated that the amount of such fines might not be fixed by the king nor even by the judges; but must be assessed by a jury of the accused man's peers, nobles for nobles and "honest men of the vicinage" for merchants, freemen, and villeins. Further, the interest of industry and commerce was safeguarded by a clause so far in advance of today's usage that it gives one a shock of surprise. "All merchants shall have safety and security in coming into England and going out of England, and in staying and traveling through England, by land as by water, to buy and sell, without any unjust exactions." In time of war, foreign merchants of enemy nationality might be "apprehended without injury to their bodies and goods," and must be held in safety if English merchants in enemy countries were "in safety there." Finally, "it shall be lawful to any person, for the future, to go out of the kingdom and to return, safely and securely, unless it be in time of war, for some short space," excepting only "prisoners and outlaws" and enemy nationals. The kinetic energy was allowed to make the long circuit; and England was on the way to world power.

On the whole, it is impossible to imagine a sounder grasp of statecraft than Magna Carta reveals, given the existing set-up and circumstances. It was rightly looked to for five centuries as a beacon and a landmark of English liberty. Its principles and some of its practical measures remained in effect to some degree permanently, in spite of abuses and the interruptions of temporary tyranny. Yet since it did not actually terminate the civil war which brought it forth, nor prevent similar and protracted disorders subsequently, it must be instructive to discover in what feature it was defective. One may say that probably, given the circumstances, nothing better could have been devised; for if it did not take full effect at the time, it laid down some indispensable axioms for future reference. The defect was the absence of the mass-inertia veto, as a national function, both in fact and in law. The enforcement of the Charter against the king was assigned to an elective committee of twenty-five barons, who "with the community of the whole land" were to seize the person, family, castles, and lands of the king, but without harming him (the latter condition would naturally be rather difficult at any time and might be impossible). They were to detain him until he redressed grievances and then resume their allegiance; another doubtful chance. What was wrong with this scheme in terms of material organization was that in the strictly feudal order the serfs and other workers on the land constituted the factor of mass, and the function of mass was exerted passively, by inertia, through the inherent limitation which feudalism imposed on production, and which restricted the feudal military effort to the resources of local circuits. The check on the king was a secondary effect.

In brief, as the barons were the "pillars of the state" resting on regional bases, their resistance should have been static to correspond with their relation to the crown. But this was impossible when the king had large revenues from the mercantile interest; while active resistance from the nobles was simply civil war. (For the same reason, the lack of legitimate control over supplies they provided, the merchants were driven to civil war against the king in the seventeenth century.) Anyhow, one can think of no measure possible at the time the Great Charter was framed, by which the general factor of mass could have been found for the whole nation and its function legitimately represented in the national government. Unhappily, even the immediate emancipation of the serfs would not have supplied this deficiency of the mass-veto and ensured stability; on the contrary, if they had merely been released from the land, the action would have thrown more men into the wage-army of the king, to smash the nation. The whole land title-system would have had to be altered, to provide individual holdings; and such a thing cannot be done overnight, and re-secured the next day firmly on a new apportionment. The procedure is impossible because it would have to be done by political edict, therefore even if it were nominally essayed, it would actually vest title in the political power and not in the individuals to whom the transfer was supposed to be made. That is, whatever power was assumed to be sufficient to take land from one person and give it to another could forever after take it back at will, and so would always have the real disposal of the land.

Thus the serfs got next to nothing in the Charter, beyond the reservation of their farming tools from fines. But the nobles, the merchants, and the yeomen got their positions on record, as validated by previous custom and law, and with the means to make a stand sufficiently secured, so that they could persist in opposition to the royal power until they did forge the necessary instrument of the mass-veto. That was to be the House of Commons, with its control over taxation and the periodic grant of supplies. In the course of that long struggle, serfdom was abolished, bought out piece-meal. Money, kinetic energy, washed it away.

There was an unexpected deflection, a side-swirl of the current of energy, as an almost immediate result of the sign-ing of the Charter. King John had been successively at odds with the nobles, the church, and the merchants, until they combined against him with the Charter. He then made a deal with the Pope, by which he was to be absolved from his signatory oath; and in exchange, he vowed temporal al-legiance to the Pope as his feudal lord, by which he pretended to bring in the whole kingdom as a fief. But there was no law nor principle of law, canonical or civil, which could cover such a transaction. True that church dignitaries could be lords of the manor, either by their own holdings or in virtue of church lands; and there were prince-bishops in Europe to whom temporal lords owed feudal allegiance. And the man who was king of England, if he were also lord of a manor in England, having no feudal superior, might conceivably have declared himself a vassal of the Pope. But this relationship would have been valid only in respect of the given manor or fief. The kingdom was no such matter; it was composed of a large number of fiefs whose holders had each sworn allegiance to the king. Such an oath is not transferable by the recipient to another person. The nature of a Christian vow is that it must be voluntary; and the person making it must be fully informed of what it covers and imports; this follows from the doctrine of free will for salvation. In the feudal hierarchy it was so understood that a tenant's allegiance to his lord went with the lord's allegiance to the king; but none of John's subjects, noble or otherwise, had agreed nor understood that the king could make them subject to any further temporal superior. In short, John promised to hand over something which was non-transferable. The deal was tempting not in its nominal terms of feudalism, but because of the money revenue. The kinetic current was so strong it almost undercut the structure of the nation in toto, threatening to lift and move it to another situation, as a stream may move a house.

Regrettably, the pope agreed to the deal, and let down the courageous Archbishop Langton and all the other eminent clerics who had wrung the Charter from John. They had exercised the proper and historic function of the church in resistance to the state; and the earthly head of the church repudiated their action. But neither king nor pope could make it stick; the immediate result was the resumption of civil war. It is at least arguable that the deferred consequence was the schism, three centuries later, of the English from the Catholic communion. Historic sequences always trace back to causes remote in time; and such a betrayal is never forgotten. Materially and morally, it left the English church in a perilous position. In the continuing struggle of the king, the nobles, and the merchants, whichever party won temporarily, the church was bound to lose a little every time, having lost its prestige as the mediatory agency. Serfdom obtained on some of the church lands, hence it would seem oppressive to the peasants, and would no longer be identified with liberty. The king still had his money revenue to support his private army. The merchants had grown strong enough to fight for themselves, and thus represent the contract society. The size of the church landholdings really weakened the nobles, by withdrawing the occupants from feudal military service. But as wealth, the church lands and revenues were an obvious temptation to plunder; while any party taking the side of the church could never again be quite sure he would not be sold out abroad. The kinetic energy flowing to the executive, the king, first destroyed feudalism, the power of the nobles over the king; then it swung the king (Henry VII) into a working alliance with the merchants, identifying their interests; then it was turned directly against the church as a landed institution, and broke up the great Abbey lands, to reconstitute a new aristocracy in conjunction with the new control agency which had been made workable in the House of Commons. Finally, the kinetic energy, under that control, was turned against the executive, the king, and it broke the royal prerogative. But in the process, too many people lost their footing on the land.

Taught by adversity in the civil war of the seventeenth century (which was a culmination of the process that reduced the too-heavy framework of the aristocracy by attrition in the Wars of the Roses, and all but destroyed it with the centralized tyranny of Henry VIII), the English nobles accepted much the same compromise as had been made by the aristocratic order in the Roman republic. The hereditary feature was retained in the upper house for the regional bases; but the effective veto was in the Commons; and the law was above the crown. In this last development, the secular government learned from the church how to fix a center, a problem which had been insoluble in the Roman empire.* The authority (since defined as infallibility) of the Pope existed finally only in ecumenical council and within a prescribed sphere (of faith and morals). So in the English form of secular government as it evolved, the authority of the king existed only in conjunction with Parliament and within the scope of law. When Charles I failed to perceive this distinction, it was imparted to him with the edge of the axe.

In mechanism, this is dead center, which is a necessity in a reciprocating action. The king does nothing; that is what he is for, being the point at which the forces meet. The crown was indispensable, given the historic set-up, for the aggregation of dominions, colonies, and dependencies of disparate types which formed the British empire, because it obviated political dealings between any two of them, or *primary* action from the center. Since they did not have to come to specific agreements, they had no occasion to disagree. At the beginning of the nineteenth century, the internal structure of England was essentially that of the Roman republic, with a modified aristocracy adjusted to an elective system; and as the English-speaking colonies began with a large measure of local self-government, the army was not an active and direct political factor in the administrative mechanism.

---

* The one serious weakness in the political *structure* of the Roman empire made this solution impossible. In the church, the diocese was a genuine regional sub-division, its representative (the bishop) being maintained directly by local revenues, of which only a moiety went to Rome. Likewise the English noble drew his revenues directly from his own local estate to support concomitant local political functions. Neither of them had to depend on a redistribution of revenue (energy) from the center. But the provincial officials of the Roman empire were thus dependent; they were paid from the center; and the stream of energy drawn off in taxes to Rome undercut them; they had no regional representative character. Therefore the adjustment at the center had to be made, as noted, by the encounter of "raw forces"—the army and the potentiality of revolt.

As with Rome, the world accepted the British empire because it opened world channels of energy for commerce in general. Though repressive (status) government was still imposed to a considerable degree on Ireland with very bad results, on the whole England's invisible exports were law and free trade. Practically speaking, while England ruled the seas any man of any nation could go anywhere, taking his goods and money with him, in safety.

But a traditional structure adapted to accommodate a high energy potential is continually under severe stress. The condition of the landless laborer poses a problem which is still unsolved.

He is a particle drawn into the energy circuit as iron filings will cohere in a magnetic current; then whenever industry slackens, which is to say the current is weaker, many of the particles must drop off again. Unemployed workmen, aggregated only by inertia, thus become a fragment of dislocated mass within the economy. As such, they are thrown against the structure, and naturally feel it only as obstruction. It is equally natural, since they are sentient being and not mere physical objects, that they should demand that the structure be abolished; or at least, spokesmen will appear for them who will make that demand, as in the Chartist movement. A man pinned against a stone pier is not likely to consider whether or not the pier is necessary for any purpose, or what else could be put in its place. He can hardly be expected to think of it in those terms.

The greatest misfortune of the productive worker who has no base is that when he is dropped by the weakened current he falls into the same material category as the habitually non-productive. The added weight makes the non-productive group feel insecure. Their uneasiness finds emotional expression in anger against the productive element. In the hope of attaching themselves more firmly to the production line, they will then demand restrictive regulation of industry and commerce, on the pretext (as Shaftesbury innocently admitted) that it is for the benefit of the working man.

But such a proposal requires status law. The peculiarity of status law is that it cuts in and diverts energy at the beginning of the circuit instead of at the end. It makes the nonproductive a first charge on production, *ahead of maintenance.* If the various taxes recently imposed in previously free economies, under the pretext of helping the indigent, are examined, their nature becomes evident. They have to be paid even though the producer goes bankrupt.

Such taxing schemes seldom or never originate with workingmen. They originate among those who draw their incomes from fixed charges—from entailed property or from endowed or tax-supported institutions—and who therefore wish to have their relation to production affirmed as a governing rule. But the unemployed workingman wants to work, to be active, to live. The demands for status law and for the abolition of structure will therefore be more or less simultaneous and both may be included in the same legislative measures.

Thus both are likely to be put in effect at about the same time. The result is now visible. The true cause of Fascism, or Nazism, or Communism, is the structureless state,* in which the whole energy of the nation, its production line, is thrown into the repressive mechanism of centralized government with status law. It is a death-trap.

The drawbacks inherent in an aristocratic order are so obvious and inherently onerous, that the fact it had a use has been largely forgotten; but it did supply structure, by maintaining regional bases. Whenever an aristocracy loses this local representative function, it is on the verge of dissolution.

* The ancient tyrannies or despotisms were nations which developed some industry without achieving any structure. This failure to synchronize inevitably causes dislocation, violence, and misery.

CHAPTER XII

The Structure of the United States

The problem then which confronted the founders of the United States was how to maintain regional bases for a political structure without an aristocracy. It was not so stated at the time, for this is a description of the practical means, when only the objective was known. In like case, it could not have been said that a keystone must be designed to complete the form of the arch, or a zero sign for the use of position in numbers, until these devices had been found; such a statement is impossible until the problem has been solved. The American revolutionaries had declared the axiom of the rights of the individual, the Society of Contract, as the reason and justification for their independence. An indigenous aristocracy would nullify their intention. Such vestige as remained, in the form of entail, which is the root of the society of status, was accordingly abolished. The separate states already existed, and had not ceded their several sovereignties to the original loose federation. Their natural resistance as political entities in being was strong enough to defeat proposals that their autonomy should be extinguished, and tended to obscure the future danger in that direction. The question immediately presented was how to bring them together in "a more perfect union"—without lapsing into democracy. What was wanted was a Republic.

The objection to democracy was clear and cogent; but for quite opposite reasons from those of the Old World. It was obvious that democracy must dissolve the European order of society, which was hierarchical, framed to hereditary rank. The premise of democracy is supposed to be natural equality.

The Society of Status claimed to derive its moral sanction from the family, extended by analogy in political organization; but this hypothesis ignores the prime fact that everyone in due course becomes adult. In such extension the feudal pattern became fictitious; outside of domestic affairs it did not and could not correspond to the facts, either in respect of blood relationship or simple seniority. It resolved into the rule of the few over the many, by the arbitrary convention of descent through "old" families. In nature, one family cannot be "older" than another. Age is personal. But maturity, the *condition* of being adult, is equality within its definition. By this conclusion, the few can have no hereditary claim to command the many.

On the other hand, this is a mathematical order applied only to chronology. It describes men as equals when they have reached a given span of years, the presumed period of maturation. Outside of that single classification, it has no positive or intrinsic significance.* The Greeks were never able to validate their hypothesis for democracy because it is a materialistic concept, and materialism will not admit human equality, nor any other principle of human association. Materialism must regard mankind as simply an animal species whose behavior is predicated and determined by instinct and expedience. On those grounds, there are no rights and no moral questions; whatever happens must happen, and whatever must happen does happen. But even if this dead-end in materialistic determinism is ignored, and equality sought in respect of phenomena, it cannot be found in human beings,

---

* Equality in itself signifies nothing, implies no values; two zeros are equal. Liberty attaches value to it. The argument that conscription is right because it is applied equally would justify torture if applied equally. This argument has been carried further by a pseudo-liberal: "The voluntary system sounds well. In practise it is a moral horror ... since no one can tell by looking at a young man whether he is doing essential war work, or is married or has children, or is perhaps not in good health. The voluntary system is not voluntary. It is in practise the worst form of compulsion ... excellently designed to make young men unhappy." Then slavery is not slavery, because the world is peopled with moral imbeciles, all equally terrified of the casual glance of a stranger.

regarded as "higher" animals or as objects in nature. Strict materialism must finally deny that a human being is an entity; it resolves him into a lump of plasmic material "conditioned" to various "responses" or "reactions." In materialistic terms, psychology becomes a branch of physiology, behaviorism. Then if the responses (attributes or qualities) are compared, one man may be demonstrably stronger than another, or gifted with some ability (music, art, or whatever) which another lacks or exhibits in less degree at a given time; but there is no general equation for the diverse endowments, even if they could be fully discovered. The only definition of equality by measure is that of Euclid: things which are equal to the same thing are equal to one another. This calls for a fixed objective standard, a perfect typical man, embodying quantitatively all human attributes in absolute scale and proportion as a norm, and with an unimaginable common denominator by which such qualities would be translatable into number for points which could be added together. Thus men as they are could be estimated by comparison and each one assigned a rating. (The Platonic theory of archetypes, or the Ideal, was an unsuccessful attempt to get around this difficulty.)

But the American axiom asserted political equality as a corollary of the inalienable right of every man to liberty. Democracy was inadmissible because it must deny that right and lapse into despotism, as it has always done. It does so abstractly, by its own logical contradiction; and in practice because logic is a statement of sequence. *It is not liberty and equality that are incompatible, but liberty and democracy.*

The distinction is that between a principle and a process; the confusion arises from an unwarrantable identification of a negative proposition with a positive. It is falsely assumed that when the claim of the few to command the many is refuted, the converse claim of the many to command the individual is proved. This is quite untenable except in strictly materialistic terms; and in those terms, right must be ruled out altogether. Right as a concept is necessarily opposed to force; otherwise the word is meaningless.

Liberty is a truly natural condition; for life itself is possible to a human being only by virtue of his capacity for independent action. If any living creature is subjected to absolute restraint, it dies. Human life is of an order transcending the deterministic necessity of physics; man exists by rational volition, free will. Hence the rational and natural terms of human association are those of voluntary agreement, not command.

Therefore the proper organization of society must be that of free individuals. And their equality is posited on the plain fact that the qualities and attributes of a human being are ultimately not subject to measure at all; a man equals a spiritual entity.

But democracy is a collective term; it describes the aggregate as a whole, and assumes that the right and authority reside in the whole, though derived from the adult condition of the individuals comprised. Then it must be supposed that at an unknown moment by an unknown sanction and for no reason whatever such right and authority was irrevocably transferred from the individuals to a group which is nothing but a numerical sum, or particles merged into mass. The authority then is not in any part, nor is any part of it in any part of the mass. Thus democracy resolves into pure process, and even the process is fictitious, for individuals cannot actually merge, though a group can exercise the function of mass for a given purpose at a given time, by inaction, a negative. The fictitious process imagined as operating in democracy is of a physical and mathematical and non-moral order, beginning with an arbitrary number delimited by accident of residence or descent.

But if the authority resides in the collective whole, it is evident that with the disagreement of even one person, the whole is no longer existent or operative; in which case no general action whatever could be legitimately undertaken.

The prime presumption has vanished. In practice then democracy must abandon its own pretended entity of the collective whole, and rely upon majority. But majority is only a part; thus majority rule implies inconceivably that the part is greater than the whole. Furthermore, even majority is not always obtainable; only a plurality may favor a given course of action; in which case one minority must command several other minorities which if added together are greater in number or weight. Such is the inherent contradiction in the theory of democracy. In any event, personal liberty is wiped out at the very beginning, with the theoretic transition from particles to mass or from the unit to the sum. Slavery of a minority, or of "foreigners," is quite consistent with majority rule.*

But in reason, if one man has no right to command all other men—the expedient of despotism—neither has he any right to command even one other man; nor yet have ten men, or a million, the right to command even one other man, for ten times nothing is nothing, and a million times nothing is nothing.

The material objection to democracy is that it has no structure, the practical defect corresponding to the moral defect. Gravity determines the movements of an aggregation of separate particles over a given surface; with every disturbance each particle is subject to the discontinuous hazard of chance; if a number of them move together under the same impulsion, it is as dislocated mass. Active difference of opinion in democracy is either the detachment of a particle or dislocated mass. As Madison said, "it affords no remedy for the evils of faction." Faction is fragmentary mass, the several fragments being thrown into collision by whatever force occasioned the cleavage.

---

* The modern cliché, "This is a democracy, I am the government," is nonsensical. Even as an agency, the government is a formal organization with an authorized personnel, of which the private citizen is not a member. When several persons employ an umpire, they are distinctively not the umpire, although he holds that office by their agreement.

At various times, various nations have exhibited certain aptitudes to an unusual degree. Different periods and places have been marked by a splendid flowering of special talents. Such manifestations are vaguely credited to racial genius, but the phrase will not bear analysis. The elements are usually mixed in origin, so that a somewhat eclectic culture has become homogeneous by development, while still open to new ideas. (Even the rigorously enclosed society of Japan acknowledged an esthetic inspiration from China.) But the prerequisite must be the conditions, or mode of association, which *do not hinder* such development of innate faculties.

Now if the works and thoughts of the men who founded the United States are examined, it is evident that they had a highly developed structural sense, a remarkable feeling for and understanding of form, proportion, perspective. However it came about, they were a nation of architects; and they thought in mathematics as "naturally" as in words. It is by no means an accident, but an indication of the intellectual context of the period, that George Washington was a surveyor (though a gentleman by family); that Thomas Jefferson, a lawyer by profession, was passionately interested in architecture; or that Benjamin Franklin, a tradesman and craftsman with no nautical connection, was given to scientific experiment, and saw nothing out of the way in proposing to work out by himself a formula for finding a position at sea. Indeed, the standard textbook on navigation was composed by a New Englander, Nathaniel Bowditch, who had no special advantage of education and was not a navigator. This predisposition was nowise exceptional. Roger Sherman, though bred to the humble occupation of a cobbler, taught himself mathematics so well that he could calculate a lunar eclipse. Once he was invited to speak on the occasion of opening a new bridge.* "He walked critically over the structure," and delivered his oration in one sentence: "I don't see

* BULWARK OF THE REPUBLIC. By Burton J. Hendrick. Little, Brown & Co.

but it stands steady." When New Englanders habitually used the phrase, "I calculate," that was what they meant. They did calculate. Roger Sherman was responsible for the dual method of representation in the two houses of Congress— by popular vote in the House of Representatives, with congressmen allotted in proportion to population, and by equality of the States in the Senate. His structural sense was sound; he hit on both the regional bases and the mass veto function at once. He knew what would stand steady.

To understand why bases cannot be established on popular suffrage, with no property qualification, it is only necessary to try an equivalent with any other physical materials. Let the substance on which the structure must be supported be composed of separate particles of equal size and weight, and each susceptible of movement—obviously nothing can possibly stand on it. A pillar or cornerstone cannot be fixed on a heap of buckshot, or a mound of sand. There must be something solid, self-contained, and immovable. A regional area answers that description, and will sustain a permanent base of political representation. The area must be definitely circumscribed, and the representation must pertain to it, not to the mobile inhabitants, who may wander about and cross the boundaries at will.

Failure to discern that a political organization consists of both structure and mechanism, that is, a fixed base to which agencies of action are attached, has caused untold disaster throughout the ages. These components were hopelessly confused in the feudal theory, where the regional areas were the real structural base while the family was supposed to perform that function. When it came to the point that there were no heirs to a territorial family, another succession was established; but still men did not see the point. Needing an immovable base, their almost incredibly irrational recourse was to bind men to the land, crushing living bodies under the weight of the pillars. But all that was actually necessary was to allot the representation to the area. To do this, however, the area must be established as a political entity, and represented as such; which can be done only by having the representative appointed by the local political organization, not by the popular vote. There must be delimited local sovereignty in the area.

On the other hand, the direct representation of the voters in a definite agency of government is necessary to utilize the function of mass, that is, of the aggregate population. The representation of mass can be effected only by delegates in proportion to numbers, regardless of the several areas which form the bases.

Thus by using the materials available, in accordance with architectural and mechanical principles, the founders of the United States solved the problem on which the Roman empire had failed. The Constitution of the United States is an architectural and mechanical drawing, in which the design is laid out on its broad general principles. They are as simple as the design of a foundation, an arch, a piston cylinder, or an eccentric transmission; and like those fundamentals, they embody *relations;* and are thus capable of infinitely complex application. *But the intrinsic design must always be maintained.* If the foundations are removed, or the keystone withdrawn, the arch must fall; if the piston cylinder head is blown out, the action will cease; if the eccentric rod is detached at one end, it can only flail about and smash the whole mechanism. A greater volume of energy does not and cannot alter the necessary *relations* involved. The belief that it does is the fatal delusion of today. Increased volume of energy has been made the pretext for destroying the regional bases, when they should rather have been strengthened.

Let the Constitution as it was originally drawn, including the Bill of Rights, be examined strictly on its merits and in the light of performance, as an architectural plan and a mechanical apparatus of an earlier day might be studied by modern architects and engineers. It will be found amazing in its correctness, in respect of the relation of mass and motion, operative through the association of human beings; and the release and application of energy.

The Bill of Rights and the treason clause taken together establish the individual as the dynamic factor. The Bill of Rights withdraws entirely from political control both the faculties and the instruments of initiative and enterprise. No law might be passed against freedom of the mind, whether in religion, in speech, or in print; nor to restrict interchange of ideas in peaceable assembly; nor to prevent the expression of private opinion from individuals to the government, by petition. No law might deprive the individual of the right to bear arms. Soldiers must not be quartered on citizens in time of peace; nor even in time of war unless under civil regulation. No man's home might be entered except on formal warrant in pursuit of a specific charge authorized by law and confined to the named purpose. No person might be tried unless formally indicted for a crime, nor condemned by secret trial or without witnesses and counsel. And most important for the maintenance of these rights, private property might not be taken for public use without just compensation. Finally, forestalling attempts on the part of the government to nullify these safeguards by indirect means, excessive bail, excessive fines, and torture (cruel and unusual punishments) were forbidden. (Excessive bail can only mean bail fixed in a sum that would be beyond the means of the average person to procure. An excessive fine would be a larger sum than the offense could involve; otherwise a fine would be an easy way of confiscating anybody's property on the slightest pretext.) *

The treason clause remains unique in all the long record of political institutions. In the first place, it declares that there is no such crime as treason in peace time. "Treason against the United States shall consist only in levying war

---

* The constitutional prohibition of excessive fines has been completely ignored in recent legislation, without one word of protest from citizens or any attempt to appeal on the issue in court.

against them, or in adhering to their enemies, giving them aid or comfort." Nothing but armed rebellion or joining with an enemy nation—and nations are by definition enemies only when at war—can be treason. No peaceful or personal opposition to government or to members of the government, comes under the head of treason. Even the forcible attack or resistance of a *single person* as such (having no connection or agreement with other persons or a foreign government to the same end), could hardly be construed as "treason," as it would not constitute "levying war." Treason must also be "an overt act," not merely an expression of opinion; and a conviction cannot be had on circumstantial evidence; two witnesses to the act are required. In the European theory it was treason to attack the person of the king even for a non-political motive. The man and the office are held to be inseparable. A like attempt against a member of a true republican government is a strictly personal criminal offense. By this unprecedented limitation of treason, the government or administration was debarred from imposing silence while making encroachments. Its members were allowed no means of reprisal against criticism or exposure.

But the treason clause also contains another unique and significant provision. "No attainder of treason shall work corruption of blood, or forfeiture except during the life of the person attainted." It is doubtful whether the average American today would readily understand the meaning of the phrase "corruption of blood," or of the limitation of forfeiture to the lifetime of the person indicted for treason. But the first restriction defined guilt as personal; and the second defined private property as belonging to individuals. Both are in opposition to the collectivist theory of the group as superior or antecedent to the individual. It is evident, from the bewildered comments of our contemporary press, that Americans have quite forgotten the historic fact that until the United States came into existence, the laws of Europe allowed punishment of all the members of a family for the crime or any one member. Since the family was the political unit, and honors were inherited and privilege pertained in some degree to all the members of the family, it appeared equitable and logical that the whole family should suffer proportionately for the delinquency of any member. The capital penalty was seldom visited upon all, even in earlier times, but lesser penalties, such as exile or imprisonment or demotion in status, were not uncommon for nothing but kinship; likewise the family property was held to be forfeit altogether by the fault of the head of the family, even if he escaped from jurisdiction or died before being brought to trial. It all went together, family honors, family ownership, family guilt, and family forfeiture. The church doctrine of private property was naturally difficult to maintain against the threat of the state, although the church never yielded that position. Family property is of course private property, differentiated from state or communal ownership as a norm; also by Christian doctrine guilt is personal. But with a charge of treason, the secular ruler could use the family unit as a pretext for confiscating all the family property; and under cover of this procedure, the secular ruler could also fall back on the political system of feudalism, and claim that property was not really privately owned, but held in tenancy from the crown or overlord, and that the tenure lapsed when the tenant failed in allegiance. Land titles did go so far back, and had so often and long been held on such tenancy from local lords or conquerors, the question was extremely complex.

On the other hand, during the period of settlement of the American colonies, the actual practice of severe penalizing of families for the guilt of a member had long tended to fall into disuse, especially in England, whence it largely vanished with serfdom. But even in England, treason might be imputed for a wide range of actions or for mere words; and forfeiture might follow after death.

But the American Constitution said, by its treason clause,

that private property belongs to individuals by indefeasible title. If a person indictable for treason, or convicted of it, should escape, his property might be sequestrated (in forfeit), as long as he was alive, a fugitive from justice or unpardoned; but at the moment of his death, the title passes unimpaired to his legal heir. Nor could any member of his family be punished for mere kinship; none could be held guilty of the deed of another. This is the meaning of the ban against "corruption of blood." Until the resurgence of Communism, even Russia had largely conformed to the American practice; but America first declared the principle as absolute.

This also prevented the State from having an invisible and unspecified power over an accused man by means of threats to his family. A man of integrity may face death for himself calmly, yet he might quail before the prospect of torture or even of penury for his wife and children, his parents, his brothers and sisters. It is disgraceful to our educational institutions and to the political intelligence of Americans, that in discussion of the notorious "Moscow trials," not one comment indicated any knowledge of the American constitutional safeguard against trials of that type, and of the base of that safeguard on individual private property; nor even of the collectivist political theory which admitted the Russian procedure until the example of the United States shamed them into desuetude.

To Americans, and by the moral axiom of the American political system, such trials are an abominable perversion of justice. But with the return of collectivism the legal imputation of collective guilt inevitably returns also.

All these provisions in the Bill of Rights and the Constitution are of the utmost importance in relation to the flow of energy; the fact which they express accounts for the unparalleled expansion of the United States in territorial extent in the given time, by accounting for the even more extraordinary extension of the field of physical science and mechanical invention. In a hundred and fifty years, men suddenly enlarged and corrected their knowledge of scientific principles which had taken many thousands of years to discover at all; and devised means of application which made possible a concurrent increase of population and a rise in the standard of well-being beyond even the dreams of humanity in the past. Nothing of the sort had ever occurred in the world before; history reveals nothing comparable to the United States as a nation. It may be pointed out reasonably that the contributions to scientific knowledge and practical invention did not originate only in the United States. But it was the *existence* of the United States, and the consequent demonstration and spread of liberty, which made the achievements of science possible in Europe.

What happened was that the dynamo of the energy used in human association was located. It is in the individual. And it was withdrawn from political interference by a formal reservation, along with the means and material by which it can organize the great world circuit of energy. The dynamo is the mind, the creative intelligence, which our Bill of Rights and the treason clause assert to be free of political control. The material means on which intelligence projects by initiative is private property. Nothing else will serve.

Likewise the structure of government was established on its enduring base, without pinning men down under the foundation. Regional areas were delimited to which the instruments of political action were attached, without confining any person by law to the given area, or confiding the power of wielding such instruments to persons by hereditary rule, or making such power unlimited. The instruments were properly defined as agencies. They pertained to the several states as such. This effect was secured by the method of appointment to the Senate. Senators were chosen by the legislative bodies of the states; that is, their office was *attached to the state,* being derived from the state; unlike the Roman provincial governors who were appointed by the central authority. The thrust was against the center, instead of from the center; therefore it countered the weight of the superstructure. On the other hand, the Senator had no political function *within* the state he represented, hence the office had no intrinsic tendency toward separatism. It took effect only at the center. The stresses were doubly equalized. The several states also preserved their political integrity by keeping to themselves the primary authority to qualify voters in Federal elections.* Nevertheless citizenship, as a general condition, was a Federal attribute; that is, a citizen of any one state had the rights of citizenship in all the other states. This effected cohesion of the particles to form a nation, without prejudice to the regional bases. The states were limited to a "republican form of government" by the Federal authority.

The citizens, by the institution of private property, were given resistance against all the agencies of government. Private property is the standing ground of the citizen; there is no other. As the state had to be a regional area with its representatives, to preserve its basic function, so it was necessary for citizens to have a direct vote for the mass inertia veto; hence the two legislative chambers, the Senate for the States and the House of Representatives for the citizens as individuals. The possibility of legislators using their office for a direct grab from the public funds was forestalled by debarring them from such action in respect of a current term of office.

The Senate, having the longest term of office and representing the states as continuing bodies, was given control of foreign relations by ratification, with negotiations entrusted to the executive. The executive was given no specific means of initiating domestic legislation, and only a provisional or delaying veto.

The House of Representatives, elected by direct vote of

---

* The proposal to abolish by Federal legislation the poll tax imposed by some Southern states as a franchise qualification is absolutely unconstitutional.

the citizens, was enabled to express the property and function of mass, the ultimate veto by negation, being entrusted with the initiative in laying taxation and granting supplies. All supplies were required to be granted only in denominated sums for allotted purposes; any such grant must therefore be used up in time and would have to be granted again. If no grant is made, the veto of inertia is in force. It is only necessary to do nothing.

To prevent the larger, wealthier, or more populous states from throwing their weight against smaller states, their representation as states was made equal. To prevent the smaller or poorer states from ganging up and fleecing the more opulent states—throwing their joint weight—the popular representation was made proportionate to the number of citizens. To prevent the central authority from mulcting the wealthy states in order to buy out poor states, it was provided that Federal taxation imposed upon persons could be levied only in proportion to population; while taxes on goods (tariffs, excise duties, imposts) must be uniform throughout the United States. That is, no favor could be shown to any one state in respect of manufactures, port dues, or the like. This prevented the political monopolies which were the bane of Europe. And the states could not impose port or border tariffs at all.

The several states were forbidden to coin money or emit paper currency ("bills of credit"), or to make anything but gold and silver legal tender. Therefore the transmission line of energy could not be cut or tapped by the political agency of any state. And the Federal government *was given no power to issue paper currency*. Though it has done so, the authority is not in the Constitution, while it is expressly stated in the Constitution that powers not delegated to the Federal authority are reserved from it. Neither is the Federal government granted any power to impair contracts, though it has lately done so; while the states were forbidden in set terms.

The Federal judiciary was to be appointed for life (subject to impeachment for misuse of office), in order to keep a check on the legislative and executive branches. The endlessly debated question of "judicial review" is mere stultification; for the jurisdiction of the Supreme Court is specified as covering only cases "arising under this Constitution, the laws of the United States, and treaties made under their authority," while "this Constitution, and the laws of the United States which shall be made *in pursuance thereof,* shall be *the supreme law* of the land." No sophistry can evade the proposition that the *supreme* law must govern the verdict; that is what supreme means. But after arguing for a hundred years against this proper and indispensable function of judicial review, the pseudo-liberals have invented a singularly vicious hypothetical perversion of it. Justice Frankfurter expressed it, writing of "the dangers and difficulties inherent in the power to review legislation. For it is a subtle business to decide, not whether legislation is wise, but whether legislators were reasonable in believing it to be wise." Judicial review *is not* concerned with deciding whether legislation is wise or legislators reasonable in believing it to be wise. Judicial review is confined to finding whether or not a given law contravenes the Constitution, the supreme law; as it does if the legislature exceeded its Constitutional power in passing the law in question—the legislature has no authority except in the Constitution.

The Constitutional provision for armed defense was consonant with the political structure. The originating authority of the Federal government was sufficient to enlist and provide for a standing army, without direct reference to the several states; but supplies could be appropriated only for a term of two years. This would tend to keep the professional army of reasonable size. As the original method was by voluntary enlistment, obviously that was the intention. On the other hand, the primary right to bear arms and form militia companies was reserved to the citizens; but if such bodies of militia were to serve in a declared war, their officers must be appointed by the states; after which they were subject to call by the Federal government. Throughout, initiative remained with the individual, as a free man; but formal action rested with the political authorities, as having the formal inhibitory power. Though a defensive war is just and necessary, war involves destruction; hence the inhibitory power must regulate it. But creative action must be free.

For its realization of these moral relations and structural embodiment of them, the Constitution of the United States has been justly described as the greatest political document ever struck off at one time by the mind of man.

CHAPTER XIII

Slavery, the Fault in the Structure

The three great ideas were brought together at last without impediment; the individual and immortal soul, exercising self-government by law, and free of the universe to pursue knowledge by reason. After two thousand years, the resources of science were released for productive application. The Declaration of Independence and the Constitution were the temporal instruments of this event.

But in its original design the Constitution had to admit one prime defect, an irreconcilable contradiction. Chattel slavery was an existent institution. Whatever form of government was adopted for the Union, it must either extinguish slavery *ab initio* (as contrary to the moral order of the universe), or tolerate it by default of such axiomatic statement. Here the federal form, which is indispensable for stability, unhappily admitted an ambiguous expedient. It was temporarily possible to leave slavery to state jurisdiction. No doubt the opinion of slave-holders was weighted by their wrongful possession; but there was also colorable pretext for delay. It was honestly feared that the Negroes, many of them newly brought from Africa, might prove a burden and a danger if liberated immediately. There was then no question of the vote, which was rightly by property qualification; but only of the difficulty of assimilating savages to civilized life in other than a servile relation; though even that was felt to be none too safe. Nobody knew just how it was to be worked out ultimately, whether by gradual education of the Negroes or sending them back to Africa. Meantime, as the Federal government must control the external borders, it had authority to forbid further importation of slaves from abroad, and indicated that intention indirectly. The implied sentiment was against slavery. On the other hand, slavery caused the inclusion of a clause in the Constitution providing for the extradition of slaves who escaped across state lines. That the subject was embarrassing is perhaps indicated by the language; the words slave and slavery are not used. The phrase is a "person held to service or labor." (At that time, the description would include free white apprentices during their terms of indenture.) Slaves then were at least persons; and are also counted as persons in apportioning for the House of Representatives. But the brute fact remained that they were slaves; and the Constitution did not pronounce them free by right.

The lasting injury inflicted by this inclusion of slavery was that it vitiated the principle on which the new nation came into being. Emancipation by slaveholders as an act of generosity, or by states as an act of authority, could never be exactly equivalent to starting with liberty as the universal right from which authority was derived.

Further, the continuance of slavery made it impossible for the Bill of Rights to limit the state governments as well as the Federal government. The existence of slavery necessarily impairs the exercise of their rights by free men. If the state power makes a man a slave, of course it abridges his freedom of speech and assembly, leaves him no security of person, and no right to property; so it can hardly be forbidden to do those things to anybody. The alleged distinction between "human rights" and "property rights" is a verbal muddle; property rights are human rights. The true issue is between the individual and the collective. The only arguments ever offered for slavery call upon the collective, either race or state, for authority and enforcement; whereas if rights inhere in the individual, no man can be owned, and every man must have the right to own property.

This moral defect caused an equivalent structural defect,

as it was bound to do. Logic was stultified, so that discussion was worse than futile. The slave states claimed that their state sovereignty sufficed to make a man a slave. Then the same sovereignty in a free state should have made any person free on crossing the border. But the extradition clause ceded this attribute; for the extradition of a slave *as such* is entirely different from the extradition of a criminal. The criminal is no less guilty after he has crossed the border, whereas the slave is presumed to become free; in delivering him up, the free state is obliged to violate its own basic law.* True that the free states had accepted the inequitable condition to begin with; union seemed so desirable that the point was yielded. The slave states could say that the free states could have and extradite slaves if they wished. Yet all the states had fought for liberty. Both sides had compromised their moral position hopelessly. If the free states said that slavery was wrong, were they still to abet it, or denounce the Constitution? But the slave states must rest their case on the Constitution, and the Constitution was open to revision. If it came to that, would they be willing to abide by it?

The conflict remained in abeyance, while the hope remained that slavery would be gradually extinguished. Yet from the first apprehension was felt for the permanence of the Union. This was evident in the prosecution of the misty Burr-Blennerhasset conspiracy, which was so largely sheer energy driving westward that nobody quite knew the intention, not even the alleged conspirators. The impulse was to continue until it reached the Rio Grande and the Pacific Coast up to Puget Sound and leaped to Alaska. And the premonition was true; it tore the nation apart.

But where was the real weak point? Unless the question

---

* Civilized nations do not permit extradition of political offenders because the offense is strictly local; a state which hands over a political refugee is thereby acting as the agent of the other state, in derogation of its own sovereignty; whereas in delivering up a criminal, it is acting as the agent of justice.

is put in relevant terms, there can be no answer. Though the Civil War occurred seventy odd years ago, the controversy is still open; did the break occur on slavery, state rights, or the cleavage between an agrarian and an industrial economy? Did the states reserve or claim too much in state sovereignty; and if they did, was it on account of slavery?

Division of sovereign powers between a Federal government and its component states is no simple matter; the past is strewn with the wreckage of leagues and federations. The whole question of sovereignty is exceedingly complex. In practice there is always a debatable margin, on which the gage of battle is thrown down when claims are pressed rigorously. Territorial sovereignty is delimited by the boundaries. This is the virtue of nationalism; it is a spatial restriction on political power, an ultimate safeguard for the individual, a chance of escape from local tyranny. The rise of "internationalism" always connotes a corresponding encroachment on personal liberty; but it really does so by leaving no sovereignty anywhere. Sovereignty rests in the nation; its powers are exercised by the government. By ordinary, all stipulated powers are accounted strength in a government; and the absence of any conceivable power in government is considered a degree of weakness. The truth is that powers which are essentially improper, being contrary to the moral order of the universe, are weakness; and so are powers allotted to an inappropriate agency. They impose weight, stress, or thrust which no structure can support. When "weak" or "strong" government is in question, the usual connotation of the terms relates only to the superstructure; and the usual recourse is further centralization of powers, which is to say, an increase in the bulk of the superstructure and the diversion of more energy into it. Beyond the correct proportions and powers, this is fatal; unless the resistance from the base is greater than the weight or strain of the superstructure, the whole must fall. Feeble governments are those which have no adequate and legitimately instrumented opposition from the regional bases and the mass veto. Utter incompetence in government is finally achieved by what is called absolute political power, whether under the name of democracy or as candid despotism.*

Then both the states and the Federal government were too weak by the claim of improper powers and the improper allotment of a proper power. The latter error nullified a vital attribute of sovereignty, its space dimension. Unless this distinction between stipulated powers and intrinsic strength is understood, there can be no relevant discussion of the subject.

The function of states in a federation is to supply bases and vertical structure; this function is static. They are required to stand against pressure from above which tends to thrust them apart, make them buckle outward. Strictly speaking, no part of a foundation or the verticals resting on it can have too much static strength, true local autonomy. A structure collapses from weakness, not from strength. If it is torn apart violently, it must be from uncompensated thrusts and stresses. These must occur because of unequal bases, faulty cross connections, or excessive and unequally distributed superstructure. Now if slavery had not been admitted to the Constitution on tolerance, its original design was marvelously sound; but the inclusion of slavery introduced all three faults. Primarily it made the bases unequal. With this, it caused an uncompensated cross-thrust; for the extradition clause concerning slaves gave the slave states a point of pressure against the free states. And in the long run, slavery afforded an excuse for adding excessive weight to the superstructure and distributing it unequally.

Thus all three of the disputed causes of the Civil War entered into it, being one cause. And as a crowning evil, again the apparent problem masked the real problem. The apparent problem was the preservation of the Union. But

* Exemplified in the collapse of the old regime in France, in Czarist Russia, in Turkey, etc.

the antecedent condition of federal union is the existence of the states. The real problem was the preservation of the states. If that were impossible, the Union must presently disintegrate or solidify into mass.

If a structure is defective, the fact that it was the best the builders could do, or thought they could do, will not avert the physical consequences. Yet since human affairs are in the realm of moral law, which is of a higher order than mechanical law, the outcome may confound all measurable probabilities. Once a machine has been devised, its performance is calculable. But no pre-estimate is possible of what machines man may invent. Machines have no independent active existence, and being creations of the human mind, the system in which they operate must correspond to the nature of the prime mover. It is now a popular cliché that the internal combustion engine has somehow brought about or necessitated some alleged new principle or form in political organization. This is ridiculous. Man himself is an internal combustion engine; he is the determinant, and his devices are only multiples of his own faculties and powers. The internal combustion engine increased the volume of production, of energy, on the already existent long circuit, that is all. The relations are unaltered. The necessary transmission line is the same; it is private property. The necessary condition of human beings is the same; it is liberty. The only change is in degree, which can involve only a requirement of more of the same thing, absolute security of private property, full personal liberty, and firm autonomous regional bases for a federal structure. For this reason the potential of a nation cannot be appraised quantitatively. It consists in abstract ideas, in its axioms of human relations expressed in organization, not in material wealth computed at a given date. The Civil War exemplifies this principle.

In the early years of the Republic, all of the measurable factors were preponderantly in favor of the Southern slave states. They had ample and varied natural resources. Their staple products, cotton and tobacco, were in demand by a world market, affording cash and credit. They had the prestige bequeathed by their great statesmen as a political asset. Practically, they had the Federal government, the wealth, and the legal leverage.

The North had the personal enterprise of a free population. As northern industry got under way, it seemed to be contributing to Southern dominance, by commerce and inventions which swelled the profits of slave-owners and enabled them to extend slave territory.

The appearance was delusive. Suddenly the free economy reached out and began to take over a greater territory than the area which had accrued to slavery. The wealth and power of the free states increased by geometrical progression, doubling and redoubling. Just before the Civil War, William Tecumseh Sherman warned his Southern friends not to provoke war, saying that an agrarian economy cannot match an industrial economy in armed conflict. But the truth is that the South was not a real agrarian economy either; it had no economy whatever of its own, lacking the generator for a local circuit. Looking further than the hazards of a particular war, it was incapable of becoming an independent nation in such conditions.

The South lost the Civil War, as it was bound to; and the question of state sovereignty was dismissed as a technicality set aside by the verdict on slavery. In resorting to war, the slave states committed the moral error of repudiating a contract after taking special advantage through it. The Federal government was clearly obligated to maintain itself against aggression or disruption; having received its authority by delegation, it had no right to abandon its deputed function unless legitimately dissolved by the same means through which it was instituted. The benefit of union to all the states is so overwhelmingly evident that its dissolution then or now wears the aspect of violent lunacy; but if the events were described as pure phenomena, an intelligent spectator would realize that there must have been a fault in the structure, as in a falling house.

So the operation and consequences of the Reconstruction Act must raise grave doubts whether there could be moral authority for perpetuating by force a union of voluntary origin. Nor is it justifiable to alter the terms of contract when one of the parties is under duress.

Being made by force, the rebuilt structure still contained a physical defect corresponding to the moral defect. The Reconstruction Act was immediate evidence; it wiped out the states as political entities.

Though the Act was terminable, and ceased in time, the damage was done. In political organization the specific act implies a continuing power. Even if it be denominated an exception, a temporary expedient, the rule has been laid down that such expedients may be used. The Northern states could not consent to any extension of Federal power over the Southern states without making themselves liable to the imposition of the same power in the future.

It was not the liberation of the slaves which extinguished state sovereignty. Liberty is a pre-condition, a universal, which the Constitution should have recognized as primary. The destruction was done by the usurpation of state powers by the Federal government as by right of conquest.

If the Federal government had fought and won a war of conquest, then the states, north as well as south, must have lost it. In place of genuine regional bases, the Civil War resulted in a factitious division with factional interests which would inevitably seek to use the Federal power for partisan advantage. And in that lesson the Western states got their first political training.

CHAPTER XIV

The Virgin and the Dynamo

The United States was bound to affect the mind of Europe because it was a projection of European experience and hopes, put to the proof in the supposed conditions of nature, as a test case against tradition. The early settlers brought to this country their crafts and tools, arts and letters, theology, morals and science, customs and law; but they left behind most of the apparatus of enforcement. They did not bring either the closed economy or sacramental religion; and the wilderness afforded sufficient recourse against the remainder of official authority. Whatever survived on its own might be assumed to have validated itself. Liberty emerged and triumphed.

A subtle critic has said: "The Declaration of Independence blew Europe off its moral base." * The phrase is exact; for Europe was not placed on a new base. The American *idea* never got back to Europe at all (as in like circumstances the idea of Roman law was never comprehended in Asia). Instead, the attendant phenomena encountered a profound misinterpretation, being fitted to a divergent European theory. The physical consequences of this moral discrepancy became immediately evident in the French Revolution, with the Terror and the Napoleonic outburst; but the full effect was delayed until this century. At one remove, the United States has caused the present explosion and disintegration of Europe. None of the harm was done in enmity. On the contrary, while the antagonism indicated by the Monroe Doctrine persisted, Europe had a chance of adjustment. The

* FROM THESE ROOTS. By Mary Colum.

friendship of America, which turned in the torrent of energy, was fatal.

While the United States was in the making, as a few happily neglected colonies, something queer happened to European thought; by way of science, it reverted to determinism in the social and political sphere.

Free will as positive doctrine was the original affirmation of Christianity. Death is the one inevitable event in every human life; so it had been taken by the pagan world as final evidence that "the fate of every man is bound about his forehead." When death was regarded rather as an event in time emancipating the soul from temporality to a wider sphere, free will entered into faith. (The major heresies from Christianity have always been lapses back toward fatalism.) * Christianity tended toward Rome as its center of organization, because in the Roman political system free will was given legitimate play, not on a precarious margin, but as the operative principle, in contrast to the mass determinism of Greek democracy or the dead-end of Asiatic despotism.

But the thousand year regime of status in Europe, in spite of the modification maintained by the church, had bred in its subjects a deep weariness. The breakdown of the Roman empire was hard to forget, since men had struggled unavailingly to keep it going; their failure left them dubious of their own abilities and faculties. The figure of the Noble Savage signalizes the discrediting of status government, but only by negation. The gradual merging of church and state —which occurred in the Protestant no less than in the Catho-

---

* The tendency might not be visible at once in these variations, but would develop by a secondary aberration of logic. The larger doctrine of Christianity embraced both Divine Law and natural law acting upon a grand general principle, and an Intercessor to temper justice with mercy in consideration of human imperfection and human striving toward truth and right. The lapse into fatalism might occur in either direction; the explicit dualism of the Manichean heresy handed this world over to the dominion of evil; and on the other hand, absolute unitarianism could be construed into a mechanistic view of the universe. Even the Jansenist interpretation of the doctrine of grace made grace a compulsion rather than an opportunity of liberation by choice and acceptance.

lic countries—deprived the church of its function of opposition to the secular administration, and facilitated the rise of the Absolute State. At the same time, Galileo's exposition of the solar system, on first view, lent itself to a mechanistic philosophy. Applied science in mechanical invention seemed to confirm this implication; and it was carried over into speculations on social relations, including political economy. Altogether, free will practically disappeared from the intellectual context of Europe.

Not quite consciously, but in the back of their minds, Europeans felt that they had tried both politics and religion, and neither would "work." This is the undertone of Montaigne's deceptively noncommittal reflections. He did not reach the conclusion, but he stood at the turning point. He would never attack either church or state directly; he sought a by-pass instead; his outward conformity was a tacit escape. When he said that if he were accused of stealing the towers of Notre Dame, he would fly the country sooner than attempt to defend his innocence in court, the inference is plain; there was no justice to be had from the law. The attitude is legitimate as a starting point for inquiry, but rationally it should lead to an examination of the existing system of law and the proper axioms of law, a course which was to be pursued subsequently with useful results. What Montaigne was doing was to assemble bit by bit fragments of evidence of human behavior from which "natural" man might be synthesized. But he never said that either; though his evidence tended mainly to indicate that man was a product of environment. Later, when the theory of "natural" man was formulated, the mechanistic theory of the universe had gained credence in European philosophy. God was a mathematician; Descartes and Newton were His prophets. To be sure, Descartes allowed man to be an exception in his mathematical philosophy, man being "continually in touch with the Divine Idea," but Cartesians of a later generation went so far as to assert that animals were mere machines, incapable of feeling pain.* One step further, and strictly "natural" man is also reduced to mechanism in such a mechanistic universe.

At this point, some social thinkers said that if the artificial restrictions of society were abolished, man as mechanism would function perfectly and precisely as he was designed to do; but they did not attempt to explain how an absolutely natural mechanism in a strictly mechanistic universe could have devised and imposed "artificial" restrictions on himself, contrary to his own nature and machinery. When the question was put, how could the rigidly mechanistic school deny that "whatever is, is right," because it could not be otherwise? Yet if they wished to change "society," they must suppose something was wrong with it. At the moment, they were obliged to ignore this difficulty; and when Marx came up against it later, in his dialectical materialism, his alleged solution merely burked the issue, by postulating that some parts of the mechanism could obey the advice of the whiting to the snail, and move a little faster if they chose, or hang back, if they were obstinate. The perfect and absolute universal machine had a propensity to go haywire.

Meantime, it is singular that the English settlers in America, of the Puritan strain, who were predestinarian by religion, should have stood by free will in their secular affairs, against the drift of Europe, but they did. They were able

---

* It is reported of a group of Cartesians at Port Royal (the Jansenist center): "They beat their dogs without remorse, and laughed at those who were sorry for the beasts when they whimpered. 'Mere clockwork,' they replied, saying that these yelps and cries were the result of a little hidden spring inside the animal, who was no less devoid of feeling." Holding this opinion, they vivisected animals to study the circulation of the blood. These were the extremists; a moderate enquirer protested that one need only observe his turnspit dogs—one was lazy and would hide when it was time for him to go to work, while the other would hunt out the delinquent and fetch him to the task—to realize that something more than clockwork was involved. . . . When Berkeley got lost in a maze of argument on whether anything existed objectively, Dr. Johnson made a similar appeal to commonsense, with pardonable exasperation, kicking a stone as refutation. It was a cogent answer; subjective my foot. The subjective is inconceivable without the objective.

to achieve this intellectual feat by narrowing predestination to its exact and literal meaning of an ultimate destination, heaven, or hell. On this earth, they had managed to get to America by their own efforts in the teeth of authority; then they conquered the enormous odds of the wilderness, incidentally setting up local government. So they could hold the conviction of political or temporal free will; and in good time they proved it, with the grand demonstration of the revolution. (It is not suggested that none but the Puritans or their descendants contributed to this result; but they did their share, whereas in Europe men who were originally of the same persuasion pressed the determinist doctrine into the service of the Absolute State.)

The mechanistic philosophy is a very late importation to America; and it is wholly imported. It did not derive from our machinery, any more than it created the machine age. When Americans began inventing and using machines, they were of the firm opinion that they did make and run those machines at their pleasure, with no nonsense about the machines "determining" or "creating" anything whatever. Machines to an American are still an expression of free will. It is difficult for an American to ride in a motor car as a mere passenger; mentally he drives it.

But what Europeans wanted was something that would run itself and humanity with it, requiring nothing of men except passive submission. Refusing to recognize that even the life of a savage calls for extremely active, voluntary adaptation, Europeans rationalized themselves back below savagery. "Nature" became personified in "enlightened despotism"; before the end of the eighteenth century, Europe was asking in plain words for a dictator.

"The central clue to the reform program of the philosophers was their faith in natural law. . . . All that was needed to unlock the millennium was a supreme legislator, a Euclid of the social sciences, who would discover and formulate the natural principles of social harmony. The mathematical generalizations which formed the ground plan of physics had been propounded by a few bold thinkers, and it seemed a reasonable surmise that the fundamental laws of human society would likewise be discovered by some inspired genius rather than by a parliamentary assembly." *

Though they talked of science, they did not give themselves the trouble to use the scientific method of definition of terms; they used the words monarchy, democracy, and republic interchangeably, and most conveniently for any dictator who might take advantage of their standing offer. Napoleon was the answer. "By leaving the ideal form of government undefined, they made it possible for Napoleon to unite the republican and monarchical tradition in a formula of democratic despotism."

Napoleon was the creation of the academic planners. But he was by no means the first attempt, though his predecessors are generally unrecognized. The consort of George II, Queen Caroline, held the same doctrine, and believed she was putting it into execution, unknown to her subjects, with Walpole as her agent; but no harm was done, since Walpole had to get his policies carried out by Parliament; the roundabout method, by which Caroline managed George and Walpole managed Caroline, merely completed the transfer of power from the crown to the Commons, though the landed gentry still retained, during the process of transition, the main share of executive offices. Caroline had got the idea of "benevolent despotism" from her grandmother, the Electress Sophia, who had learned it from Leibnitz. By another channel, it was subsequently imparted to George III, who tried to fill the bill as the "Patriot King." His well-meant efforts were incomprehensible and infuriating to the English, who had not divorced reason from commonsense; and when George became certifiably insane, nobody was surprised.

But on the Continent, it was in consonance with this theory of an autocratic lawgiver inexplicably empowered to dispense

* EUROPE AND THE FRENCH IMPERIUM. By Geoffrey Bruun.

"natural law" that Voltaire made friends with Frederick the Great, and Diderot with Catherine the Great; and Madame de Stael was eager to flatter Napoleon, and told Alexander of Russia: "Your character, Sire, is a constitution." Turgot is credited with the statement: "Give me five years of despotism, and France shall be free." Since France had had a hundred years of despotism, and was not free, it would seem that the only objection the philosophers had to the Bourbons was that they were not despotic enough. These were the advance guard of the modern "liberals."

Europe has never given up this fantasy of the deus ex machina; it reappears at every turn of events. It is revealed in the words of the Empress Eugenie, speaking of the ephemeral empire of Maximilian in Mexico, when she said that Maximilian should have set up a dictatorship on the pattern of that of Napoleon III, "a dictatorship which should bring liberty, and a man able enough to maintain them side by side." The words mean nothing at all; she had them by rote. Maximilian himself explained that he "needed a strong force in order to impose reforms and improvements; the people here have to be compelled to what is good." His empress Carlotta, when she went mad, dreamed of Maximilian as "king of the earth and sovereign of the universe."

During the French Revolution, Burke remarked of the French royalist exiles in England that excepting for professions of attachment to the persons of the King and Queen of France, these aristocratic refugees "talked like Jacobins." Obviously they were unaware of it; and Burke might have added with truth that the Jacobins, along with most of the European revolutionaries of the eighteenth and nineteenth centuries, talked like absolute monarchists. The slogan of the English Chartists was: "Political power our means, social happiness our end." The Marxian "dictatorship of the proletariat," after which "the State would wither away," was a later repetition. The current version of this fatal twaddle was echoed by an American journalist after a visit to Communist Russia; in his version, "Russia was laying a new foundation for an evolutionary society, which was to pass through foreseen and planned for stages of growth from an absolute and political dictatorship through industrialism to liberty, democracy and peace. . . . A *scientific*, not a moral culture." The slaughter and starvation of millions of people, selected as victims specifically because of their productive character and free intelligence, was the long-term result of the mechanistic theory of the universe. And the attendants of the Sacred Juggernaut form a remarkable procession: Frederick, Catherine, Caroline, Mme. de Stael, the two Georges, the two Napoleons, Eugenie, Carlotta, Marx, Lenin, and an obsequious train of journalists.

In the meantime John Stuart Mill, professing to be the champion of liberty, sold it out again to "society." That is, he assumed that personal liberty was justifiable only if it served the collective good. Then if a plausible argument can be put forward that it does not—and such an argument will seem plausible because there is no collective good—obviously slavery must be right.

The persistent dreams of humanity are of eternal youth and beauty and absolute power. The first two must be sought for their own sake, since they cannot be disguised by a moral pretext. In the early mythologies they are imagined as gifts of the gods to some fortunate mortals. With the dawn of science, the hope was transferred to expectation of an Elixir of Life, to be discovered by research. Neither of these wishes could do much harm. Bishop Berkeley, the philosopher, was mysteriously convinced that tar-water was a panacea for almost every bodily ailment. One cannot guess why he endowed this irrelevant prescription with such magical properties; he had no ulterior motive. The significant point is not merely that tar-water cannot do what Berkeley thought it could. Nothing can. What he desired is unrealizable in the nature of things. There are deadly drugs; but there is no elixir of life for the physical body. Yet the desire has a residual intelligence, which yields beneficial results in the improvement of health and comeliness through rational study of biology and hygiene.

In mechanics a similar impossibility was imagined, a Perpetual Motion Machine. Here genuine science confronts a difficulty, so far unsolved, in defining energy or discovering its ultimate properties. Strict science is confined to measure; its findings must be quantitative. Dealing with inorganic matter, science postulates the Second Law of Thermodynamics, which says that energy "runs down," by conversion from a kinetic to a static manifestation. The two aspects of energy are exemplified in a man walking, moved by kinetic energy, and bumping into a stone wall, in which he encounters static energy. The wall has resistance, which is measurable in terms of energy by the force required to break through it; and the kinetic energy conversely is measured by what it can move, in static form.

Now if the energy of the whole universe, by which it moves, is considered to be fully defined in terms of its properties as manifested through inorganic matter, the universal energy must be a fixed quantity; and must also be subject to the Second Law of Thermodynamics, by which the whole universe is bound to "run down" ultimately, to become a motionless frozen lightless mass, absolutely static, so to remain forever after. Certainly the Second Law of Thermodynamics is valid in respect of energy utilized through inanimate materials; engineering and mechanics must be governed by this principle to get results. But if the same principle is assumed to govern the universal energy as such —instead of being merely a phase of its transmission through certain inorganic elements—it evokes an initial phenomenon, the "starting" of the universal mechanism in the first place by the primary existence of a fixed quantity of kinetic energy: how or from whence the hypothesis cannot pretend to explain nor even contemplate.

The religious hypothesis of the nature of the universe is

actually much more rational, postulating a First Principle
(God), the Source of energy, which does not "run down,"
is not measurable, and is manifest to our rational faculties
in both eternal and temporal aspects, by the measurable phenomena of inorganic matter, and through the rational faculty itself, which is of the nonmeasurable order, indicating
a divine element in man, the immortal soul. On such a First
Principle, the universe need not run down; the phases of
inorganic elements which are subject to the Second Law of
Thermodynamics would be secondary to the Creative First
Principle which completes an eternal circuit, eternally self-
renewing, through further processes man has not yet fath-
omed.

Now the "perpetual motion" crank, in a muddled manner, is approximating the absurdity of the strict quantitative
mechanistic view of the universe, which does imply that
somehow the cosmic machinery was set up *in posse*, and then
kicked into gear with a given quantity of kinetic energy
which has to be assumed as "there" already; after which it
went on running "of itself," with no further supply, and
must continue to do so until it runs down, by exhaustion of
the quantity. Thus the perpetual motion crank, approaching
his alleged problem, admits that he has to get his engine
started by a normal introduction of energy from an external
source. After that, he says, it will keep on running on its
own indefinitely.

This is the claim and the demand made by all the promisers of eventual felicity through an initial despotism. A few
years of external force, the dictatorship of the proletariat
or the élite, absolute government—and then no more effort,
no need of intelligence, a machine running on—to a dead
end. The theory of Marxist Communism is precisely that
of the Perpetual Motion Machine, point by point, for it
stipulates that the productive system created by free enterprise is a pre-requisite, to be taken over by the Communist
machine.

Thus the dream of power is also susceptible of two interpretations, one incalculably beneficial, the other vicious, the cause of infinite misery. When it is directed toward the mastery of nature, the ordering of inorganic matter by knowledge of natural law, it is creative, not only in material goods but in enrichment of human personality. The latter development occurs because in man, the being who thinks, *reason is the individuating attribute.* Acute observers have found that primitive peoples, such as the Eskimos, do exhibit a "collective" psychology, to such degree that in group actions the consciousness of individuality is blurred. Whatever reason lies in the action has been merged with instinct by habit. It is neither the joint action nor thinking alike in conscious reasonable terms which induces this collective "unity"; it is *not thinking at all* at the given moment or occasion. The exercise of intellect in abstract reasoning will lead intelligent men to like conclusions through logical sequences, and at the same time develop their individuality; because thinking is an individual function.

Therefore the collectivist, to attain his objective, the collective society or state, seeks the one type of organization, the political agency, which is directly prohibitory and must tend to stop men thinking. This is the evil interpretation of the dream of power, its perversion into the lust for power over other men, instead of mastery of nature.

The lust for power is most easily disguised under humanitarian or philanthropic motives. It appeals naturally to people who feel a sentimental uneasiness for the misfortunes of others, mixed with the craving for unearned praise, and most especially if they are non-productive.* An amiable child wishing for a million dollars will usually "intend" to give away half of this illusory wealth. The twist in the motive is

---

* The tax farmers in France lent their patronage to the proponents of rigid political systems, such as the Physiocrats, and other absolutist theorists who brought on the Terror. Incidentally, at least a few of the tax farmers were strung up to the lamp posts when the Terror broke loose—but only a few.

shown by the fact that it would be just as easy to wish such a windfall directly to those others without imagining oneself as the intermediary of their good fortune. The child may imagine earning the money, though even so imagination might as well extend to others earning theirs; but as a rule it is to come from some undefined available effortless supply already extant—a perpetual motion machine. The child does not even conceive that persons in need of help can also imagine a million dollars for themselves. The double gratification, of personal wants and of power through "doing good," is innocently stipulated. Carried into adult years, this naïve self-glorification turns to positive hatred of any suggestion of persons helping themselves by their own individual efforts, by the non-political means which imply no power over others, no compulsory apparatus. The hatred has a deep motive back of it; for it is true that *nothing but the political means* will yield unearned public adulation. Let it be asked how any person wholly devoid of talent, skill, accomplishment, wit, beauty, charm, or even the practical ability to earn a living by routine labor, can conceivably become an object of flattering attention, greeted with applause and given a hearing for the feeblest inanities—obviously nothing will serve except political position. A large private fortune may procure a private circle of sycophants; but only the imperial decree could have gained Nero an audience for his singing or extorted applause for Caligula from the crowd.

But the rationalized dream of the Absolute State has a special historic connotation on its recurrence. The periods in which it has crystallized in literature are vastly significant.

The three most famous paper schemes of this type are Plato's "Politeia," or ideal state, mistranslated as the "Republic," * More's Utopia, and Marx's nameless Promised Land

* If any meaning is to attach to language, it is by distinctions. Rome supplied the form and meaning of Republic, with the word; and the Greeks of democracy. Plato's model of organization was the Spartan collective, a democratic military Absolute State. The distinction between a Republic and a Democracy was made

to come after the destruction of capitalism. What they have
in common in their form is that all of them are final; they
are arrangements in which human beings fit as specialized
parts of a pattern. Their social and economic relations admit
neither the biologically natural but mathematically irregular
and interwoven order of the family, nor the unpredictable
creative faculty of the individual. The mold is set, to pre-
clude variation or change. They are static societies. Plato and
More made the individual subject to the civic organization,
and Marx made him subject to mechanized industry.

But what they have in common in respect of the times
when they were imagined reveals their true significance.
Each of the three marks an era in which new developments
had already occurred *which must make a static society impossible.* The men who wrote these dreams were seismo-
graphic. They had felt the impending change, as if the earth
had shifted beneath their feet; and their minds took refuge
in a fantasy of a world which should not be subject to change.
Plato lived in the age when the Greeks were formulating the
basic principles of science. Sir Thomas More lived in the
dangerous years of the Renaissance, the revival of science.
Marx witnessed the industrial revolution, the application of
science. All three fantasies are reactions from the Age of
Energy.

Plato was a literary man; it was his artistic sense of form
which was disquieted, and which he sought to compensate
with a rigorous design. More was an intelligent man and a
wit; he labeled his creation frankly for what it was: Utopia
means Nowhere. Marx was a fool; he offered his scheme as
a prediction of the future.

It is through this imposed model for clockwork that

in the very words; democracy literally means the rule of the people, a concept
which will not admit any limitation in the political power. A Republic signifies
an organization dealing with affairs which concern the public, thus implying that
there are also private affairs, a sphere of social and personal life, with which
government is not and should not be concerned; it sets a limit to the political
power. The facts in each case corresponded to the meaning of the words.

Europe has observed the United States since its inception; stultification could go no further. The principle of social harmony is liberty, the rights of the individual; that is the natural law of man, which the United States had discovered and formulated, before the French Revolution.

Henry Adams, who witnessed the Energy Age after it was well under way, spent his life endeavoring to trace the connection between the last century of the Middle Ages, and the modern outburst of energy in kinetic uses. He picked up the clue, pondered it, and let it slip. What was the relation, he asked, between the Virgin and the Dynamo? His question was neither irreverent nor irrelevant. He perceived that after the majesty of Divine Law had been established in medieval philosophy by severe logic, the image of the Virgin then became more prominent in religion, as the recipient of honors and petitions. He recognized that this was because the Virgin represented an unconstrained element, grace or mercy, which implies free will in man, being available to continual choice. Then man was not to be bound by any irrevocably determined sequence, as a machine is. Man is not a machine. But at this point Henry Adams failed to realize that it is by freedom of personal volition that man is capable of pursuing his intellectual inquiries and making his inventions. This is the genesis of the dynamo. Being constructed according to the laws of mechanics, the dynamo itself is deterministic; that is to say, left to itself, it will stop. Then if it is to run, it must be by the will and intelligence of man. *A machine economy cannot run on a mechanistic philosophy.*

CHAPTER XV

The Fatal Amendments

The United States is the Age of the Dynamo. By carrying over the axiom of free will from religious to political doctrine, a Niagara of kinetic energy was released. The swelling flow calls for maximum firmness of the bases and of tensile strength in the structure, and the minimum obstructive form or action. Unhappily every alteration, except two, in the Constitution, subsequent to the Bill of Rights,* was of a contrary type.

The test may be applied to any amendment by general questions: Does the amendment deny the rights of the individual? Does it weaken the bases by impairing the states as political entities? Does it add to the gross bulk or tend to improper distribution of the weight of the superstructure? If it does any of these things, it must turn the beneficial operation of a high energy system into a danger of equal magnitude.

Further, all these injurious effects are interacting; one amendment may inflict dual damage; and one impairment will cause occasion or excuse for another. As the structure cracks, sags, or sways, disrupting the private economy, the

---

* The Bill of Rights is integrally of the original Constitution, being "the price of ratification." It is an itemized safeguard of the rights of the individual, and of state sovereignty. The only objection then offered to it was that enumeration of individual rights might be construed as limiting them to the issues named or as implying that the primary right of the individual is not comprehensive—the European idea of "liberties" instead of the American liberty. The point seemed far-fetched; it was certainly far-sighted, for of late that very perversion has been proposed, in a cheap parody, with the phrases "freedom from want, freedom from fear," etc. However, it is impossible to make any instrument fool-proof; and the Bill of Rights has served admirably in practical application.

alternating attack by the zealous amenders will be plied more furiously. There is a progressive increase in chronological frequency of amendments to the Constitution. And the full consequences are compounded and cumulative, becoming manifest after a lapse of time all at once in a general collapse. They are also aggravated by a concurrent drift in judicial decisions, and extensions of the political power by simple usurpation. A sedition act is such usurpation; there is no authority for it in the Constitution, and there was wrathful protest on the first occasion; now it is accepted casually, with little comment except suggestions to enlarge it, frequently at the behest of alleged "liberals."

An early usurpation long forgotten as an event, yet still in force, took effect after over a century, in 1933, with the confiscation of private property in gold. When John Jay was Chief Justice, the first to hold the position, and as one of the authors of *The Federalist,* surely acquainted with the nature of the Constitution, he gave a verdict sustaining the right of the citizen to sue the government. Jay said that the American theory, origin, and form of government was a departure from the European idea on just that issue, the precedent right of the citizen over the state. By the American theory, Jay said, the government is the agent of the citizen, having only delegated authority; and it is absurd to hold that a person may not sue his agent. Subsequently Jay was reversed, though he cannot be refuted. But since then the citizen has been at the mercy of government in the United States as if he were the subject of a king; he cannot even plead for redress of wrong done him by the government, without permission. And the very first amendment (Article XI) after the Bill of Rights extends this usurped prerogative to the several states as against citizens of other states. The next amendment (XII) is technical.

Sixty-two years elapsed without further alteration, until the one positively right amendment was made, the Thirteenth, which limits the political power by debarring slavery.

The Fourteenth Amendment confirmed Federal citizenship and the civil rights of citizens throughout the Union. But it would have been better if the Bill of Rights had been explicitly extended to bind the state governments. This would not have relegated various issues to "implied powers," a wretched and dangerous subterfuge.

The Fifteenth Amendment fatally perpetuated the destruction wrought by the Reconstruction Act. It deprived the states of an indispensable attribute of state sovereignty, the exclusive power to designate the qualifications of voters, originally reserved to them by the Constitution.

The proper use of a necessary power and the proper agency for its use are entirely different questions. Control of the external borders of the nation rightly pertains to the Federal government, the organization representing the full territorial extent. The Federal government has certainly discriminated between races in quotas for entry. Possibly the line drawn is morally wrong; it may be unjustifiable even to reject refugees. Great nations have always been liberal in admission of persons. Nevertheless, it is necessary that the Federal government should have the power of the border; otherwise the nation cannot remain in being.

To form a true and workable federation, the component states must cede the attribute of sovereignty of the border. But they must retain a legitimate control over admission to the state's body politic, to preserve their political entities. This is the power to admit to the franchise. Race, color, or previous condition of servitude are irrelevant. They ought not to be considered disqualifications. The correct qualifications lie in local residence and allegiance and real property. Only in these requirements can a moral principle be found. If the franchise calls for qualification at all, it is clearly conditional, not absolute. So far as the conditions are practical, they must relate to the function of the instrument. The action is that of measured extension from a permanent base, so it must be attached to immovable local property. Liquid capital will not do.* These qualifications are moral as well as material, being all within the competence of the individual; a responsible person can fulfill them by his own choice and efforts. But it is absolutely necessary that the power to designate qualifications should also be in the state. If the Federal government has power to fix or alter any particular, even negatively, it has the ultimate full power of fixing all requirements by particulars. And a defect running through the whole structure is much more grave than a localized error.

Interference in this manner is by decomposition. It was forty years before the decomposition of the bases became fully apparent; but it made the next attack possible, when a national function was nullified, by the income tax amendment. Previously no direct or personal tax could be laid except in proportion to the population. Then the action would be equated in every voter and representative. If a tax were proposed, each would know that he must pay a proportionate share; while if any region were to receive an extra share in expenditure (as in river or harbor works, etc.), its influence would be greatly outweighed by that of the other areas. Mass inertia is the stabilizing function; it inheres in any ponderable material; but it is best understood when it is supplied separately, as in ballast. The weight (gravity) is the power; its use is in a constant relation to a center of gravity. When the interest of every voter must be practically the same, the center of gravity was a constant even though the particles of ballast were mobile. But when the Federal government could mulct a wealthy state in taxes disproportionate to the population, to buy out a poor state by expenditures disproportionate to the population, the equation vanished. The mass-inertia veto was lost. (The weight, the interest, thereafter took effect in unbalance, as uncompart-

* The ownership and residence in a slab shack with a potato patch is a *sound* qualification for the vote, while ownership of every share of stock in the Standard Oil Company is not.

mented liquid ballast surging from side to side, dislocated mass.)

Probably the majority of people had no comprehension of these altered relations. They thought of it in simple terms of taxing the rich, perhaps with a vague infantile further expectation that the proceeds would be "given to the poor." Money obtained from the rich in any form except wages is never given to the poor. If it is taken by an ordinary hold-up man, it goes to the hold-up man. If it is taken by a philanthropic organization, it goes to the organization. If it is taken by the government, it goes to the politicians. Neither does increased taxation of the rich lower the rate of taxation on the poor; it is bound to cause an increase in all taxation, reaching down inchmeal until it expropriates a portion, not merely of the last dollar of a poor man, but of the first dollar he can earn. The tax will have to be paid before he can even touch his earnings. The present tax on wages, accurately described as "the Social Security swindle," could not have been imposed under the original Constitution; it is validated only by the income tax amendment. There is no means by which "the rich" can be taxed without ultimately taxing "the poor" far more heavily. And one tax tends to increase all other taxes, instead of lessening them, because tax expenditure goes into things which require upkeep and yield no return (public buildings and political jobs). Kinetic energy has been converted into static forms, which then necessitate the diversion of more kinetic energy to carry the dead-load.

The final and formal stroke in disestablishing the states was the Seventeenth Amendment, which took the election of Senators out of the State Legislature and gave it to the popular vote. Since then the states have had no connection with the Federal government; representation in both Houses of Congress rests only on dislocated mass. The simultaneous abdication of both Houses in 1933 was the result. They were not thrust apart, they did not even fall apart, because they

were no longer in any structural relation whatever, neither
to mass nor to each other nor to the superstructure. They
had simply ceased to function. The immediate appearance of
an enormous bureaucracy was the natural phenomenon of the
structureless nation.

Concurrently and by interaction with these political events,
the productive economy was distorted, and energy diverted
into the political channel. The Civil War precipitated the
sequence. The looting of the defeated Southern states (under
the direction of philanthropists as usual in collaboration with
crooks), was most demoralizing because the political power
pretended to legitimacy in the acts of extortion. Scoundrels
were immune within the law, while honest men were forced
to revert to the primitive pre-legal mode of association; the
chief, informal council and *posse comitatus*. There was no
government, there was only force, the moral control having
been disconnected. People lived by the moral order; they
cannot survive otherwise; but the ancient and erroneous
identification of government with force became plausible
again. Likewise politics became lucrative.

Generally speaking, up to the Civil War any man seeking
political honors expected to do so at some financial loss to
himself; he lived by his private means. It is only when
this condition prevails that men of intelligence, integrity, and
good taste—the productive character—will be inclined to
enter public life. Lord Acton was referring to political power
when he said: "All power corrupts, and absolute power corrupts absolutely." Political power has this effect by its relation to production. The productive man is aware that political
expenditure is a charge upon production, net expense. He
does not like to live at the expense of others. If he is obliged
to forego in his private earnings more than he receives in the
remuneration of office, though he may not be sure that he
has earned his salary, he is at least certain that he did not
seek office as a parasite. It is to be observed that today the
men who refuse to accept any pay for government positions

are without exception those who have been most actively engaged in production, industrial managers. The previous "social workers," professional politicians, and persons with unearned incomes, are distinguished by the eagerness with which they attach themselves to the political payroll, or turn their political position to incidental gain. They are not aware of any objective in political life except parasitism. The parasitical view of politics was formulated unconsciously when the argument began to be heard that larger salaries, perquisites, more ostentatious public buildings, embassies, and uniforms must be provided to maintain the dignity of office. If a position is rated by its expense or display, obviously it must be deemed wanting in intrinsic dignity or worth. The ambassadors who feared that in ordinary clothes they might be taken for waiters were probably right. No one would have taken Franklin, Adams, or Jefferson for a lackey.

It is this derogation of values that the productive man dislikes. Further, he knows he will be constantly importuned for favors he has no right to grant, by the parasites he would never meet in productive life. Hence the best men are found in public life only when it is dangerous, burdensome, and at their own expense.

The cost and display of government is always in inverse ratio to the liberty and prosperity of the citizens, as with the impoverished nation and magnificent monarchy of Louis XIV. Today, when our agriculture is in distress, the Department of Agriculture grows like a monstrous fungus. The huge Department of Commerce grew as international trade dwindled and internal commerce dived into the depression.

Further, political power has a ratchet action; it works only one way, to augment itself. A transfer occurs by which the power cannot be retracted, once it is bestowed. In the lowest illustration of this, a candidate for office may promise the voters that he will reduce taxes, or the number of offices, or the powers of office. But once he is elected, he can use the taxes, the officeholders, or the powers to ensure re-election;

therefore the motive of the promise is no longer operative. By cutting down expenditure or the number of officeholders or graft, he will certainly create enemies, so the reverse motive, impelling him to evade his promise, is doubled. The voter can only vote the incumbent out; but the next officeholder will come into those augmented powers, and be still harder to get rid of in turn. The difficulty of taking back powers once granted is illustrated in the repeal of the Prohibition Amendment; although it was demanded and carried by overwhelming sentiment of the citizens, the article of repeal contained a proviso which would retain numerous Federal jobs; it was impossible to make a clean sweep of the pernicious usurped power. The Prohibition Amendment was an assertion of absolute government, the indication of complete decomposition of the body politic. The "lame duck" amendment is a triviality indicating nothing but the degradation of the charter, a scribble on the margin.

CHAPTER XVI

The Corporations and Status Law

Concurrently with the specific extension of political power, the production system is disorganized, directly and indirectly. The Civil War had far-reaching consequences in economic life. The "reconstruction" of the South loaded the Southern states with debt contracted by the camp-followers of government by conquest, the carpetbag administration. Repudiation ensued; whether or not the bonds could have been paid, the Southerners felt no moral obligation, and it is not difficult to understand their position. They may have been in error none the less; repudiation of debt grounds the transmission line of energy, and the South remained economically prostrate while the rest of the nation went ahead.

The Civil War also prompted the Federal government to finance railroads, by land grants and cash subsidies. With this the era in which business was charged with corrupting politics was well under way. Now business cannot corrupt politics. The glib retort would be that corruption cannot be corrupted. But political organization is not corruption within its right limits, which are approximately indicated by the margin where the alleged corruption by business begins. It is certainly politics that corrupts business, and must do so to the degree of its over-extension. Business consists of production and exchange. These are spontaneous activities, which must be carried on in freedom. Hence individual private property is requisite for a high energy system; the owner does not have to wait for permission to put it in use. The field of business is primary.

Politics consists of the power to prohibit, obstruct, and expropriate. Its field is marginal; but for this reason it always tends to encroach on the primary field of freedom, in such manner that the producer may be compelled to obtain permission before he can get to work. Where permission is required, or expropriation possible, a consideration may be extorted. Does the element of corruption inhere in business or in politics?

Is it wrong to produce something or to process or exchange the products? No. Then it cannot impart corruption to anything else. Is it wrong to restrain, obstruct, or seize the goods of another? Yes. It is always wrong if done by initiating action (instead of recoil action). The potential of corruption then lies in politics, not in business. When politics are notably corrupt, it is an infallible indication that there is too much political power, extending beyond its proper marginal field of action.

The political power, both obstructive and expropriative, was so extended in respect of the railroads. To bring in the West, the Federal government made huge land grants and gave a cash subsidy for a transcontinental railway. But for the Civil War, probably the Federal government would not have taken such action. If it had not, no one can say how long it might have been before a transcontinental line went through, if ever; but indisputably there would have been some years' delay. Here is the combination of circumstances and sequence of events which lends plausibility to argument for political action extending into the primary field of economics. Was there not a positive gain, at least in time? Indeed, how could a transcontinental line have been built at all, through the long stretch of wilderness, without Federal subsidies?

To dispose of the last question first, if the political power had merely permitted anyone who wanted to build a transcontinental line to acquire title to the necessary right of way on the same terms as any settlers in virgin territory, whether by purchase or by entry, use and record, a railway would have been built as soon as there was a reasonable prospect of sufficient traffic, or perhaps a little too soon.

Still, in the existent circumstances, there was the chronological "gain in time." Development by private capitalism works on a self-adjusting time space equation of local energy circuits and the long circuit. The solitary frontier trapper was an advance guard capitalist. He might bring a pack of furs to trade only once a year; then they went by wagon freight. It might be said that he was a year or more away from the market. On the other hand, a year was his production and exchange time anyhow, more or less; he could get along for a couple of years if he had to. But if fur prices and freight rates warranted, competitive transport would be attracted, in a year or two.

Farming also advanced into the wilderness by private enterprise at a self-adjusting rate, whatever the surplus production would pay for in time and distance (transport). If a group of farmers had "gained" time, in terms of distance, into the wilderness, they would have been that much worse off. Throughout the private economy, the costs and risks are self-evident, and the conditions are open to choice. Errors are self-liquidating.

There was a peculiarity of the slave economy, that it was incapable of pioneering, being unable to go beyond the limits of established political authority, of its own kind. If a slave-owner had compelled his slaves to assist in conveying himself and his goods beyond the scope of the collective power by which he enforced his commands—which in fact made them slaves—he would have had no further control over them. He could not have got back nor sent his goods back on the same terms as he came. So it would have been with anyone who used the slaves in like manner by favor of the owner. Travelers in Africa have recounted how they were supplied with bearers by command of some native chief, and the bearers carried the burden for a certain distance, and then ignored further orders. Whether the travel-

ers had "gained time" or not can be reckoned only by the
time it took them to find some other means of transport to
get out of their plight.

The peculiar position of the Western farmers becomes
apparent when their complaints are examined. Railway freight
rates were so much lower than wagon freight would have
been, over the same distance, that there is no comparison.
Railway freight was also ten times speedier. Yet the farmers
denounced the railways for their high rates; and if any delay
occurred, it caused intense exasperation. Had it been suggested to a Western farmer that if he thought such charges
excessive, he should use some competitive line or method
of transport, he would have been indignant. There was none,
nor could he wait until competition arrived. The time and
distance which seemed to have been "gained" was simply
the measure of his distance in time from competition; which
means, from the market. The political power had intervened,
and such was its necessary effect. The Western farmers, who
willingly took what appeared to be the advantage of it, in
so doing had surrendered their power of choice for an indefinite future period. The intervention of the political
power had created a monopoly. And even its supposed beneficiaries found it odious.

Curiously, people made the correct distinction emotionally,
though they failed to translate it into reason. There was a
marked ambivalence in the feeling toward the railways.
The sight and sound of a locomotive is still evocative to
Americans of wonder, romance, and hopeful anticipation. In
rural districts and small towns, everyone liked to go on a
train journey. People went down to the station to see the
train come in. They knew the expresses by number, listened
to the whistle as a friendly sound, waved as the trains went
by. They hated "the railway" only as an abstraction.*

---

* Except perhaps in California, notably in San Francisco, where it is no
exaggeration to say that people loathed even the train, the tracks, and the railway station, with objective animosity. There were special reasons for this local

What was it then that they hated? Certainly they did not wish to abolish railways, never see one again. The distinction emerges clearly. *Everything that was the creation of private enterprise in the railways gave satisfaction.* Private enterprise mined, smelted, and forged the iron, invented the steam engine, devised surveying instruments, produced and accumulated the capital, organized the effort. In the building and operation of the railways, whatever lay in the realm of private enterprise was done with competence. The first transcontinental line was the greatest engineering job ever tackled as one undertaking. It went through with the unprecedented speed of the high potential long circuit of energy to which it belonged. The same genius for organization of high energy systems went into the operation of the lines. No previous type of business called for one-tenth the ability of this type; schedules had to be exact, continuous, and yet instantly adjustable in every detail, over time and space, handling unpredictable numbers of persons or units of goods in transit between thousands of intermediate points in a branching system, both ways, at maximum velocity. Probably the railways still represent the peak of efficiency in operating management, because no greater demand has yet been made by any other business. And, on the whole, the public respected this achievement.

What people hated was the monopoly. The monopoly, and nothing else, was the political contribution.

Even in its proper application, the political power tends to cause irritation; much more so when it is unwarranted. Life protests instantly against compulsion, arrest, or expro-

---

sentiment. California had an independent existence before the advent of the railways. Then certain railway magnates lived .there, in visible enjoyment of large fortunes gained by the political subsidies which went into the railroads. Further, there were flagrant local cases of farmers positively defrauded by one railway corporation on land contracts, and they never got redress; in which again the political power was used to perpetrate the injustice. Men were actually killed for defending their property rights. The mixture of political power in economic life had the usual effect of insolent corruption.

priation of its creative product. The black cloud of sheer hatred, vindictive despair, which obscures the civilized world at present, is evoked by the omnipresence of political agencies. The Gestapo and Ogpu or Cheka are the slimy spawn of the Absolute State.

The direct consequence of the encroachment of political power on the primary field of free enterprise, in respect of the railways, was that new states were admitted to the Union before they had time to develop true regional interests and political entities. In one instance at least, a state was designated solely to secure a political majority in the nation. Being in effect creations of the Federal government rather than of the citizens of the state, the newer states tended to look to the Federal government for special legislation, including charity.

The indirect consequence was quite as bad. Obviously, if public funds have been granted to endow anything whatever, on the pretext that it is for the benefit of the citizens at large, every citizen must have the right to use the resultant facilities on equal terms. (He may not want to use them at all; he might even be ruined financially in his private fortune by being unable to compete with the government-endowed corporation; but he isn't asked about that.) Then the government must have authority to enforce such equality. (It has already destroyed the natural power of the individual to bring the corporation to terms by competition.) "Government regulation" is imposed. To be sure, it won't do the citizen any good; the result is that the railways are not allowed to make desirable improvements or discontinue wasteful expenditure.* But the power is there, and is bound to be used. (It does no good simply because the "mixed economy" leaves no basis of equity; there is no ethical reason

---

* The actual improvement of railway service, and economy of management, has kept pace with the development of a competitive method of transportation, in motor cars and planes. At the same time, the railways have not been superseded, because the different modes of transport feed into one another, each having a special function.

why anyone should be entitled to a ten dollar subsidy from the public funds, any more than to a million dollars.)

Successful management and productive enterprise had always been admired and respected, as they should be; presently they became liable to suspicion and resentment. The change of sentiment is easily traced to its origin. If any one business may be named, after the railroads, as having incurred this obloquy, it was the Standard Oil Company. Yet, like the railways, Standard Oil by its ordinary business operations steadily increased the comfort and convenience of existence in America—from oil lamps to gas stations. It has been managed with amazing competence; it has met every financial obligation unfailingly through hard times and kept solvent; its products have been excellent and reliable. It might be cited as a model corporation—if it had not used the political power, at one remove, by taking rebates on railway freight rates. The charge of ruining competitors would have had no point but for the means employed, which were deemed unfair, as they certainly are. If one department store prospers and another fails, the public rightly realizes that better judgment has been used in locating or managing the successful store, and that there is no sound reason why they should subsidize bad judgment. They know that capable competition does not tend to extinguish competition, but enlarges the market; the possibility of choice is what people want. But the individual taxpayer had no choice about giving rebates on a tax-subsidized "public utility." Standard Oil had used the political means; it became an object of execration. Demonstrably there was no other cause of offense, since the people who denounced it still purchased its products willingly. They approved Standard Oil as a business; they were enraged by its political connection.

Now the sole remedy for the abuse of political power is to limit it; but when politics corrupt business, modern reformers invariably demand the enlargement of the political power. There was a time when people had either more sense or more honesty; but perhaps it was only that the issue could not be mistaken, as it then appeared. The corporate form obscured the transaction. In an earlier day, monopolies were granted by kings to their favorites. It was evident that a law aimed at individuals would be absurd; the effective course was to prohibit the political power from granting monopolies. But the proposal to "regulate" corporations to prevent monopolies seemed plausible. If it were mere folly, it would leave things no worse than they were; but it contains another element—it reintroduces status law.

This was done by diverting attention from the cause to the effect, and finally legislating against the natural process which had been injuriously affected—a triple perversion.

As freak legislation, the anti-trust laws stand alone. *Nobody knows what it is they forbid.* Their professed object is to prevent or dissolve (with penalties) "combinations in restraint of trade." What is a combination in restraint of trade?

The railroads could not be charged with that imaginary crime unless two or more railway corporations combined; but their monopolies existed anyhow, and they never restrained trade anyhow. They took all the traffic they could get, and did a good deal to create traffic, by drumming up immigration.

Standard Oil did not restrain trade; it went out to the ends of the earth to make a market. Can the corporations be said to have "restrained trade" when the trade they cater to had no existence until they produced and sold the goods? Were the motor car manufacturers restraining trade during the period in which they made and sold fifty million cars, where there had been no cars before? Or did the railways restrain the motor car industry? They had no means of doing so; what they really did was to bring the raw materials to the motor car manufacturer, and then transport the finished cars everywhere for sale.

If two corporations do combine, and carry on all the business both of them previously handled, enlarging it if possible, are they restraining trade? The accusation has been brought against the corporations that they don't produce more than they have a reasonable expectation of being able to sell by strenuous efforts. This is "limiting" and therefore "restraining" trade. But, in the first place, any one season's production is intrinsically limited by the capital available, as well as the prospective market; and, in the second place, if they stretched that limit to its utmost one season, and did not sell the whole product at a net profit, they would not be able to produce anything next year. They would be bankrupt. They can't even eat up their capital by degrees, so much a year. Generally, their paid-up capital is in plant and equipment; while materials in process of manufacture, or in stock, represent credit (bank loans or bills payable). Even if a manufacturer were to operate strictly on his own capital, owing nobody and with money in the bank, his stock is liquid capital; and would be depleted the second year. As for borrowed capital, credit, if interest is not paid and bills for materials met, the loans must be called and no more material will be delivered; then the whole business stops at once; not by successive percentages; and the plant is rendered non-productive. If the management should disregard these imperatives, they would be eligible for Matteawan. It is difficult to believe that anyone could make such a suggestion in good faith.

Then what was the offense to be? Other complaints against the corporations comprised a triple contradiction. They were variously accused of charging too much, of underselling competitors, and of price-fixing (agreeing on prices with competitors).

Exactly how much, in comparison with what, is "too much?" Is it too much if the owner asks more than somebody is willing or able to pay? Then the great majority of us ought to have a legal case against Tiffany's. Is it asking more than someone else asks for the same kind of goods? Then that other person is guilty of "underselling"; both should be haled into court. But if they agreed to set the same price, they would be criminals as price-fixers. Nor would it be an innocent course for them to sell nothing more and starve to death peacefully; they would certainly be "limiting the market" if they held their goods or did not go on producing.

Altogether, the only acts which could be alleged against the corporations in their business transactions are simply the necessary acts of production and exchange; the Neolithic man who chipped out a flint arrowhead and swapped it for a clamshell ornament was guilty of the same crime—except that one charge of "combining" two or more corporations. Now it would have been quite possible to pass a specific law to prevent such mergers; all that was necessary was to limit their charters, and forbid one corporation to buy another, or any shares in it. Such a law might have been either senseless or somewhat harmful; it would certainly have been in restraint of trade, but the political power is restrictive; and the law would have been specific in naming the act proscribed.

That was the one thing the legislators would not do. Least of all would they admit or name the real offense—the use of political power. Their object was to secure control of the corporations. It was attained by using a phrase which could be construed as covering any business transaction whatever, if a corporation were concerned in it; with the implication that such acts were to be deemed crimes, in the particular instances, according to their effects, *although those effects could in no case be shown or proved.* Take any such case, real or imaginary, and let the question be asked: Exactly where, when, and how was trade restrained? Was the volume of trade diminished? Was any person actually restrained from offering an article for sale, or buying an article offered if he chose to do so? What article? And what person?

When an individual is indicted for embezzlement, theft, or the like offense, the money or goods involved must have actual existence, and the owner must be named; with the

burden of proof on the prosecution, the accused needing only
to refute the evidence presented, if he is innocent. If a person
were simply charged with "dishonesty," or "immorality," and
required to account for his whole life, to bring all his correspondence into court on demand, and prove a general
negative, he would be subject to the same *kind* of law as the
anti-trust laws. Individuals were subject to that kind of law,
in the Society of Status. Its modern name is Administrative
Law. During the nineteenth century, it survived only in
Russia, under the Czars (and was there called administrative
law; travelers from free nations heard of it with astonishment and indignation). It is still the law in Communist
Russia, but it is no longer confined to Russia.

Surely, if an earnest endeavor had been made to decide
upon the most imbecile accusation possible against anyone—
such as arresting a rabbit for practicing birth control, or a
Marathon champion in the middle of the race for loitering,
or Brigham Young for celibacy—nothing more preposterous
could have been imagined than to fix upon the American
corporations, which have created and carried on, in ever-
increasing magnitude, a volume and variety of trade so vast
that it makes all previous production and exchange look like
a rural roadside stand, and call this performance "restraint
of trade," further stigmatizing it as a crime!

Another aspect of the imposition of political "regulation"
on economic effort is the pretext that the corporations had
too much power, an economic power which also influenced
politics. This is likewise imputed to large private fortunes,
as an excuse for heavy death-duties. As a matter of fact, the
danger inherent in large fortunes is their weakness against
political power. But if it were proved that the corporations
did have and exercise such undue power culpably, and a serious proposal made to remedy this condition by handing over
the government to the corporation management, would it
not be manifestly a lunatic scheme? Yet that is the net effect
of government regulation, beyond the enforcement of con-

tract law as it applies to any commercial transaction between private persons. The political and economic powers are merged, brought under a single control. Thereafter it is immaterial which group of persons exercises the joined powers (though the politicians will inevitably get the upper hand); the sum of power will be the same. Whether three is added to two, or two to three, the result is five. "Totalitarian government" is nothing but political control over economic life. The cry against "competition," the senseless phrase, "production for use and not for profit,"—as if there could be any profit if the product were not used; did Standard Oil pour its products down the sink? or did the management of General Motors wear their product on their watch chains?—are all approaches to political control and absolute tyranny. Competition cannot be eradicated; in productive or creative effort it is beneficial. If it is penalized in such desirable manifestations, it finds mean and futile expression. At royal courts, where status is rigidly defined, and there is no productive field, trifles become objects of competition; courtiers will stand on their feet all day so that sitting down may become a privilege; princes will squabble ignominiously over the distinction of walking first through a door. A man who makes a better car than another, or makes it at less cost, is competing usefully; even a man who wants to make more money than his neighbor, in a free society, will find the largest fortunes are made by large-scale production. It is only in the political field that competition is for power over other men, even to slaughter more of them in war. Individualism alone gives legitimate and creative play to the competitive instinct to increase and improve production.

Government cannot "restore competition," or "ensure" it. Government is monopoly; and all it can do is to impose restrictions which may issue in monopoly, when they go so far as to require permission for the individual to engage in production. This is the essence of the Society of Status.

The reversion to status law in the anti-trust legislation

went unnoticed. Probably the politicians did not know exactly what they had done; but they knew what they wanted. They had secured a law under which it was impossible for the citizen to know beforehand what constituted a crime, and which therefore made all productive effort liable to prosecution if not to certain conviction. Because it was imposed at first through corporations, its actual incidence was not realized. Whoever said that "a corporation has neither a body to be kicked nor a soul to be damned" had a glimpse of the truth, which is that any law whatever must bear upon *persons*. The acts of a corporation are necessarily performed by persons; the assets of a corporation belong to persons; the punishment must fall upon persons. And if such acts are liable to penalty, the law can and will shortly extend to include strictly individual effort in its scope.

It is in that extension that the naked purpose becomes apparent. The full import of any extension of the political power consists in the field of action which it covers, not in the particular act first forbidden. I.e., if government is morally competent to prohibit the sale of intoxicating liquor, it must have power to prescribe every item of diet to citizens. After centuries of freedom, such an assertion will seem vaguely absurd; but it was put in practice in Sparta. The field of action which the anti-trust laws invaded was that of production and exchange; the first crime alleged was "restraint of trade." But the power invoked was necessarily comprehensive; and when it was applied to individuals, the charge was "over-production!"

Once again, it is deemed a crime to work, a crime to produce. It is even a crime to give away food grown by the donor on his own land, by his own labor. It is not yet a specific crime for a man to eat the food he has grown—as it is in Russia—but that is the inevitable next step. Already the primary right of human beings to mere existence has been denied; since farm quotas, priorities, and ration cards cover all the processes of production and exchange, by which existence is supported, life is made to depend upon daily and hourly permission.

In the famous Dred Scott case, which men understood correctly as defining the issues on which the Civil War was precipitated, the decision rested upon a stated axiom; and the axiom repudiated the Declaration of Independence. Technically, it was found that the Court had no jurisdiction; and the reason given was that a Negro could not be a citizen, not even by birth nor though his parents were not in formal bondage. He might indeed be allowed to reside in the country, and to hold property, but only by favor, not of right. If he were not a citizen, he must be liable to deportation. Yet having been born in the United States, he had no other country, no place to which he could claim admittance. Then he could nowhere enjoy the first benefit of property, which is standing ground. There was no place on earth where he had a right to be; which is to say, *he had no right to be*, if that decision contained the truth.

In Dred Scott's case, his material condition was deduced from a primary assumption, a denial of the birthright of a human being. By the opposite approach, when the acquisition, possession or use of every material object is made permissive, then every productive action of which a man is capable can be performed only by permission. As such actions constitute a man's mode of being, the primary assumption is implicit; he has been reduced to the nameless plight of Dred Scott. If he has no *right* to act, to produce, to exchange, *he has no right to be*.

So the ruling upon Dred Scott has been pronounced upon all humanity, by the denial of every attribute of birthright. Men are presumed to exist only by permission. At long last, the persistent purpose of the non-producers has been attained, with no reservations, no limitations; and most extraordinarily, with no other claim than that of their own incompetence. They have got a strangle hold on the producers.

CHAPTER XVII

The Fiction of Public Ownership

As language is the faculty which distinguishes man from the lower animals, it is also a ready index to the intellectual level of cultures and persons. The confusion and vagueness of terms always found in collectivist theories is not accidental; it is a reversion to the mental and verbal limitations of the primitive society it advocates, the inability to think in abstract terms. This defect is strikingly evident in the collectivist arguments concerning property.

Property is ownership. Things which nobody owns are not property; they are merely objects in nature. Perhaps the most senseless phrase ever coined even by a collectivist is that of Proudhon: "All property is theft." It is indeed remarkable in its own way, for the variety of errors compressed into such brief utterance; in four words it confuses objects, acts, attributes, moral values, and relations, as if they were interchangeable. Theft presupposes rightful ownership. An object must be property *before* it can be stolen.

Savages and collectivists are notably ignorant of the severely logical branch of language, which is mathematics. The savage does not go beyond simple addition and subtraction of digits. The collectivist may learn formulas by rote, but cannot grasp the principle of their application to physical phenomena. He will reckon upon processes and results which could be obtained only from a factor he has theoretically excluded from the problem he is proposing to solve. The problem is to define the conditions necessary to a productive society. They must answer to the world of physical reality; nothing may be assumed to exist in physical reality which does not so exist; nor may any aspect of physical phenomena be excluded which will inevitably enter into the conditions in reality. But when the collectivist rejects private property from his theoretic economy, he excludes those aspects of material phenomena which mathematics recognizes by the third dimension. "The three dimensions of a body, or of ordinary space, are length, breadth and thickness; a surface has only two dimensions; a line only one." With the third dimension, cubic measure is possible; and the construction becomes capable of solid content. It would never have been possible to conceive of measure abstractly without the previous reality and concept of a unit of measure. The unit of measure of physical energy is established from solids, in terms of time, space, and mass resistance or displacement (gravity). Real physical energy cannot exist except in a three dimensional world, nor without its real existence could it have been conceived abstractly.

Two bodies cannot occupy the same space at the same time. This is the reason why private property belongs to man as a creative being (a right both natural and divine). Individual ownership anwers exactly to the conditions of physical phenomena. Public ownership is fictitious; its verbal terms do not correspond to reality, to the properties of physical objects and the conditions of time and space. A number of persons may reside in the same house, but only by allotment of objects in space and time to each, either specifically or by precedence. Nobody could live in a house if the general public were assumed to have the right to go in and out, to sit in the chairs, sleep in the beds, cook in the kitchen. Ten men may be legally equal owners of one field, but none of them can get any good of it unless its occupancy and use is allotted among them by measures of time and space. No agreement can obviate this necessity. If all ten wished to do exactly the same thing at the same time in the same spot, it would be physically impossible, whether they agreed or not. Private group ownership necessarily resolves into manage-

ment by one person, with division of the product, and ultimate recourse to division of the actual property, in case of
irreconcilable disagreement.

Theoretically, public property belongs to everybody
equally, indivisibly, and simultaneously, which is absurd; if
this assumption were applied, the result would be that any
person presenting himself to use the property could be asked:
"Are you everybody?" and he would be bound to reply:
"No"; while he could not assert any claim to use any
particular division of the property. The actual use of public
property by the public is therefore limited to approximately
two dimensional conditions, in which cubic measure, or solids,
need not be taken into account, so that a man is regarded
as a point in a line which is divisible into an infinite number
of points; and with any number of lines intersecting without
interference, on a plane surface. Thus it is practicable—
whether or not it is necessary or advisable—to make roads
public property, because the use of a road is to traverse it.
Though the user does in fact occupy a given space at a given
moment, the duration is negligible, so that there is no need
to take time and space into account except by negation, a
prohibition: the passenger is not allowed to remain as of
right indefinitely on any one spot in the road. The same rule
applies to parks and public buildings. The arrangement is
sufficiently practicable in those conditions to admit the fiction
of "public ownership." To be sure, even in the use of a road,
if too many members of the public try to move along it at
once, the rule reverts to first come, first served (allotment
in time and space), or the authorities may close the road. The
public has not the essential property right of continuous and
final occupancy.

"Public property" which is used for other purposes than
transit is not available to the public at all in any way. Part
of the Executive Mansion is open to the public for transit
part of the time; but the conditions were pointedly expressed
when two children wandered into the building without per-

mission and intruded into the forbidden space. The wife of the Chief Executive deemed it advisable to print a warning that such conduct was unsafe; the children might have been shot by a guard. "Public domain" which is leased for revenue is used by the lessees as private persons; and the rent is not distributed to members of the public; it is used by officials. Whatever "public" property admits of tenure in occupancy, or bears usufruct, officials occupy it or consume the usufruct, while the public pays the upkeep. "Public utilities" are not available to the public as owners. Any citizen who wishes to obtain electricity from a municipal plant must pay out of his private resources for the measured quantity of electricity he gets. He is not the owner; an owner does not have to buy the product of his own property. At the same time, a citizen who does not use any electricity is nevertheless charged indirectly with a fraction of the upkeep in taxes, though he cannot exercise any property rights whatever in the plant. He can't even go into the premises of right, which is the first prerogative of an owner.

Public property then admits of *use by the public* only in transit, not for production, exchange, consumption, or for security as standing ground. Where all property is "public," under Communism, government ownership, the officials appropriate to their personal use whatever they like, with funds for upkeep; while the public exists perpetually in the condition of passengers on a road, having no right to remain in any one spot or to use any object; all the activities of members of the public must be by permission of compulsion.

It is impossible to imagine any practical method by which the use or the product of any kind of productive property whatever can be made available to "the public" as such. Though anyone who comes along may use a road (unless it gets jammed), it is not possible to devise any means by which anyone who comes along can help himself to electricity, or for the matter of that to potatoes, as a member of the public, "according to his needs." The phrase has no application to reality *in a productive society*. It is an idea limited to the conditions of wild nature, in which primitive man lives on whatever he can catch or pick up in the way of game, berries, fish, or insects.*

The collectivist is incapable of understanding this because his concept of the "collective" *has no dimensions*. The society founded on private property is organized for a man of three dimensions, occupying a space of his own in a world of three dimensions, through which energy flows in action and is put to use for production. The collectivist society is "planned" for a world of two dimensions, in which nothing is conceived as occupying space or causing displacement. Man is conceived to be everywhere at once and nowhere in particular, in the collective. The concept is that of a world and a society *in which there is no energy*, neither kinetic nor static.

But since in reality every object must occupy three dimensional space, and moving objects do cause displacement, whenever communists seize the political power to try their alleged experiment, Communism is always said to be still in the future, never in the present. The present is described as "a period of transition." The commonsense of colloquial speech recognizes the facts, with the advent of collectivism, when people complain that they are being "pushed around."

Perhaps the collectivist has a dim notion of his logical difficulty with the no-dimensional collective; for all collectivist theories begin with the assumption of a productive machinery and system *taken over* from the society of private property and personal enterprise. Collectivists must feel, though they do not acknowledge it, that their hypothetical society is non-productive, for production creates its own means of production. To obscure this difficulty, they lay stress on distribution and consumption as the crux of their schemes. But still they

---

*Even in a hunting economy, where a good kill of game is distributed among the members of the tribe, it is the individual hunter who gives it for distribution, and his own property right is observed in that he keeps for himself the portion he prefers.

cannot imagine any practical method which approximates to their promise; they can only offer a paper copy of the forms of distribution devised by the society of private property, while eliminating the moral and physical relations which made those forms workable. That is, they must use quantitative measure for goods, and of time for labor (measures unnecessary to the savage living on the bounty of nature); and a medium of exchange. But they deny the right of the owner and producer to his property and product. In so doing, they necessarily deny the right of a man to his own labor, which is to say, to his own person. All collective societies demand forced labor. With this there can be no true exchange, but only expropriation and doles.

Collectivists use the word "right" but never in any context which corresponds with reality, and is capable of specific application. By the Marxist theory, of course they ought not to use the word "right" at all, for Dialectical Materialism is deterministic; therefore it admits no right nor wrong. The use of speech is communication, but Marxists use words with the intent of causing confusion; yet they assume that a productive society, which depends primarily on exact communication, can be organized after they have destroyed that means. In this they revert below savagery, and even below the animal level. They have got down to the premise of mere mechanism. Cogs in a machine need no language.

Thus collectivists talk of civil rights in a collective society, where in fact civil rights cannot exist because there is no *place* in which they can be exercised and no materials on which they can take effect. How can a man speak freely if there is no spot on which he and his audience have the right to stand? How can he practice his religion if he has no right to own a religious edifice, or to his own person? How is a free press to exist if the materials are not in private ownership? With state ownership, *nothing can be done except by command or permission.* A slave is under command and permission. He is not free.

Collectivists talk frequently of "the right to work." What does that connote in terms of physical reality? In a free society, any man has by nature the right to work. No one may force him to work; nor may anyone stop him from working on his own property or in contract with another. But if he has no property, or not enough to yield him a livelihood, he must seek employment from others. It is never within the worker's power to exact his own terms in full, any more than he can find in nature everything as he would have it; but since the employer must need to hire labor (else he would not be at the trouble), there is a basis for bargaining and agreement. If neither is willing to meet the other's terms or to compromise, each may look elsewhere, to another possible employer or workman. But it is said that the workman without property (land) is in more urgent need than the prospective employer; he cannot afford to wait, hold out a length of time for his terms, as the employer can. (It is not conceded in theory that employers go broke, though they certainly do in fact; it is rather assumed that they can sit tight forever if they choose.) Therefore, because land exists in nature and all the raw materials of production are of natural origin, it is said that if a man cannot demand and receive employment at a living wage as of right, his natural right to work has been denied.

But is there any imaginable production economy in which the contingency of unemployment will not occur with much harsher terms attached to it?

Certainly in a savage nomadic society, the raw resources of nature are directly available to every man (as to the lower animals), "according to his abilities." But the moment he begins to utilize those resources in any manner beyond the abilities of the lower animals, by making weapons or tools, private property in such objects is necessarily established. Still, any other man can presumably make similar tools from the resources of nature. Likewise, when land is brought under crude cultivation, marginal to a hunting economy—as some

North American Indians grew corn at their summer camps—
there need be no exact boundaries; and presumably any person might make his own tools and scratch a fresh plot of
ground. But natural causes bring about recurrent famine. The
hunter has the right to hunt, but he finds no game. Animals
may devour the corn; there is no fence. Buildings are not
tight nor durable; there is no way of storing food. Then
everybody starves, and that is that.

With permanent settlements, permanent landholdings are
recognized, in regular cultivation. The higher the form of
production, the more necessary it is to fix ownership, and
ownership may take various forms, by persons or local groups
or families or other allotments, possibly subject to reappor-
tionment. The two extremes of property title are government ownership and individual private property. The
question is, by which system does a man retain his natural
rights?

With group ownership, a man must be born or formally
admitted as a member of the group, else he has no property
right. If he has, he may in certain circumstances be bound
to the soil. Such was the feudal system. It was a three dimensional concept; a man had a place, a right to work on a
specific portion of land. But he was subject to forced labor so
many days a year; he had no right to change his employment; and he had little chance of increasing his production,
by improvement of tools. His natural rights were severely
restricted; he lost mobility and choice. The presumed compensation was stability, with a local energy circuit of production. But he still suffered recurrent famine, as in a state
of nature. The feudal system could not form the long circuit
of energy. A runaway from one feudal group could find no
place in another; he had to seek the contract society. Many
did, a proof of which system they found preferable; others
bought their freedom.

With individual private property, every man has a natural
right to own property. He may inherit it or earn the price

and purchase it. Such acquisition is reasonably possible for any able-bodied and competent person, in a natural lifetime, by labor and thrift. When he has got it, it is his own, with the usufruct. He can try out his own ideas, to improve or increase production, build on it for income, or otherwise please himself. He can accumulate provision for his old age or against vicissitudes of any kind. Further, in the contract society, if he has special abilities in management, or creative ideas, he can obtain capital on credit, with no guarantee on his part except honesty of conduct, and repayment if the project succeeds, the owner of the capital taking the financial risk of failure, while the borrower has a chance of considerable gain, and of knowing that he has earned it fairly by increasing production. These are the advantages peculiar to individual private property.

Then let the case against private property, its possible disadvantages, be stated with the utmost rigor, at its possible worst. Many persons may have inherited no property, nor yet have had time to accumulate any from their earnings before encountering hard times. True that some might have had the chance, and neglected it; but it is never true that all the unemployed had that previous chance. Some are young; others worked productively but met with sickness or loss. And even the imprudent cannot be deemed to have forfeited their natural rights. That opportunity may recur in the future does not soften the immediate pangs of want. Part of the lifetime of such persons will be a period of hardship, which may seem rather worse because others are more fortunate by no effort on their part.

But is it true that the unemployed are in this condition because they are denied access to the land?

In Europe, during modern times, practically all the usable land was owned. There was no wild land to which an unemployed man could have "access"; and the owners of land were unlikely to permit the unemployed to use it rent free. But in the United States, there was never a day, in "hard times," when the unemployed could not have had "access" to wild land, or even to owned land which the owner would have let them use for production. Yet in hard times men did not go into the wilderness. The statement that the land frontier took up the slack of unemployment during industrial depressions is a wholecloth falsehood. On the contrary, the frontier was settled from the capitalist production overflow of good times. During hard times men withdrew from the frontier, even abandoning homesteads, and turned back toward the areas of more advanced development, the towns and industrial regions. They looked for wage jobs.

So it is said that the unemployed are denied "access to the means of production," which includes the land. But the means of production of an industrial economy are not to be found ready made in nature. The man who wants employment then requires something more than his original natural right. He requires the use of the tools, accumulated capital, and organization of a high productive economy, to apply to the resources of nature.

But this definition still does not cover the whole difficulty. The owners of industrial property occasionally run at a loss, to keep up their plant and business connections for the future. In the United States, during times of stress, many employers would certainly be glad if they could run in full employment for the time being at the bare cost of materials, maintenance, and wages of labor and management. Dividends can wait, and often are deferred. But if an idle plant, including even a stock of raw materials, were handed over to unemployed workers, thus giving them free "access to the means of production," the workers would be unable to get continued production out of it, to pay for their labor, because that depends on continued exchange at a profit; they could only use up the stock and stop work.

Then the unemployed man in a private property economy has not lost his natural rights, and is suffering no greater hazard or privation than he would in a state of nature. He is free to quest for what he needs, but it is scarce for the time being, hard to find. Would he be willing to return to a state of nature as preferable? No. His refusal is rational. The hazard has in fact been greatly reduced; for the United States, the one great free economy the world has ever developed, has never known famine, although the Indians in the same territory were subject to it. There is no loss, but net gain. The hardship of the unemployed man is not that he has been denied his natural rights, but that for the time being he is not provided with something he did not have in nature.

But what he lacks cannot be defined merely as access to the land or to the means of production; it is an immediate connection on the *long circuit* of energy.

The gravamen of the collectivist complaint is that in hard times, there are goods undistributed, productive machinery standing idle, and men in want of work and goods. Though the goods are in fact rapidly distributed, at a loss to the owners if need be, and productive employment resumed, this is not deemed to constitute an optimum for a working system, allowing for possibilities of improvement in its specific operation to get better results along the same main line. Then the real accusation against private capitalism must be that it does slow down occasionally; breaks and stoppages occur along the line. It does not function with absolute, unvarying, mathematical regularity to supply everybody's wants continuously and unfailingly and without exception, regardless of the infinite risks of human fallibility, moral and intellectual.

The collectivist promises an organization that will never break down even temporarily. He insists that he has the plan of the perfect, "automatic" machine. On its own terms, this theory is insane. If reduced to specifications, it must be like the wonderful One-Hoss Shay, in which every material, part, and detail was exactly as strong as every other item, so that no part could break down. The imaginary One-Hoss Shay did wear out, but all at once, completely, in utter disintegration. The collectivist absolute government is expected to "wither away" and disappear in the same manner; but although the government is the only specific form the collectivist has in view, he insists that on its dissolution there will be some other kind of organization to take its place automatically, he can't say exactly what—the proposal trails off into incoherencies and mutterings of revelations to be made later.

There is just one more alleged objection advanced by the collectivist, his final argument, against private property. It is said that after a given stage of capitalistic development there will necessarily and always be more men seeking employment than there will be jobs; therefore the workman will have no real power to bargain and get a fair wage, but must take whatever the employer offers. This is a variant by reversal of the Malthusian theory. Malthus thought there was a "law" by which population tends to increase faster than production, so that workers must be forever "pressing against subsistence" (as animals might in nature)—nothing but immediate limitation of population could remedy the evil. Theoretically, of course, the world could be overpopulated, beyond what its natural resources could support; but Malthus was arguing particularly about the problem of poverty with a going productive system in a world which still had plenty of unoccupied space. Now his supposed law does operate in a collectivist economy, because that economy will not admit improvement in the means of production; hence collectivist societies have legitimized infanticide in the past. Although Malthus lived during the period when industrial production was getting under way, he seems to have fallen into an arithmetical catch, like the fallacy of Achilles and the tortoise; or else he thought production had already reached or almost reached its highest capacity, and could be so figured. Anyhow, the collectivists were forced to admit that production had refuted Malthus, increasing prodigiously, year by year. Then they had to say that the trouble was "overproduction"; the workingman would work himself out of a job pretty soon! This theory has evoked the phrase "technological unemployment," which is said to be caused by mechanical improvements in the means of production. That is, if a machine is invented by which one man can do the work previously done by ten men, it must put nine men permanently out of employment. It sounds plausible, but is it true?

Malthus imagined a fixed limit of productive capacity per person, an arbitrary quantity. (He must have had that in view, for there certainly is a limit to the number of children any adult can bring into the world.) The collectivist, with the theory of "technological unemployment," assumes a fixed number of jobs, another arbitrary quantity. In the feudal system there was such a fixed number of jobs, established by allotments of land in a given area, and ratified by the feudal lord and the community. This condition did not have to be stated in theory, it was factual and inevitable in the circumstances; but unhappily it has been carried over into theorizing on free enterprise, in which it has no meaning. In feudalism, the specific limitation on the number of jobs might stretch or shrink a little, but it was fairly constant.

No such rule can be applied or even imagined as applicable to a private capital free enterprise system, if the facts are examined.

In the free economy, *there can be no fixed number of jobs*, not for one minute. Employment, production, and consumption *in a free enterprise society* cannot be figured on the same ratios or relations as are assumed by collectivists (which have in fact obtained in collectivist societies). The ancient collectivist societies assumed that a given number of persons could produce a given quantity of goods; which could then of course be divided pro rata. (What it always came down to in practice was bare subsistence.) Then if all the available land or materials were in production, the maximum number of jobs were filled; somebody would have to be put out of a job before another could be taken on. And if an extra quantity were produced, on total reckoning, for the given quantity of labor, it would diminish to that extent the demand (necessity) for labor. Theoretically, it would put somebody out of employment. This reckoning is really made on a strict subsistence basis, in which "consumption" is just what people eat and wear.

But in a free enterprise economy, *increased production increases the number of jobs*. It might be said that one job creates another, which is true as far as it goes, but open to misinterpretation; for only productive employment does that. If a man were paid to pick up pebbles on the beach and throw them into the ocean, it would be just the same as if he were in a "government job," or on the dole; the producers have to supply his subsistence with no return, thus preventing the normal increase of jobs. Putting the unemployed on the dole does not *increase* "purchasing power." The dole divides up whatever is already in production. "Purchasing power," *per se*, is exchange. Increasing production does increase "purchasing power," and therefore creates jobs.

Are there fewer men employed in the great steel industry than there were in hand forging? or in rail and motor transport than in wagon and pack transport? or in the building trades with steamshovels, concrete mixers, and so forth, than in handicraft building? No. The real result is not only that people have more tools, larger houses, and travel more, which must tend to maintain employment—they also want and have things they never had before. Motor cars need tires, roads, gasoline; houses are equipped with new conveniences; when people travel they want hotels, amusements, more clothes— all of which means the creation of *more jobs, new jobs*.

Nothing increases the number of jobs so rapidly as labor-saving machinery, because it releases wants theretofore unknown, by permitting leisure. In a pre-industrial economy, jobs are made by simple division of labor; acquired skill and organization permit some economy of effort; but on the whole people literally have not enough surplus *energy* to want much. What does any person who is thoroughly fatigued want? The answer is just nothing. And if he works very long hours, he has no time either, to use what he might conceivably want. By conserving human bodily energy, multiplying the production from a given expenditure of muscular strength, the free economy enables men to want things which are unimaginable in a state of nature.

Here is a strange exemption of human organization from the general implications of the Second Law of Thermodynamics. Physical energy manifested through inanimate mechanism—gasoline introduced into a motor car, electricity in a vacuum cleaner—does not cause that mechanism to want, or require, either more or less than a given quantity, known beforehand, which it can accommodate, of which a fixed percentage will be "lost" in transmission, and the rest will go through to perform a measured task. A man can absorb only a limited quantity of physical energy in food, but at the level of well-being his wants increase progressively and incalculably for other things: and he himself is capable of creating devices to augment his energy and then to put it in use for his novel purposes. His circuit is intrinsically different from any specific circuit composed wholly of inanimate materials. Strictly quantitative mechanical calculations, by ratio or number, *cannot be applied beforehand to human free productive organization as a whole.*

The free enterprise system starts correctly with a concept, corresponding to reality, of a three dimensional man in a three dimensional world, having free will, the moral capacity for contract; therefore it predicates individual private property, by which he may secure his own place, from which point his relations in time and space are left to agreement and self-adjustment. The economic sphere is reserved from the static political clutch, because it is understood that the quantity of production and changes of position are *not calculable in advance.*

The collectivist theory starts with a no-dimensional man in a no-dimensional collective and a two-dimensional world, excluding private property, yet it assumes three-dimensional production and division of the product. It is impossible to elucidate the innumerable contradictions implicit in this muddle. The collectivist doesn't even try to work out a practical system of his own, consonant to his theories; he merely goes back to barbarism for distribution by edict, while at the same time he says he will use the productive machinery of free enterprise, which in fact can operate only by the inductive pull of distribution by free exchange.

In arguing against free enterprise capitalism, the collectivist always adopts the false assumption of a fixed number of jobs in that system. Conversely, in arguing for collectivism, he always assumes that there will be as many jobs as there are workers. The government will make the jobs.

The one definite and unequivocal stipulation of the collectivist is that all property shall be in government ownership for the collective. In that case, *everyone must ask for work from the government;* and *no one* can have any resources which would enable him to make better terms by waiting. Neither is there any other employer to whom the worker might apply.

In free enterprise, the jobs are spontaneously created by the productive system. The person who wants to work is hired directly by the person who wants work done, each being free to seek the other; each is interested personally in the benefit. (If it is said that a contractor hires men to do some work someone else wants done, it is still a fact that the contractor also wants the work done, for his own benefit.) Every want operates directly to stimulate a supply; every supply is a stimulus to discover a want. (Supply creates demand as much as demand brings out supply.) Throughout the longest series of exchanges, every person has a direct interest in getting the goods through, or producing them; so that the general sequence creates the long circuit of energy, by an unbroken transmission.

The collectivist's theory of inevitable "class conflict" in the free economy rests on the economic fallacy of the "wages fund." It assumes a fixed quantity to be divided between "labor" and "capital," so that neither can get any more except at the expense of the other; therefore their interests must be diametrically opposed and antagonistic. Certainly individuals must always have their separate interests; but in the free economy, there is nothing to divide until "capital and labor" have come to an agreement, hence their separate interests draw them together. And increased production can increase both shares, not one at the expense of the other.

Where the government is the sole employer, someone may certainly want to work, or want work done, or want a certain product; but he is never in direct exchange with any other person who has a like interest in the transaction. The man who wants work must ask the government for some kind of a job and for a portion of the alleged "general" production. Thus between what he offers and what he wants an agency intervenes which has no interest in the transaction. The immediate incentive is really the other way; officials won't want to be bothered by taking on more people for whom "jobs" must be "made." Then the government distributes the product. It is of no interest to the persons employed in distribution whether the quality is good or not, nor whether the stuff is handled for the convenience of either the producer or the consumer; because neither the producer nor the consumer has the power to decide which distributor he will patronize, or how much he will pay for an article. He must go to whatever depot his ticket indicates, and take whatever there is, on the fixed terms; or do without; while the persons employed in distribution will wish to handle less rather than greater quantities. The officials will get theirs first and best.

Yet all these persons must ask the government for employment all their lives. It is idle to demand it as a right, for they have not the least power to enforce such a demand. They cannot accumulate materials and land by which to make themselves independent; and certainly they cannot pick up any tools offhand and go to work upon the first material or plot of land they come upon. *They must ask for everything, day by day, hour by hour.*

If it is true that with private property some persons, having no property at a given time, have no "access" to the land or to the means of production, and are thus at a disadvantage in seeking employment, then under collectivism everybody is in that condition. Every workman has lost *all* his natural rights, and gained *absolutely nothing* in return. He is still subject to famine, and gets at best bare subsistence; but he can neither stay in one place of right, nor move about of right. Long trains of prisoners transported in cattle cars to a place where they do not wish to go are in the logical condition of members of the collective.

It is specifically against the interest of officials in a collective to increase production above bare subsistence level, for "the people." It would only give them more bother; and it would (if consumed) tend to increase the energy of the miserable population, and make "the people" unruly.* Even when the interest of the officials does call for increased production of war materials (the officials being desirous of saving their own necks), the need has to be met by importing machinery and goods at the cost of a reduced margin of subsistence, or on credit, a debt which will never be paid.

What power, in what circumstances, can the individual have against government? In a free economy, there is a government of limited powers. Individual citizens own the productive property. Whether or not it is expressed in a formal charter, the limitation of the power of government is kept in

---

* This is true of all administrations seeking to *perpetuate* their tenure. Robert Owen said he was told by "a veteran diplomat" in 1817 that "the governing powers of Europe" were aware that science could improve the lot of the human race, so they must be against it—"if the masses became well-off and independent, how were the governing classes to control them?" The modern method of prevention of general well-being has been stated. "We will tax and tax, and spend and spend, and elect and elect."

effect by the fact that the government must get its supplies from the citizens by taxation, and the taxation can be kept within limits by a proper division of the political agencies (checks and balances) and a proper representative system, the representatives being obliged to seek re-election. Nobody is presumed to have the right to demand employment from the government, because it is well understood that government "jobs" are non-productive. However, if he has a vote, the citizen without property has a means of bribing the government to make a job for him, by expropriating the property of another citizen. Such bribery depends entirely upon the ownership of private property by other citizens. If the process is carried on until all property has been expropriated or made subject to expropriation, no citizen, no voter, has any power left against the government, or any bribe to offer to the government.

In the collective, where there is no private property, the government owning everything and the individual nothing, the power of the government is absolute; and it is immaterial what claim the worker may make, he has no means of obtaining it.

The government certainly can "make jobs," but there is no connection of supply and demand, no induction on the flow of energy. The only effective demand is that of officials for what they personally want; but as they are under no necessity of producing in return, there is no exchange; it is simply a net charge on forced labor. The circuit of energy is cut with every transaction.

Further, if the no-dimensional concept of the collective did approximate to reality—which is impossible—the "right to work" would be utterly meaningless. No part of the collective could act without the whole acting in accord. If a person is supposed to be only a component of the collective, and one person wants to do even one thing, he must theoretically get the consent of every other person, be it a thousand, a million, a hundred million, or two billions. It is ridiculous. Of course, what the person really has to do is to get the consent of certain officials. Now in the free society any person wishing to undertake an enterprise in which capital and various persons will be employed, must obtain the consent of the owners of the capital and of the persons who will do the work. That is not always easy, but he can apply directly, and those concerned can make their own decision according to their view of their own interest. Very few original ideas return production immediately; innumerable ideas fail expensively; but those concerned have the right to take a chance and the loss. How can any official even be granted explicit authority to take a similar chance? He cannot. The matter requires personal judgment on every single proposal. Can every official of the collective have authority to dispose of all available materials? No. Can each official have authority to dispose of a given portion of available materials for—what? For a proposal of an experimental innovation, made by anybody, while nobody knows what the result will be? Of course not. What is the official to do? He may deal out a favor, but it must be at a risk to himself with no particular inducement in the prospective returns. And what inducement is there to the innovator, the man of creative ideas? None.

Hence the collective society is static. Whatever productive machinery it contains must be inherited or borrowed from a primary field of freedom elsewhere, a free economy. With such borrowings, nobody in the collective need be responsible for the decision and expenditure involved in the period of original invention. The machinery can be taken over at a fixed cost. It can even be copied at a fixed estimate; but it can't be invented.

The history of small nominal collectives within a free economy leads to extremely misleading conclusions because the relation to that free economy is not recognized. Many fail forthwith, but few such group experiments have "succeeded" in a remarkable way. Where the founder of such a collective prescribed a rule which cut the group off from social relations with the free society—as by celibacy among the Shakers or the "community marriage" of the Oneida community—a strict internal limitation on consumption and a discipline of regular labor could also be prescribed. In these "successful" experiments, the communities not only got a living; they actually got rich. Why, then, it may be asked, is not collectivism at least a practicable system by which people can be secure and rich at the expense of their liberty, if they are willing to surrender their liberty?

The answer is, because there would be no surrounding free economy from which they could get rich. These enclave groups sold their products to the free economy and converted the gain into real property, land and buildings, static forms. But the individuals concerned never surrendered their liberty; it was impossible to do so, while the free economy existed. Any member of the collective could walk out any minute he chose. No member of the collective could really be subjected to personal punishment, imprisonment, or even the prescribed discipline of labor, as by deprivation of subsistence, by the collective, while the free economy existed. Only those who voluntarily submitted to it were in the collective, and only for such time as they chose. Nothing in their economic procedure was peculiar to the collectivist system. Anyone in the free economy could get rich by the same labor, thrift, and accumulation as the collectivists practiced. *Everything* in these groups which is pointed to as the fruit of collectivism was owing to the free economy: the means of production; the market whereby production was converted into static wealth; the laws by which life and tenure were secure; and even the habit of self-discipline by which the rules were observed and labor performed. Above all, there was *no power whatever* of actual compulsion, of the brutalities, torture, starvation, exile, execution, which collectivism inflicts when it has the power.

Altogether, private property is the only basis of a productive society, the only means by which *anyone* can *ever* have free "access to the means of production," not of permission but by natural right. In any society, or if there were but one man on a desert island, work must be done; that is a law of nature. But only in a society of individual private property can a man have a say as to the conditions in which he will work, or acquire property on which he can work just as he pleases, or accumulate property by which he may ensure subsequent leisure, or improve his skill or the means of production for his own benefit.

The incidental hazard of a free society, which is that of nature, that some individuals may be temporarily unable to command a livelihood, is the permanent condition of every man in a collective society. In giving up freedom, the individual gets nothing in return, and gives up every chance or hope of ever getting anything.

Private individual property is not only the most favorable condition for a high production economy. *It is the only transmission line by which high production is possible at all.*

What does any collective society promise even in its most extravagant propaganda? Simply that it will copy the production of the free societies—which in fact it cannot do. In the nineteenth century some Socialists promised a return to handicrafts, although handicrafts developed with private property, not government ownership. Workingmen were not attracted. The Communists then promised machinery.

During the past twenty-five years, collectivism has been imposed on one European nation after another. During that period considerable improvements in machinery have been made in the United States. Has any collectivist nation made any improvement in machinery? None. The Nazi collective promised workingmen in Germany cheap cars, which American workingmen have had in increasing numbers for twenty-five years. Has even one cheap car been produced for or obtained by a workingman in Germany? Or in Russia? Or in Japan? Not one. Has the standard of living risen in either country? No, it has fallen far below the nineteenth century level.

As a reasonable test of the respective claims and performances of the collective society and the free society, when they exist simultaneously, which will individuals join if they have the choice? Millions of persons came to the United States and remained gladly, as long as they could gain entry; they stand in line now for admittance under immigration quotas. How many persons have sought admission for citizenship and permanent residence in Russia, Germany, Italy, or Japan under collectivism? Have professed collectivists from Germany sought admission to Russia? No, they seek the United States none the less, if they can contrive to get here. The borders of the collectivist nations are closed—to prevent their own people escaping, as from a jail. And the happy collectivists crawl through barbed wire to get out.

CHAPTER XVIII

Why Real Money Is Indispensable

Another statement about property reveals the primitive mental level of collectivists: the proposal to "abolish inheritance of property." Since property is in tangible objects,* there are only two ways by which inheritance could be abolished. The objects must be destroyed or else declared to be no longer property, debarred from use, a dead man's land let go back to wilderness. Savages or barbarians sometimes adopted this course, as when the goods and gear of the dead were buried with them and their huts burned, or the Viking's ship became his funeral pyre, or former camp sites were abandoned.

What the collectivists mean, but do not say because if it were stated truthfully it would hardly appeal to any rational person, is that on the death of an owner the government should seize whatever property he had, a piecemeal expropriation which would take in all existent property in the course of a natural lifetime. No moral or intelligible reason can be adduced why Hitler, Stalin, or any other government official should inherit the product of every man's thrift, labor, and care, rather than his wife, children, or whomever he wishes to have it; but that is the proposal. Death and taxes arrive hand in hand.

The economists who advocate fiat money (paper currency not redeemable in gold), or else an arithmetical sign which they call a "commodity dollar" (perhaps because it is neither

* Property in copyright relates to tangible objects, reproductions; with a copyright song, the right takes effect also when it is sung for remuneration, the remuneration being tangible.

a commodity nor a dollar),* are below the mental level of savages. The savage applies number, but he has not advanced to the abstract concept. The advocate of fiat money has forgotten how to apply number.

Sir Isaac Newton was asked by the British Treasury officials and financiers of his day why the monetary pound had to be a fixed quantity of precious metal. Why, indeed, must it consist of precious metal, or have any objective reality? Since paper

* The "commodity dollar" was supposed to be found as an equation of exchanges on a "sliding scale" for a given period. Whatever the *process* might be, if it were *applied*, fixed quantitative units of measure must be used; and quantities of goods of different kinds can be equated only by a fixed unit of value, a real dollar. Apparently the idea was to vary the hypothetical content of the dollar periodically by the equation found in the previous exchanges; perhaps with only paper currency in circulation. It is impossible to make sense of the theory. As all units of measure are determined arbitrarily in the first place, though now fixed by law, obviously they can be altered by law. The same length of cotton could be designated an inch one day, a foot the next, and a yard the next; the same quantity of precious metal could be denominated ten cents today and a dollar tomorrow. But the net result would be that figures used on different days would not mean the same thing; and somebody must take a heavy loss. The alleged argument for a "commodity dollar" was that a real dollar, of fixed quantity, will not always buy the same quantity of goods. Of course it will not. If there were no medium of value, no money, neither would a yard of cotton or a pound of cheese always exchange for an unvarying fixed quantity of any other goods. It was argued that a dollar ought always to buy the same quantity of any description of goods. It will not and cannot. That could occur only if the same number of dollars and the same quantities of goods of all kinds and in every ·kind were always in existence and in exchange and always in exactly proportionate demand; while if production and consumption were admitted, both must proceed constantly at an equal rate to offset one another. Money *is* the equation in a production and exchange system. It has been suggested (by Muriel Rukeyser, in "Willard Gibbs: American Genius") that Professor Irving Fisher, a leading proponent of the "commodity dollar," was trying to apply to economics the Gibbs method of Vector Analysis (applied in the Phase Rule to thermodynamics "to interpret physical phenomena"). But Vector Analysis or the Phase Rule do not change any unit of measure. Miss Rukeyser herself quotes good authority on that point, Dr. W. R. Whitney (of General Electric), who refers to "this group of mathematico-physical expressions of *measured facts* which Gibbs had so scientifically co-ordinated." The fixed unit of measure for the facts is pre-requisite to the theory of Vector Analysis; and correct application of the method necessarily depends on the same units of measure being observed throughout. If the unit of measure were changed between operations, it would be impossible to proceed from one set of calculations to the next. The "commodity dollar" fallacy was thoroughly exposed some years ago.

currency was already accepted, why could not notes be issued without ever being redeemed? The reason they put the question supplies the answer; the government was heavily in debt, and they hoped to find a safe way of being dishonest. But Newton was asked as a mathematician, not as a moralist. He replied: "Gentlemen, in applied mathematics, *you must describe your unit.*" Paper currency cannot be described mathematically as money. A dollar is a certain weight of gold; that is a mathematical description, by measure (weight). Is a piece of paper of certain dimensions (length, breadth, and thickness, or else weight) a dollar? Certainly not. Is a given-sized piece of paper a dollar even if numerals and words of a certain size are stamped on it with a given quantity of ink? No.

They took Newton's word for it, possibly conceding that the greatest mathematician of their age might know the primer of his science. But the fact that educated men were ignorant of the first rule by which they carried on their own business, commerce, and finance; and the further fact that Newton's answer has since been forgotten many times, in spite of the disastrous consequences which ensued each time, indicates a very grave problem of civilization.

Mathematics is the world language of the energy age. Its use goes far beyond that of Latin in the Middle Ages; while it expresses international relations, it is also the instrument of practical thought and communication in daily life. Anyone who operates power machinery has to think in mathematical ratios—time, speed, distance. The men who organize and perform the practical tasks by which modern civilization is kept going—whether they are truck-drivers or aviators, mechanics on the assembly line, engineers, or industrial managers—think correctly in the practical language of modern civilization while they are on the job. If they reverted for one day to the primitive level of intelligence in respect of their work, at the end of that day the whole country would be a scene of wreckage.

But if those who are entrusted with the general direction

and political organization of a vast system which depends throughout on the correct knowledge and use of the language of mathematics actually do not know, or do not understand, the most elementary statement in that language, how can the system function? If politicians and financiers will believe neither logic nor evidence for a rule as primary as that two and two make four, what will convince them?

The verbal language of a high civilization is also a precision instrument. When words are used without exact definition, there can be no communication above the primitive level. If those who are supposed to express or influence "public opinion," the writers, economists, social theorists, and pedagogues, think in the concepts of savagery, what can be the outcome?

What is most astonishing is that when the enemies of civilization have openly declared their intention to destroy it, to break down the circuit of the high-energy Society of Contract, and have explained how they mean to do so, those who are to be destroyed will deliberately carry out the program of ruin. The explicit threat is cited by J. M. Keynes: "Lenin was certainly right. There is no subtler, no surer means of overturning the existing basis of society than to debauch the currency. The process engages all the hidden forces of economic law on the side of destruction."

The requirements of a sound currency are simple. If five apples are exchanged for a pound of cheese, and the cheese for two yards of cotton, and the cotton for a peck of potatoes, and the potatoes for two hours of labor, by what common measure can these various items be reckoned? Each is worth any one of the others, and all of them are worth five times what any one of them is worth; but it signifies nothing to say that any one of them is worth one, or that five of them are worth five. One what? Five what? Things which are equal to the same thing are equal to one another. As the several items can be ex-changed, they must be equal; but in what terms? Not in pounds, yards, or hours; they are equal in value. Then what is wanted is a unit of value to reckon by. Any of the items could be designated as the unit of value if the sequence of transactions were considered closed on the spot. But these are perishable goods, and have been considered as fixed quantities. General exchange must go on in an endless sequence through time and distance, to include variable quantities of raw materials existent in nature, labor applied to them, and end-use, consumption or inactive possession.

Then what is wanted is a medium of exchange, something for which everything else can be exchanged, so that it enters into every transaction as the unit of value, and serves for an indefinite number of transactions, an endless use. If the pound of cheese had been exchanged for a certain weight of precious metal, a dollar, and the dollar for two yards of cloth, and then again for a peck of potatoes, and again for two hours of labor, and again for five apples, each item would be worth a dollar and all of them would be worth five dollars. If all the goods were consumed, the dollar would remain, to continue the sequence of exchanges. Further, if a man who has perishable goods, say apples, does not want any other goods immediately, he can sell his apples for money, and the money will keep, enabling him to buy a sack of flour the next year; though the wheat which went into the flour was not yet sown when he sold the apples. That is the use of money. It facilitates immediate exchange; it is a repository of value; and it carries exchanges through time on the long circuit of energy.

The use of things depends upon their intrinsic qualities. Cheese is edible. Leather is used for shoes because it is pliable, tough, long-wearing. So the material used for money must be durable, divisible, incorruptible, portable, not easily imitated, and found in nature in sufficient but limited quantity. Nothing but the precious metals answer to these intrinsic requirements. There is never "enough money" in the Society of Status. The free economy produces its money as it produces steel, by going and getting it, digging the ore out of the ground. Neither is it an accident that the supply of real money increased as production of goods increased; the advanced methods of production permitted low-grade ore to be smelted at a profit. Nevertheless, the quantity of gold available is always limited.

Gold was not and is not given value by fiat, any more than cheese or cotton or leather were given value by fiat. It has value because it serves a vital need. *Nothing can be given value by fiat.* If a gold coin of the Roman Republic were dug up now, it would have its original value, though the Roman Republic perished two thousand years ago. So would a Russian gold rouble minted under the czars, or a gold coin of Germany or France dated before 1914; though the last czar was shot in a cellar, the last German emperor fled the country and died in exile, and France has suffered invasion and conquest. But paper currency of Russia, Germany, or France before 1914 is now waste paper.

A dollar is a certain quantity of gold. That is not a matter of opinion; it is so by definition and by law, Federal statute. All the gold held by the government belongs by right and law to individual citizens, who placed it on deposit originally; just as money in a private bank account belongs to the depositor. A dollar bill is a certificate of deposit, a warehouse receipt for a dollar. The value is in the metal on deposit, just as the value indicated by any warehouse receipt is in the goods it calls for. If the goods do not exist, or are destroyed, or will not be delivered, the paper has no value. That is what happened in Germany when paper currency was printed though there was no gold to redeem it; and a cartload of paper currency would not buy an egg. Neither are checks money; they are promises to pay money. Otherwise anyone could write a check and obtain goods for nothing.

If it is said that anything will do for money, as long as people accept it, let it be asked, why will not people accept "anything?" Offer the man who says "anything will do for money," a handful of pebbles in payment of a debt.

The absolute necessity of real money, the unit in precious metal, for any extensive sequence of exchanges, has been proved by the very theorists who said it was a mere convention, and by the nation whose agents are still spreading propaganda to persuade other nations they wish to destroy that a "managed currency" consisting of nothing but printed paper is just as good or better. Communists and other advocates of government ownership argued for a century that vouchers for labor would be the "just" medium of exchange, and that real money was a capitalist device to exploit the workers. Then they tried their own scheme in Communist Russia, and could not make it work even by terror and starvation. It was not that people would not accept "labor vouchers"; the poor wretches were forced to accept them; it was simply that the necessary application of arithmetic to goods and labor could not be made at all without real money. *In applied mathematics, you must describe your unit.* Communist Russia had to go back to the gold unit.

Why cannot even slave labor and forced transfer of goods be carried on with labor vouchers instead of real money? The transactions need only be followed through to discover the reason. To be sure, if a single slave-owner held land with natural resources to supply every need and slaves to perform all the work of production, he could distribute to the slaves whatever he pleased, but he would not need labor vouchers. But suppose ten men, slave or free, should work to grow wheat in a certain field; it is perfectly possible to divide the product by vouchers for the number of hours of labor. Then suppose ten other men work in the adjoining field growing sugar beets; the same division can be made. And a labor-hour portion of wheat could be exchanged for a labor-hour portion of beets. But the quantity of wheat or beets which a labor-hour voucher represents has been established only for the given product of the given fields for that one season. In other fields beets or wheat grown by other groups would yield different quantities per labor-hour. Further, when the wheat went to the mill or the beets to the sugar factory, more labor hours would have to be included, not to mention the labor hours represented in the machinery. Then what quantity of goods would a labor-hour voucher call for? The whole scheme is impossible. Nobody but a collectivist could be so feeble-minded as to imagine such a system. *In applied mathematics, you must describe your unit.* With a gold unit of value, labor hours and material and depreciation of machinery and everything that goes into the whole process can be reckoned by a common measure; and they *must* be reckoned somehow, in order to move anything at all from field to factory to shop; so the prices on the goods will show what can be bought for any given sum in currency.

But if the paper currency is not actually redeemed on demand in real money (gold), if the citizen cannot regain possession of his own property when he presents the certificate of deposit, because the immediate incumbents of political office, members of the government, refuse to obey the law (as they have refused), then what difference does it make whether the gold really exists or not? What difference would it make if all the gold in the world should vanish utterly, dissolve into air, or be sunk at an unknown spot in mid-ocean? Or if there were only one gold dollar in existence to be described as the unit of exchange, would not that do?

There is in that question—which has been put by those who should know better—an implicit assumption that seizure and sequestration of gold by governments, does not or need not "make any difference." If that is true, why do governments seize gold? Unless the action is to be imputed to a kind of hoodlum idiocy, like that of street loafers who snatch things at random, obviously it must make a difference.

Probably most people do not recognize any difference between temporarily suspending payment of gold and seizing gold; although the difference is precisely that between a bank suspending payment and a banker going through a depositor's pockets for whatever he may have left after the bank has failed. When money is left on deposit in a bank, there is the contingent risk that the bank may not be able to pay promptly on demand. That is default. The bank has assets which may be sold to pay depositors. The citizen who holds a dollar bill has real money on deposit with the government. Somebody brought in raw gold to the mint; for which by law he was entitled to receive coin in the same quantity minus a small percentage for the cost of minting. But instead of taking the real dollar, someone accepted a certificate of deposit. The government never owned any gold; but was permitted to hold it until called for. As the government also borrows large sums on bonds, and spends the money, if many people want their own money at one time, the government may be unable to pay; it is in default. The government has no assets with which to meet its debts; government property would not bring much even if it were sold, because it is non-productive; and besides, the creditor has no recourse in law. The contingency of suspension of gold payments by government is unavoidable as long as governments are permitted to issue paper currency and borrow money. These are intrinsically dangerous powers; but it is doubtful if the question will ever receive intelligent consideration; or at least, not until men learn to think more boldly. At present it is taken for granted that governments must have such powers, just as it was formerly thought necessary that kings and nobles should have certain powers which are abolished in a republic. Be that as it may, it does make an immediate difference when governments seize gold; it is the prevalence of this government gold monopoly, held by force, that made the Second World War inevitable. It enables governments, as in Germany and Russia, to subvert the private economy into a war machine, rendering the citizens powerless. The method by which the surreptitious objective is achieved is a steady abstraction of value from the money, and an increase of the national debt through borrowing from the banks.*

Still, why is it necessary that the gold should actually exist, once it has been expropriated by the government?

---

* When France was bankrupted by the Mississippi Bubble, "the agents of the Mississippi Company were empowered to search houses and confiscate all the coined money they found.... Heavy fines were imposed in addition. It is astonishing that people should have borne this oppression so patiently." (Saint-Simon.)

Let the governments bear witness. Even in Russia, at the time the Communists said gold was merely a convention, and that they would not use it, they took care to seize the gold nevertheless. The pretext is offered, by the paper currency theorists, that people are simply accustomed to gold, and persist in using it only by habit; therefore it must be taken away from them for their own good. True that no one government could get hold of all the gold in the world and sink it in the sea, and close all the gold mines; but government could prohibit it, sink whatever gold there is in the country, and stop the entry of any more. The problem would be much easier than it was with liquor, because gold cannot be manufactured. Why does the government keep the gold, after it has taken it away from the owners by force?

Because real money is indispensable; the exchange values, prices, are established by the total quantity of gold existent. Roughly speaking, if there were in exchange fifty pounds of sugar and ten pounds of butter, five pounds of sugar would be given for a pound of butter; one quantity divided by the other. As gold is the medium of exchange, the quantities of goods are divided by the quantity of gold (dollars), to find the price. The process in general exchange is immensely complicated by the numerous kinds of goods, the varying supply and demand, distances which add cost of transport, and deferred exchanges; but the total quantity of gold is nevertheless the determinant of prices, by comparison of quantities. If there were only one gold dollar in existence, it could not be used as the unit of value, because it would not give any number for the divisor. How many paper notes should be printed? One? An unlimited quantity? There would be no proper number. If the ancient dreams of the alchemists had been realized, so that gold could be manufactured in unlimited quantity, gold would also have become useless as a medium of exchange.

There was once a government which really prohibited gold, and kept none itself, in the belief that gold was bad for people. That was Sparta. But the Spartans believed that comfort, convenience, industry, were bad; and work was ignoble. The Spartans used iron for money, because nobody could carry enough of it around for general exchange. The object was to keep the nation poor, to keep the citizens on a bare subsistence economy. The plan succeeded perfectly. That is just what the prohibition of gold will effect; it will reduce a nation to a dead level of poverty and keep it in that condition. But the rulers of Sparta were willing to remain poor themselves. They enjoyed no more luxury than anyone else; no more than the very slaves who did the work. Yet even in Sparta, where food was doled out at a common soup kitchen, *something* had to be used for money, and that material had to have intrinsic value.

The modern despots do not wish to be poor themselves. They wish to grab every luxury an industrial economy can supply. What they want is to keep the producers poor, by taking the product and doling a little back again for subsistence. That is why governments seize and keep gold.

When paper currency is depreciated, the difference has to come out somewhere; and the main cut is in wages. The fact is that heavy government expenditure must always be taken from the workingman's wages; there is no other possible source. But the depreciation in currency comes out of wages immediately; whatever anyone gets in his pay envelope will simply buy him that much less in goods. Conversely, increased production raises wages even though the sum in money is the same; it will buy more.

Aside from the immediate loss, the worker is deprived of a *repository of value*. Whatever he gets, he cannot save any part of it for the future, if it is in depreciable paper currency. Real money is the only means by which the worker can have any independence. That is the difference it makes when governments seize gold. It makes the worker helpless. He can only live from day to day, with an expectation of getting less and less as time goes on. Nowhere in the world now is any worker as well off as he was before governments seized real money.

That is true even in respect of high-wage labor in the United States; if the workman has any possessions, they are wearing out—his car, for example—and he does not know when or how he can get another. If he has insurance, he does not know in what valuation of money it will be paid.

In a free enterprise economy, the products first put on the market as luxuries tend steadily to come within reach of everyone, and are then regarded as necessities. That is one general benefit of considerable private fortunes, which must be invested for income, which means increased production. The remaining margin will be spent to buy things of recent invention which are still expensive, but capable of being improved and made at less cost. The whole process is most evident in the development of motor cars for general use. Related accurately, the story has elements of comedy. First, various inventors and engineers put together a lumbering contrivance nobody could want except to gratify his taste for mechanics. Presently it was "improved" into a luxury; that is, it was still expensive, inconvenient, and of no practical use, because there were no suitable roads, no gas stations or repair shops; and a car was more than likely to leave the owner stranded a long way from home, an object of derision. Those were pleasure cars! Wealthy purchasers paid for the period of experiment, first putting up the capital (of which an enormous sum was sunk without return), and then buying the cars. Presently various ingenious men thought they might make cheaper cars. Throughout, those who had put in money and time were impelled to go on in the hope of getting a return. So the rich supported the nascent industry until cars were good enough for people of moderate means. When the cheap car got into mass production, the manufacturer saw that he had to have a correspondingly extensive market. If the workingman was to buy a car, wages must be higher. The manufacturer raised wages voluntarily, and so forced other employers to do the same. Where, in such a sequence, would any *government* have had the same inducement? Nowhere. More than that, if currency had been subjected to depreciation during the given period, the process must have stopped, because the rise in real wages was necessary, along with lowered costs in materials. At a given time, a manufacturer in a growing enterprise has most of his capital in materials; if he cannot replace his stock at the same cost, he must raise his prices for the product. At the same time if the cost increase is by depreciation of the currency, real wages are lowered, so that his market is gone; nobody can afford to buy the product. Production must cease.

But the most dangerous fallacy regarding money which has been put forward recently pretends to find an argument in the German war gamble. It has been variously expressed, but one statement covers all the points.

It is that Germany is "winning the war because it has been fighting with an industrial and engineering economy," while the Allies "have been fighting with a money, or financial, economy." * It is further said that "Thorstein Veblen knew all about" this economy, and "in Germany Walther Rathenau tried to put it in practice" first. It is described as "taking the heavy financial boot off the brakes, and letting the productive machinery run freely. . . . Liberated machines will always beat liberated money."

The mental level of savagery is again evident in the terms used; they are animistic. A savage might, on first seeing a motor machine, think of it as a kind of Djinn in a bottle, a captive creature. But the idea is nonsense. A machine cannot be either enslaved or liberated; the terms apply only to human beings. It is true, however, that Rathenau did all he could to organize Germany so that it was bound to go to war, willy-nilly. (He thought that only government should have so much power. The power he helped to give to government has expropriated, exiled, or put to death the Jews in Germany; they owe their misfortune largely to one of their own race. It is unlikely that the fact will ever be acknowledged.)

But what kind of economy is Germany actually running on?

* Carl Dreher (who, also quotes Dorothy Thompson) in *Harper's Magazine.*

All the resources that Germany is using in war were produced by a money economy. The machinery was invented in a money economy; Germany was equipped with factories, the science of chemistry was developed, technicians were trained, by a money economy. While preparing for war, Germany borrowed all the money she could get, and bought on credit all the goods she could get, for which she did not pay. These resources were embezzled from the money economies. Incidentally, it was the action of governments elsewhere which enabled Germany to embezzle on such an extensive scale. For three years in succession, Germany "bought" the South African wool-clip, by the intervention of the South African government which "financed" the deal; that wool went into uniforms for the German army; and Germany never paid. It was a dead loss to the producers, who thought their government was making a nice deal for them!

The Nazis took over an economy which included agriculture and industry, both using machinery and money. So did the Communist government in Russia. Also in Russia, all the modern machinery had to be supplied from money economies elsewhere, and paid for (so far as it has been paid for) in gold. In both Germany and Russia, real money is still used; and both sides are fighting the war on the production from a money economy. What kind of economy have they got?

If a bandit holds up the owner of a motor car at the point of a gun, takes the car, and rides off in it, and then obtains gas, repairs, and whatever else he requires by the same means, what kind of an economy is he running on? If a sufficient number of bandits should seize the whole economy in the same manner, but "legalize" it by compulsion of the courts and legislatures; and if they should also "pay" for what they take in paper currency, in whatever sums they chose, what kind of an economy would it be?

In an electric power plant, there is a generator and other equipment for the conversion and transmission of energy. It might be from water power, or from fuel; in the latter case, the supply of fuel must be continuous, and in either case, there is maintenance. As the energy is taken off, a meter records where it goes. It is paid for; and money brings back the necessary supplies; the figures on the money are also a meter. A savage, observing that operations are carried on with constant regard for these two records, might say: Why do you not take off the meter, and never mind about the money? Then you could use all the power any way you pleased. Liberate the Djinn, instead of cutting it off the way you do, here and there; it's all cooped up.

A dishonest person could conceivably introduce hidden wires to take some of the current off without any indication on the meter; or he could make false entries in the money accounts.

What kind of an economy would that be?

An engineering and industrial economy is a money economy. It cannot work any other way. A bandit can certainly operate a stolen motor car for a time, but he has not thereby devised an engineering economy. He is running on a stolen portion of the capital of an industrial, engineering, money economy. Germany is running on capital embezzled from abroad, and on the capital of Europe, looted by military force. Russia is running on capital seized from the industry already existent at the time the Communists took over, and on machinery supplied by free economies elsewhere, notably the United States. Some of it was paid for, in money; some has simply been given to Russia, at the cost of the free economy.

When the Indians obtained guns from the white men, and used the guns to get their food, game, what kind of an economy were they running on? When the military Turks seized the profits of traders and the product of conquered farmers, to make war, what kind of an economy were they running on? Was it a military economy? Certainly not. It was an agricultural and commercial economy. They turned the proceeds to war, and were for a time victorious; but they were running partly on capital, and the economy ran down.

Veblen's alleged idea, as cited, was that "the guild of engi-

neers, supported by the massed and rough-handed legions of
the industrial rank and file, should disallow private ownership
of the machinery of production and operate it at maximum
capacity."

How? Were they to take over machinery in existence? But
why should they do that? Machinery in existence has only
a short life. It would have to be replaced in no long time. If
it can be replaced—new machinery made—without regard for
money, what is the point of stealing machinery already somewhat worn? Why could not the "engineers and massed and
rough-handed legions" make what they need—without
money? There is the perpetual motion machine again; they
have to get it started. After that of course it will go on running. What is most curious is that even if this absurdity be
admitted, surely the scheme could be started with only a small
amount of money. Henry Ford had very little money to begin
with. Aren't the "guild of engineers and massed and rough-
handed legions" together as smart as just one middle-aged
mechanic, in a Michigan small town?

The truth is that they are not. No group is as intelligent as
an individual. No group, as a group, has any intelligence; all
intelligence is in individuals.

And money is the means by which the intelligence of individuals can be brought together in free co-operation, on large
productive enterprises. Money is the only means by which
machinery can be invented or used at all. What engineers
and labor can accomplish under state ownership (which is the
only way private ownership can be disallowed) is to build the
pyramids, useless and ponderous masses of rock piled up as
a memorial of the Veblens of an earlier day. Herodotus relates, hundreds of years later, that "the Egyptians so detest
the memory of those kings (the pyramid builders) that they
do not much like even to mention their names."

Even before Germany surrendered entirely to the power
of government, German technicians and engineers could not
equal those of the United States in finding and developing

natural resources. (The United States was the great money economy of the world, with land as well as goods in the market.) Private property, money, freedom, engineering, and industry are all one system; they are the components of the high potential long circuit of energy. And when one element is taken out, the rest must collapse, cease to function.

CHAPTER XIX

Credit and Depressions

Since production is carried on through time, credit arises as a natural consequence. Credit is patterned on the processes of nature. When a man plants something in the expectation of a harvest, he is expending goods and labor in the present for a return in the future, with the attendant risk of loss. The next step is obvious; one man can advance goods to another for a subsequent return. There is no reason to suppose that money created credit, though they might have developed simultaneously. Money is the only means by which deferred exchanges * in goods could be effected without credit. But men give credit, and cannot be persuaded to refrain from doing so, because it is their nature to. By virtue of his mind, man works through time and space. The impulse is not greed, but the creative and expansive faculty. The added risk is accepted for the sake of quicker and greater extension of power over nature.

If mankind wished to have the soundest possible production system, money is the proper medium. In that case, no credit should be given, no loans should be made. All transactions in goods and money should be closed on the spot, including the shortest possible period for payment of labor. Money would still cover time and distance. With such a system, there could be no panics; and there need be no hard times except as incident to crop shortages. It cannot be said that there would be no poverty, because goods must be produced. Proposals to "abolish poverty," or to guarantee "freedom from want" or

* THE PROMISES MEN LIVE BY. By Harry Scherman. Random House. Mr. Scherman coined the phrase, "deferred exchanges."

"freedom from fear" are a mere confusion of terms. Fear and want are subjective; and poverty is the absence of wealth. If it were promised that from the hour of his birth no man should ever again stand in his naked skin, who is to produce the clothes? who is to have such absolute power over every person? The only condition in which no one can experience poverty, want, or fear, is that of rigor mortis. The dead neither want nor fear. With living persons producing and exchanging goods in freedom, judgment and the seasons are variables, introducing risks. All that can be said is that money is the safe means of extending exchanges of goods into the future.

The spot cash system has never been proposed by any social theorist, because it calls for no control, no compulsion, no political job or power for the reformer. It is entirely within the competence of the individual as long as there is real money. Nobody is obliged to give credit. Men can stick to cash transactions if they care to, and they don't. During the Middle Ages, when interest on money was stigmatized as morally wrong, men made loans at interest just the same, and paid high rates. The merchants and craft guilds quietly carried on a far-reaching credit system; the ultimate reliance for collection was on negative and private power, by refusal to trade further with a defaulter.

Without credit, it is difficult to imagine how the modern high energy system of production could have got under way. Accumulation of paid-up cash capital in the needed sums would have been almost impossible, or at least much slower. Though vast enterprises have been created without using all of the various modern instruments and channels of credit—as Henry Ford managed without public stock flotations—yet if there had been no such credit system as there was, with banks to facilitate payment for shipments to and from distant points and to carry deposits of current funds and give some local credit, one cannot conceive of the business attaining such magnitude.

Even without credit, there must be capital losses. Inventions and improvements may make previous capital assets obsolete; or experiments with new inventions may fail; and finally, capital enterprise necessarily pushes ahead of the immediate demand; it creates a market. Energy drives for an outlet, and human judgment is not always adequate for its direction. Dishonesty is the smallest factor in the widespread losses of a major panic and depression; mostly it enters after the fact. That is, men resort to crooked shifts when enterprises begun honestly are failing. Hence the nauseating spectacle of prominent men falsifying accounts and mumbling feeble excuses or sullen lies under investigation. This is not to palliate dishonesty; it is imperatively necessary that summary treatment should be meted out to the guilty, and that failure should result in demotion. The point is that dishonesty is never the prime cause of a collapse of credit. But it causes greater injury than the proportionate sums involved, because it diverts attention from the crucial task of getting production going again. Further, it confuses the vital issue of profit, and affords a pretext to muddle discussion with such meaningless phrases as "production for use and not for profit."

Production *is* profit; and profit *is* production. They are not merely related; they are the same thing. When a man plants potatoes, if he does not get back more than he put in, he has *produced nothing*. This would be obvious if he put a potato in the ground today and dug up the same potato tomorrow; but it is all the same if he plants one potato and gets only one potato as a crop. His labor is wasted; then he must starve, *or someone else must feed him*, if he has no reserve from previous production. The objection to profit is as if a bystander, observing the planter digging his crop, should say: "You put in only one potato and you are taking out a dozen. You must have taken them away from someone else; those extra potatoes cannot be yours by right." If profit is denounced, it must be assumed that running at a loss is admirable. On the contrary, that is what requires justification. Profit is self-justifying.

When any institution is not run for profit, it is necessarily at the cost of the producers. One way the non-producers go about destroying a free production system by degrees is to persuade men of wealth to endow foundations for "social work" or for economic or political "research." The arguments sought by such research will generally be in justification of parasitism, favoring the creation of more sinecures by extension of the political power.

It is most important to recognize just what has happened when credit collapses, causing a "depression." The energy circuit has broken down. At numerous points along the line, energy is leaking, being lost in one way or another. When the wires from an electric power plant go down in a cyclone, a similar condition occurs, but from external accident; and the necessary measures for repair are obvious. With a production system, the energy hook-up is more complex, and the breakdown is from internal causes, originating in misjudgment of the various factors and connections.

In the simplest possible example, if a man should walk eight miles in two hours to obtain supplies which will yield him only sufficient energy to walk four miles in an hour, it is a losing venture. Real physical energy has been lost, expended in the heat and waste matter of muscular effort. But for accounting purposes, the loss would have to be reckoned in time or mileage. This is the utmost simplification, which assumes that the man himself is the whole production system. If he used any tools, their cost and wear ought to be included. So with a high production system, every part of it must be maintained by surplus production; the system as a whole came out of stored up surplus. When a railway is overbuilt, extended "ahead of time" through space in which there is not enough traffic to support it, it is a tricky problem to discover the *real* loss to the energy circuit; when and where does it occur? * A

* It has been suggested, by a transportation expert of wide general knowledge and practical experience (Robert Selph Henry, assistant to the president of the Association of American Railroads) that the major business depressions of the 19th

specific loss to an investor does not necessarily signify a real loss to the energy circuit, nor even a gain to some other person; though either supposition may be true in a given instance. It might be that in one transaction, there is a real loss to the circuit, a loss to the original investor, and even a loss to the purchaser who takes over the assets and makes them pay; but none of these factors can be taken for granted. Time, space, and management are the variables. *Real* losses occur *through* time and space; and *in* physical objects. *The same loss has both aspects.*

Material is perishable in that it loses its usable form and quality with wear or mere neglect, in time. The kinetic energy of a production circuit may be dissipated without return in so many ways that it is tedious to enumerate them. It may be converted into static forms which are useless for the circuit; and these again may be simple net loss, or they may be carried as

---

century appear to have followed immediately upon periods when rapid expansion of transport facilities temporarily outran the general development of the country. Nothing could be more probable. A high energy system is a conquest of time and space, and rapid transport is the physical transmission line. Any disproportion in such facilities would have direct consequences to the whole system as a matter of course. But as long as the financing came from private enterprise capital, the condition would be self-correcting.

Mr. Henry says: "In the case of each of the earlier depressions, the new system of transportation, although created faster than it could be put to economic use, in time justified itself and paid out, because it was inherently much more efficient and economical than the transportation system which it replaced.... This did not prove true after the depression of 1929.... One possible reason for this difference might be found in the fact that the new system (super-highways, inland waterways improvements, Federal airports, etc.) upon which more money was spent in two decades than had gone into railways in more than a century, does not meet these conditions. It is not less expensive to maintain and operate than the system, which it partially replaced, but is tremendously more expensive. Another important difference is that while more than 98 per cent of the investment in railroads came from private funds, and was therefore subject to the inescapable test of economic reality, approximately 85 per cent of the recent investment in transportation plant came from public tax funds, which are relieved of that ultimate test."

In brief, a lot of energy has gone into static forms, and a continuous current still goes into a ground wire through those forms; it is not merely a net loss but a steady leakage.

dead load, at a continuing loss. (If a skyscraper is built for which there are no tenants, it might conceivably be abandoned; that would be net loss; but if it is maintained at a cost above the rental return, it is a continuing loss, dead load.)

But of all the material objects used in exchange, *real money is the one factor in which the loss cannot occur.* Of course if a five dollar gold piece were actually lost, dropped by accident and not found again, a moiety of energy is lost with it, which went into digging and minting the gold, although this is offset if the coin has been in use for a time. And gold does wear away slowly. But it is not perishable as most commodities are perishable; time has practically no effect on it. It is because, practically speaking, energy cannot be lost in or through money as a physical object, that it registers loss elsewhere, in the same manner as it facilitates transfers, serving as a meter.

Therefore real money never is and cannot be the cause of a credit collapse. Yet it is invariably singled out on such occasions for attack. The level of intelligence again is revealed in the language; it is the animistic thinking of a savage who imagines a "money devil." *

The notion that there must be something wrong with real money because it does not automatically pay bad debts is such an entirely irrational illusion that it seems to lie beyond the reach of evidence or logic. Apparently it derives from the fact that credit, which is debt, has to be computed in money. The sum of debt then may be ten or twenty or a thousand times the amount of real money in existence; because the same money can pay an infinite series of debts in sequence. If twenty million bushels of wheat were contracted for, and only ten million bushels existed, there really would not be enough wheat to fulfill the contract; but in that case, nobody would argue that there must be something wrong with wheat as a commodity; much less that the situation could be remedied by calling half

---

* The weakest point in a credit system is that a *presumed* profit is taken by the financing agency (the ʋank or investment broker) when a debt is incurred, not when it is paid.

a bushel of wheat a bushel. Certainly if one man contracted to deliver wheat which he hoped to acquire, and then failed to obtain it when the time came for delivery, it would hardly be proposed that wheat should be seized from another man who owned some, in order to complete a transaction into which the owner of the wheat had never entered. But that is what is done with money in a crisis.

Probably the underlying cause of confusion is that increased production tends to lower prices. If it did not, distribution would be impossible, for such increase. But that inescapable condition may at any time result in a temporary loss to producers of a given commodity because they have produced more. A wheat grower might get $2 a bushel one season because of crop shortage, and only $1 the next when he had grown twice as much wheat. He feels that this is inequitable; the $2 was all right, no matter how high the cash profit was; but the $1 is not enough. On the other hand, the buyer feels that he is not getting enough for his money when he pays $2, though he has no objection to paying only $1. But both of them are inclined to think the money must be at fault; the quantity must be inadequate. When it comes to paying debt, that is, meeting the consequences of credit, debtor and creditor are equally prone to this illusion on the same transaction, both being liable to loss.

In a collapse of credit, enterprises which are sound enough in themselves are adversely affected. Cash reserves are a precaution against such contingencies; they constitute storage batteries, by which the business can keep going until the long circuit is restored to sufficiently sound condition. But the only practicable test of where the leakage and loss occurs is that repayment ceases somewhere. The quickest and most drastic liquidation of a credit collapse would be the best and most equitable; because it would most rapidly reconnect the production system; but this is seldom allowed. Instead, the political power is called in to seize or depreciate money; the meter is falsified, and a general leakage all along the line is caused.

After that, no genuine recovery is possible, unless or until this power is revoked and the general leakage stopped. Under the Roman empire, after the government intervened, there never was any recovery. That was the end of the empire; and Europe was sunk for centuries.

It should be kept in mind that even in private control, misjudgment on a high potential energy circuit can and does cause vast disturbances and incidental losses in the economy. If viewed merely as physical phenomena, the effects in peace are startling enough. They are most apparent in cities, above all in American cities, because the latter are truly dynamic apparitions. The pre-industrial cities of Europe were of course local energy circuits, connected on the long circuit; but the limited potential allowed them to take form as authentic social and political organizations. The pattern is visible in the grouping of civic and religious edifices, commercial quarters, and residences, so as to indicate a center. No American city ever quite established such a pattern. From the beginning, the American city was a high potential power station, a generator of more energy than the traditional form could accommodate. As the energy flowed out to expand the nation, it shifted and transposed every aspect of the civic scene continually.

A city by origin is a crossroads; that is to say, it marks the confluence of streams of energy, and augments the flow. Immemorially, the location of cities has been fixed by ports, rivers, and highways, a port being the end of an ocean route. The advent of railways did not alter this relationship, but for the time being confirmed the natural factors. Though railways to some extent superseded inland waterways, they still followed the water level as far as possible, and therefore did not greatly change the previous trade routes. Once the right of way had been obtained and the tracks laid, traffic was tied to the line of rails. But the next development in transport was essentially different. Its effect is most strikingly exemplified in New York.

Having the port and river to begin with, and an ocean route

to Europe, New York naturally became a great railway terminus. With these advantages, it was also the financial center. Significantly, the motor car industry developed inland. New York supplied liquid capital to promote the unparalleled expansion of that industry.

But motor cars are not tied to a special track, like railways; neither do they require a set terminus, as ships and railways do. Something had happened, with the advent of the motor car, which was not immediately perceived; the trade routes were altered to a considerable degree. In the past, when the great trade routes were blocked or shifted, cities and regions fell into decay, as with Venice, the Levantine ports, the Hanseatic towns; but the cause was obvious. It occurred in respect of the routes as such. With the motor car, the change occurred in the vehicle of transportation; and what it did was to diffuse traffic and lessen the importance of the centers. Whether or not the airplane tends to centralization again remains to be seen; the plane is certainly tied to established routes, much more than the motor car, because it must have a landing field, but we do not yet know if this is a permanent condition. In any event, the railway built up great cities as it also facilitated settlement of the wilderness; it was an ambivalent factor, and on the whole it equilibrated the economy. In the development of the high energy production system, the railway is the product of an immense centralization of energy (in money, cash capital); hence its action must tend preponderantly the other way. From that point, the normal process should have been mainly toward decentralization; and the motor car came in appropriately. Another sign of decentralization was the stepping down of the size of the generating units of power, in smaller dynamos. These developments have a philosophical, social, and political meaning. *The motor car is designed for individual ownership and use.* The course of events reveals the true nature and processes of capitalism, which is not collective and cannot be brought into any system of collectivism; capitalism is the economic system of individualism. The energy age could get under way only by a preliminary concentration of liquid capital in private control, which collectivism will not permit to begin with. Thus it was assumed by superficial minds, such as Marx, that capitalism tended to concentration of wealth and a "class" division of interests. But the "interest" of capitalism is distribution. All the inventions of man have individualism as their end, because they spring from the individual function of intelligence, which is the creative and productive source. Freedom being the natural condition of man, inventions making for greater mobility resolve into individual means of transport. So far as co-operative action is useful toward the development of the individual, capitalism is fully able to carry out by voluntary association vast and complex operations of which collectivism is utterly incapable, and which are self-liquidating at the limit of their usefulness, if they are allowed to complete the process. No collectivist society can even permit co-operation; it relies upon compulsion; hence it remains static.*

That miscalculations will occur is inevitable. Though the motor car, the smaller dynamo, and other signs should have been sufficient warning that the great American cities were already somewhat overgrown, nobody read the omens. Instead, when the liquid capital from the profits of the motor car industry flowed back to New York, the stream was directed under the very foundations of the city. It shot up in steel and

---

* Paradoxically, though socialism cannot tolerate free enterprise, the political framework of free enterprise accommodates every form or type of co-operative association, *to the full extent of its practicable operation*. The socialist electrical engineer, Steinmetz, working for General Electric, did not want fixed compensation, preferring to draw whatever funds he felt he needed; and his wish was complied with, on open account—which would have been impossible in socialism! The arrangement was practicable in the given case simply because it was left to the private judgment and willingness of the parties concerned.

All the defects which may occur in a free enterprise system are positive and settled features of collectivism. If the collective (political power) debars a man from work, what can he do? If a man does inferior work in a free economy, the purchaser is the judge; who can have the right to judge under socialism? At worst, in a free society, the most unfortunate depend on charity; in the collective, they may be killed.

stone, a terrific projection of energy, in the last great sky-scrapers, "bigger and better," the Chrysler Building, the Empire State Building, Radio City. It had one effect of an explosion, shattering the previous real estate values. That profit really should have been used to decentralize the industry which produced it, and equilibrate industry and agriculture; instead it was thrown into a short circuit.

Yet these costly mistakes of the private property capitalist economy could be absorbed at private expense and forgotten if the political agency were not called in to perpetuate and aggravate them. In New York, obsolete buildings could have been torn down and the sites utilized profitably for parking space, which was badly needed; with a margin for improvement in the aspect of the city, by letting in light, air, and a few trees. Paradoxically, overbuilding would have made space. Rents would have been adjusted downward, as they should be in a high production system; and values temporarily lost would have been recovered on a fairly permanent basis. This natural process was stopped just at the point where it threatens the city with permanent paralysis, by keeping many persons on relief in undesired idleness at subsistence level, on taxes which are a burden to production and tend to drive industry away.

Likewise, when the forces in action, including the mass pressure of unions, were tending to decentralize the great industries of the middle west, political action supervened, and forced even greater centralization.

A liability to panics and depressions is inherent in a high production system using credit; just as a liability to famine is inherent in a low production system. Of the two hazards, that of the high production is obviously least, on the plain evidence of history. But the intervention of the political power greatly aggravates the hardship in any case. The nineteenth century was the first century of high energy production. It was also the first century in Europe when men did not actually perish in large numbers from hunger. The one famine which did occur in Europe was the Irish famine, where a staple crop was blighted and there was little or no industrial development because the political power did not permit enterprise to function freely. Elsewhere, industrial depressions caused severe hardship, even destitution, but it was possible to ward off sheer starvation at the very worst. And the extreme hardship was due to the partial survival of the status economy. In the United States, there were several very heavy and protracted depressions, "hard times." Practically nothing was done by the political power under pretext of relief. There was rock-bottom poverty, men tramping the country looking for work, and living on hand-outs or soup-kitchens. But prices of commodities were so low, being allowed to go down as far as they would, that very little money sufficed for subsistence. When the credit collapse had been liquidated, recovery was so rapid that the change seemed fabulous in retrospect. The frontier of freedom had not been closed.

There is a peculiar contrast between the depression of the Nineties and that following 1929, perhaps a lesson for political thinkers. A hundred years ago, Macaulay expressed apprehension that the American constitution and property rights must sooner or later be subverted by popular suffrage, because in time of distress the "have nots" would vote to expropriate the "haves." Unless one goes behind the returns it might be assumed that he was right; but what did happen? In the depression of the Nineties, an election turned on that issue, in respect of money, the "free silver" question. Certainly the majority of voters were in some distress. The vote was fairly close, although decidedly weighted against sound money by the Democratic party solidarity of the South. But the popular decision was for sound money. Again, in 1932, the popular vote was for government economy, sound money, and incidental reduction of the political power, though the country was suffering acutely from a depression.

What was the cause of the panic? Enormous government loans abroad which were not repaid; and the existence of the

Federal Reserve system, a political creation, which made an inordinate credit extension possible.

And who went on Federal relief first?

By no means the "have nots." The real cleavage did not occur on the lines Macaulay drew, between the rich and the poor. It was between the producers and the non-producers, in the main. The first measure of "relief" was the Reconstruction Finance Corporation; and the first money paid out from it went to J. P. Morgan & Co. It was the non-productive rich who first went on the dole. Had they not done so, no measure could have been passed for Federal poor relief; and the workingman accepted it only in extremity and with bitterness; what he wanted was a job. Vincent Astor, drawing a large inherited income from ground rents, sold slum property which had been exploited till there was no income left in it, to the Federal government. Owning shipping, he got shipping subsidies. Speculators urged the extension of government power to maintain the inflated values of their paper securities, by depreciation of money and by stopping "bear" sales on the market, so that huge blocks of stock at artificial prices hung over the market and made normal recovery impossible. To "save" them from the consequences of their own gambling, everyone who had not participated in the game was penalized. Laws were passed against "hoarding," so that the only action punished was prudence. By this means the normal reserves of cash which normally restore production were dissipated. Likewise, thrifty, competent, and solvent farmers, who managed to get their living from their farms, were penalized with quotas and quota taxes to subsidize speculative farming. One man in Montana drew $30,000 of government money because he had persisted in wasting seed wheat on arid land during a drought; while a poor widow in New England was forced to pay a "processing tax" because she raised a couple of pigs and made them into bacon!

The line was drawn in a striking manner, between the producer and the non-producer, with Henry Ford and Senator

Couzens. Ford was in production; he was against government intervention. Couzens, a one time partner of Ford's, who had taken his fortune out of production and put it into tax free government bonds, advocated the government expropriation of money.

Every time the production system tried to function healthily, the non-producers invoked the political power to choke it off. Ultimately, the main current of energy was forced into the political channel.

This process had already occurred in Europe. Enormous loans were made through political agencies to political agencies; and the money went into non-productive static forms, public buildings, municipal "improvements," none of which yielded any return. Then there was no work, and political control forced the workers into armament factories. In both America and Europe, misdirected energy was projected upward; but Europe did not build skyscrapers. What went up was military airplanes.

An airplane rides on a jet of energy as a cork-ball rides on the jet of a fountain. The energy is drawn from a circuit in which the cities are the center. And the planes are bombing the cities out of existence. How long can they stay up in the air when they have destroyed the source and the circuit which lifted them skyward?

None of this was unpredictable, nor was it wholly unforeseen. Ninety years ago Herbert Spencer perceived the political trend; he said: "We are being rebarbarized." He recognized the cultural level which is enforced by complete "social" control of the individual. But he did not realize that it cannot be imposed on a high energy system peacefully; and that the process was bound to result in explosion.

If a financial system is unsound, it can only be so by the possibility of over-extension of credit, and paper currency. A true remedy could only consist of limiting such facilities. Government "guarantees" merely put the property of prudent men at the disposal of speculators in case of loss. There is no such thing as a "money panic"; a financial panic occurs from collapse of credit.

In the United States, the inevitable consequence of the political power extending over money, with the Federal Reserve system, was forecast with detailed accuracy by Elihu Root. He wrote: "This is in no sense a provision for an elastic currency. It does not provide an elastic currency. It provides an expansive currency, but not an elastic one. It provides a currency which may be increased, always increased, but not a currency for which the bill contains any provision compelling reduction. . . . With the exhaustless reservoir of the Government of the United States furnishing easy money, the sales increase, the businesses enlarge, more new enterprises are started, the spirit of optimism pervades the community. Bankers are not free from it. They are human. The members of the Federal Reserve Board will not be free from it. They are human. All the world moves along on a growing tide of optimism. Everyone is making money. Everyone is growing rich. It goes up and up . . . until finally someone breaks . . . and down comes the whole structure. I can see in this bill . . . no influence interposed by us against the occurrence of one of those periods of false and delusive prosperity which inevitably end in ruin and suffering. For the most direful results of the awakening of the people from such a dream are not to be found in the banking houses—no: not even in the business houses. They are to be found among the millions who have lost the means of earning their daily bread."

Elihu was also among the prophets.

But the direful results do not always stop with a financial depression; they may issue in violence. Civil wars occur when kinetic energy is forcibly blocked or subverted by political intervention. The popular idea of revolution being made by "masses" ground down for a long period into abject penury is fallacious. Slavery has never been abolished by a slave insurrection, but only by the exertions of free men. There are "palace revolutions," in which power is forcibly seized by one group from another, without any other change; there are also factional civil wars when a form of government collapses. But in the significant type of civil war or revolution— the terms are not identical, but a given war may include both elements—both sides have colorable claims to some legitimate authority; both are energetic, with a going production system involved in the question at issue; and the larger number of producers are resisting a fresh increase of government power, as in the English Civil War of the seventeenth century, and the American War of Independence. The latter began as a civil war and ended as a revolution, establishing a new form of government to secure the traditional principle of representative self-government originally claimed. Thus any extension of government powers and increase of taxation on the pretense of "averting revolution" can only create the danger if it did not already exist, and aggravate it if it did exist.

Conversely, when a dictatorship gains power, it is by various groups conceding the power piecemeal, not perceiving what it must add up to in the end. Men enslave themselves, forging the chains link by link, usually by demanding *protection as a group*. When business men ask for government credit, they surrender control of their business. When labor asks for enforced "collective bargaining" it has yielded its own freedom. When racial groups are recognized in law, they can be discriminated against by law.

CHAPTER XX

The Humanitarian With the Guillotine

Most of the harm in the world is done by good people, and not by accident, lapse, or omission. It is the result of their deliberate actions, long persevered in, which they hold to be motivated by high ideals toward virtuous ends. This is demonstrably true; nor could it occur otherwise. The percentage of positively malignant, vicious, or depraved persons is necessarily small, for no species could survive if its members were habitually and consciously bent upon injuring one another. Destruction is so easy that even a minority of persistently evil intent could shortly exterminate the unsuspecting majority of well-disposed persons. Murder, theft, rapine, and destruction are easily within the power of every individual at any time. If it is presumed that they are restrained only by fear or force, what is it they fear, or who would turn the force against them if all men were of like mind? Certainly if the harm done by willful criminals were to be computed, the number of murders, the extent of damage and loss, would be found negligible in the sum total of death and devastation wrought upon human beings by their kind. Therefore it is obvious that in periods when millions are slaughtered, when torture is practiced, starvation enforced, oppression made a policy, as at present over a large part of the world, and as it has often been in the past, it must be at the behest of very many good people, and even by their direct action, for what they consider a worthy object. When they are not the immediate executants, they are on record as giving approval, elaborating justifications, or else cloaking facts with silence, and discountenancing discussion.

Obviously this could not occur without cause or reason. And it must be understood, in the above passage, that by good people we mean good people, persons who would not of their own conscious intent act to hurt their fellow men, nor procure such acts, either wantonly or for a personal benefit to themselves. Good people wish well to their fellow men, and wish to guide their own actions accordingly. Further, we do not here imply any "transvaluation of values," confusing good and evil, or suggesting that good produces evil, or that there is no difference between good and evil, or between good and ill-disposed persons; nor is it suggested that the virtues of good people are not really virtues.

Then there must be a very grave error in the means by which they seek to attain their ends. There must even be an error in their primary axioms, to permit them to continue using such means. Something is terribly wrong in the procedure, somewhere. What is it?

Certainly the slaughter committed from time to time by barbarians invading settled regions, or the capricious cruelties of avowed tyrants, would not add up to one-tenth the horrors perpetrated by rulers with good intentions.

As the story has come down to us, the ancient Egyptians were enslaved by Pharaoh through a benevolent scheme of "ever normal granaries." Provision was made against famine; and then the people were forced to barter property and liberty for such reserves which had previously been taken from their own production. The inhuman hardness of the ancient Spartans was practiced for a civic ideal of virtue.

The early Christians were persecuted for reasons of state, the collective welfare; and they resisted for the right of personality, each because he had a soul of his own. Those killed by Nero for sport were few compared to those put to death by later emperors for strictly "moral" reasons. Gilles de Retz, who murdered children to gratify a beastly perversion, killed no more than fifty or sixty in all. Cromwell ordered the massacre of thirty thousand people at once, including infants in arms, in the name of righteousness. Even the brutalities of Peter the Great had the pretext of a design to benefit his subjects.

The present war, begun with a perjured treaty made by two powerful nations (Russia and Germany), that they might crush their smaller neighbors with impunity, the treaty being broken by a surprise attack on the fellow conspirator, would have been impossible without the internal political power which in both cases was seized on the excuse of doing good to the nation. *The lies, the violence, the wholesale killings, were practiced first on the people of both nations by their own respective governments.* It may be said, and it may be true, that in both cases the wielders of power are vicious hypocrites; that their conscious objective was evil from the beginning; none the less, they could not have come by the power at all except *with the consent and assistance* of good people. The Communist regime in Russia gained control by promising the peasants land, in terms the promisers knew to be a lie as understood. Having gained power, the Communists took from the peasants the land they already owned; and exterminated those who resisted. This was done by plan and intention; and the lie was praised as "social engineering," by socialists admirers in America. If that is engineering, then the sale of fake mining stock is engineering. The whole population of Russia was put under duress and terror; thousands were murdered without trial; millions were worked to death and starved to death in captivity. Likewise the whole population of Germany was put under duress and terror, by the same means. With the war, Russians in German prison camps, Germans in Russian prison camps, are enduring no worse and no other fate than that their compatriots in as great numbers have endured and are enduring from their own governments in their own countries. If there is any slight difference, they suffer rather less from the vengeance of avowed enemies than from the proclaimed benevolence of their compatriots. The conquered nations of Europe, under the Russian or German heel, are merely experiencing what Russians and Germans have been through for years, under their own national regimes.

Further, the principal political figures now wielding power in Europe, including those who have sold their countries to the invader, are socialists, ex-socialists, or communists; men whose creed was the collective good.

With all this demonstrated to the hilt, we have the peculiar spectacle of the man who condemned millions of his own people to starvation, admired by philanthropists whose declared aim is to see to it that everyone in the world has a quart of milk. A graduate professional charity worker has flown half around the world to seek an interview with this master of his trade, and to write rhapsodies on being granted such a privilege. To keep themselves in office, for the professed purpose of doing good, similar idealists welcome the political support of grafters, convicted pimps, and professional thugs. This affinity of these types invariably reveals itself, when the occasion arises. But what is the occasion?

Why did the humanitarian philosophy of eighteenth century Europe usher in the Reign of Terror? It did not happen by chance; it followed from the original premise, objective and means proposed. The objective is to do good to others as a *primary* justification of existence; the means is the power of the collective; and the premise is that "good" is collective.

The root of the matter is ethical, philosophical, and religious, involving the relation of man to the universe, of man's creative faculty to his Creator. The fatal divergence occurs in failing to recognize the norm of human life. Obviously there is a great deal of pain and distress incidental to existence. Poverty, illness, and accident are possibilities which may be reduced to a minimum, but cannot be altogether eliminated from the hazards mankind must encounter. But these are not desirable conditions, to be brought about or perpetuated. Naturally children have parents, while most adults are in fair health most of their lives, and are engaged in useful activity which brings them a livelihood. That is the norm and the

natural order. Ills are marginal. They can be alleviated from
the marginal surplus of production; otherwise nothing at all
could be done. Therefore it cannot be supposed that the producer exists only for the sake of the non-producer, the well
for the sake of the ill, the competent for the sake of the
incompetent; nor any person merely for the sake of another.
(The logical procedure, if it is held that any person exists
only for the sake of another, was carried out in semi-barbarous
societies, when the widow or followers of a dead man were
buried alive in his grave.)

The great religions, which are also great intellectual systems, have always recognized the conditions of the natural
order. They enjoin charity, benevolence, as a moral obligation, to be met out of the producer's surplus. That is, they
make it *secondary to production,* for the inescapable reason
that without production there could be nothing to give. Consequently they prescribe the most severe rule, to be embraced
only voluntarily, for those who wish to devote their lives
wholly to works of charity, from contributions. Always this
is regarded as a special vocation, because it could not be a
general way of life. Since the almoner must obtain the funds
or goods he distributes from the producers, he has no authority to command; he must ask. When he subtracts his own livelihood from such alms, he must take no more than bare
subsistence. In proof of his vocation, he must even forego the
happiness of family life, if he were to receive the formal
religious sanction. Never was he to derive comfort for himself
from the misery of others.

The religious orders maintained hospitals, reared orphans,
distributed food. Part of such alms was given unconditionally,
that there might be no compulsion under the cloak of charity.
It is not decent to make a man strip his soul in return for
bread. This is the real difference when charity is enjoined in
the name of God, and not on humanitarian or philanthropic
principles. If the sick were cured, the hungry fed, orphans
cared for until they grew up, it was certainly good, and the

good cannot be computed in merely physical terms; but such actions were intended to tide the beneficiaries over a period of distress and restore them to the norm if possible. If the distressed could partly help themselves, so much the better. If they could not, that fact was recognized. But most of the religious orders made a concurrent effort to be productive, that they might give of their own surplus, as well as distributing donations. When they performed productive work, such as building, teaching for a reasonable fee, farming, or incidental industries and arts, the results were lasting, not only in the particular products, but in enlargement of knowledge and advanced methods, so that in the long run they raised the norm of welfare. And it should be noted that these enduring results derived from *self-improvement*.

What can one human being actually do for another? He can give from his own funds and his own time whatever he can spare. But he cannot bestow faculties which nature has denied; nor give away his own subsistence without becoming dependent himself. If he earns what he gives away, he must earn it *first*. Surely he has a right to domestic life if he can support a wife and children. He must therefore reserve enough for himself and his family to continue production. No one person, though his income be ten million dollars a year, can take care of every case of need in the world. But supposing he has no means of his own, and still imagines that he can make "helping others" at once his *primary* purpose and the normal way of life, which is the central doctrine of the humanitarian creed, how is he to go about it? Lists have been published of the Neediest Cases, *certified* by secular charitable foundations which pay their own officers handsomely. The needy have been investigated, but not relieved. Out of donations received, the officials pay themselves first. This is embarrassing even to the rhinoceros hide of the professional philanthropist. But how is the confession to be evaded? If the philanthropist could *command* the means of the producer, instead of asking for a portion, he could claim credit for production, being in a position to give orders to the producer. Then he can blame the producer for not carrying out orders to produce more.

If the primary objective of the philanthropist, his justification for living, is to help others, his ultimate good *requires that others shall be in want.* His happiness is the obverse of their misery. If he wishes to help "humanity," the whole of humanity must be in need. The humanitarian wishes to be a prime mover in the lives of others. He cannot admit either the divine or the natural order, by which men have the power to help themselves. The humanitarian puts himself in the place of God.

But he is confronted by two awkward facts; first, that the competent do not need his assistance; and second, that the majority of people, if unperverted, positively do not want to be "done good" by the humanitarian. When it is said that everyone should live primarily for others, what is the specific course to be pursued? Is each person to do exactly what any other person wants him to do, without limits or reservations? and only what others want him to do? What if various persons make conflicting demands? The scheme is impracticable. Perhaps then he is to do only what is actually "good" for others. But will those others know what is good for them? No, that is ruled out by the same difficulty. Then shall A do what he thinks is good for B, and B do what he thinks is good for A? Or shall A accept only what he thinks is good for B, and vice versa? But that is absurd. Of course what the humanitarian actually proposes is that *he* shall do what he thinks is good for everybody. It is at this point that the humanitarian sets up the guillotine.

What kind of world does the humanitarian contemplate as affording him full scope? It could only be a world filled with breadlines and hospitals, in which nobody retained the natural power of a human being to help himself or to resist having things done to him. And that is precisely the world that the humanitarian arranges when he gets his way. When a humanitarian wishes to see to it that everyone has a quart of milk, it is evident that he hasn't got the milk, and cannot produce it himself, or why should he be merely wishing? Further, if he did have a sufficient quantity of milk to bestow a quart on everyone, as long as his proposed beneficiaries can and do produce milk for themselves, they would say no, thank you. Then how is the humanitarian to contrive that he shall have all the milk to distribute, and that everyone else shall be in want of milk?

There is only one way, and that is by the use of the political power in its fullest extension. Hence the humanitarian feels the utmost gratification when he visits or hears of a country in which everyone is restricted to ration cards. Where subsistence is doled out, the desideratum has been achieved, of general want and a superior power to "relieve" it. The humanitarian in theory is the terrorist in action.

The good people give him the power he demands because they have accepted his false premise. The advance of science lent it a specious plausibility, with the increase in production. Since there is enough for everybody, why cannot the "needy" be provided for first, and the question thus disposed of permanently?

If at this point it is asked, how are you to define the "needy," and from what source and by what power is provision to be made for them, kind-hearted persons may exclaim indignantly: "This is quibbling; narrow the definition to the very limit, but at the irreducible minimum you cannot deny that a man who is hungry, ill-clad, and without shelter is needy. The source of relief can only be the means of those who are not in such need. The power already exists; if there can be a right to tax people for armies, navies, local police, road-making, or any other imaginable purpose, surely there must be a prior right to tax people for the preservation of life itself."

Very well; take a specific case. In the hard times of the Nineties, a young journalist in Chicago was troubled by the appalling hardships of the unemployed. He tried to believe that any man honestly willing to work could find employment; but to make sure, he investigated a few cases. Here was one, a youth from a farm, where the family maybe got enough to eat but was short of everything else; the farm boy had come to Chicago looking for a job, and would certainly have taken any kind of work, but there was none. Let it be supposed he might have begged his way home; there were others who were half a continent and an ocean from their homes. They couldn't get back, by any possible effort of their own; and there is no quibbling about that. They couldn't. They slept in alleyways, waited for meager rations at soup-kitchens; and suffered bitterly. There is another thing; among these unemployed were some persons, it is impossible to say how many, who were exceptionally enterprising, gifted, or competent; and that is what got them into their immediate plight. They had cut loose from dependence at a peculiarly hazardous time; they had taken a long chance. Extremes met among the unemployed; the extremes of courageous enterprise, of sheer ill-luck, and of downright improvidence and incompetence. A blacksmith working near Brooklyn Bridge who gave a penniless wanderer ten cents to pay the bridge toll couldn't know he was making that advance to immortality in the person of a future Poet Laureate of England. But John Masefield was the wanderer. So it is not implied that the needy are necessarily "undeserving." There were also people in the country, in drought or insect-plagued areas, who were in dire want, and must have literally starved if relief had not been sent them. They didn't get much either, and that in haphazard, ragbag sort. But everyone struggled through to an amazing recovery of the whole country.

Incidentally, there would have been much more severe distress instead of simple poverty at the subsistence line, but for neighborly giving which was not called charity. People always give away a good deal, if they have it; it is a human

impulse, which the humanitarian plays on for his own purpose. What is wrong with institutionalizing that natural impulse in a political agency?

Very well again; had the farm boy done anything wrong
in leaving the farm, where he did have enough to eat, and
going to Chicago on the chance of getting a job?

If the answer is yes, then there must be a rightful power
which shall prevent him leaving the farm *without permission*.
The feudal power did that. It couldn't prevent people from
starving; it merely compelled them to starve right where they
were born.

But if the answer is no, the farm boy didn't do wrong, he
had a right to take that chance, then exactly what is to be
done to make certain he will not be in hard luck when he gets
to his chosen destination? Must a job be provided for any
person at any place he chooses to go? That is absurd. It can't
be done. Is he entitled to relief anyhow, when he gets there,
as long as he chooses to stay; or at least to a return ticket
home? That is equally absurd. The demand would be unlimited; no abundance of production could meet it.

Then what of the people who were impoverished by
drought; could they not be given political relief? But there
must be conditions. Are they to receive it just as long as they
are in need, while they stay where they are? (They cannot
be financed for indefinite travel.) That is just what has been
done in recent years; and it kept relief recipients for seven
years together in squalid surroundings, wasting time, work,
and seed-grain in the desert.

The truth is that if any proposed method of caring for
the marginal want and distress incident to human life by
establishing a permanent fixed charge upon production would
be adopted most gladly by those who now oppose it, *if it were
practicable*. They oppose it because it is impracticable in the
nature of things. They are the people who have already
devised all the partial expedients possible, in the way of private insurance; and they know exactly what the catch is,

because they come up against it when they try to make secure provision for their own dependents.

The insuperable obstacle is that it is absolutely impossible to get anything out of production ahead of maintenance.

If it were a fact that the producers generally, the industrial managers and others, had hearts of chilled steel, and cared nothing whatever about human suffering, still it would be most convenient for them if the question of relief for all kinds of distress, whether unemployment, illness or old age, could be settled once for all, so they need hear no more of it. They are always under attack on this point; and it doubles their trouble whenever industry hits a depression. The politicians can get votes out of distress; the humanitarians land lucrative white collar jobs for themselves distributing relief funds; only the producers, both capitalists and workingmen, have to take the abuse and pay the shot.

The difficulty is best shown in a concrete instance. Suppose a man owning a profitable business in sound condition with a long record of good management wishes to arrange that his family shall have their support from it indefinitely. He might as owner be in a position to give first lien bonds yielding a certain amount; say it was only $5,000 a year on a business which was paying $100,000 a year net profit. That is the very best he could do; and if ever the business failed to produce $5,000 net profit, his family wouldn't get the money, and that's all there is to it. They might put the concern through bankruptcy and take the assets, and the assets after bankruptcy might be worth nothing at all. *You can't get anything out of production ahead of maintenance.*

Aside from that, of course his family might hypothecate the bonds, hand them over to the "management" of some "benevolent" friend—a thing which has been known to happen—and then they wouldn't get the money anyhow. That is about what occurs with organized charities having endowments. They support a lot of kind friends in cushy jobs.

But what if the business man, through the warmth of his

generous affection, fixed it irrevocably so that his wife and family had an open checking account on the company's funds, to draw just what they pleased. He might feel innocently sure they would not take more than a small percentage, for their reasonable needs. But the day might come when the cashier must tell the happy wife there was no money to honor her check; and with such an arrangement it is certain that the day would come rather soon. In either case, just when the family needed money most, the business would yield least.

But the procedure would be completely insane if the business man gave to a third party an irrevocable power to draw as much as he pleased from the company's funds, with only an unenforceable understanding that the third party would support the owner's family. And that is what the proposal to care for the needy by the political means comes to. It gives the power to the politicians to tax without limit; and there is absolutely no way to ensure that the money shall go where it was intended to go. In any case, the business will not stand any such *unlimited* drain.

Why do kind-hearted persons call in the political power? They cannot deny that the means for relief must come from production. But they say there is enough and to spare. Then they must assume that the producers are not willing to give what is "right." Further they assume that there is a collective right to impose taxes, for any purpose the collective shall determine. They localize that right in "the government," as if it were self-existent, forgetting the American axiom that government itself is not self-existent, but is instituted by men for limited purposes. The taxpayer himself hopes for protection from the army or navy or police; he uses the roads; hence his right to insist on limiting taxation is self-evident. The government has no "rights" in the matter, but only a delegated authority.

But if taxes are to be imposed for relief, who is the judge of what is possible or beneficial? It must be either the producers, the needy, or some third group. To say it shall be all three together is no answer; the verdict must swing upon majority or plurality drawn from one or other group. Are the needy to vote themselves whatever they want? Are the humanitarians, the third group, to vote themselves control of both the producers and the needy? (That is what they have done.) The government is thus supposed to be empowered to give "security" to the needy. *It cannot.* What it does is to seize the provision made by private persons for their own security, thus depriving everyone of every hope or chance of security. It can do nothing else, if it acts at all. Those who do not understand the nature of the action are like savages who might cut down a tree to get the fruit; they do not think over time and space, as civilized men must think.

We have seen the worst that can happen when there is only private relief and improvised municipal doles of a temporary character. Unorganized private giving is random and sporadic; it has never been able to prevent suffering completely. But neither does it perpetuate the dependence of its beneficiaries. It is the method of capitalism and liberty. It involves extraordinary downswings and upswings, but the upswings were always higher each time, and of longer duration than the downswings. And in the most distressful periods, there was no real famine, no black despair, but a queer kind of angry, active optimism and an unfaltering belief in better times ahead, which the outcome justified. Unofficial, sporadic private donations did actually serve the purpose. *It worked,* however imperfectly.

On the other hand, what can the political power do? One of the alleged "abuses" of capitalism was the sweatshop. Immigrants came to America, penniless and ignorant of the language and with no skilled trade; they were hired for very low wages, worked long hours in slum surroundings, and were said to be exploited. Yet mysteriously in time they improved their condition; the great majority attained comfort, and some gained wealth. Could the political power have provided lucrative jobs for *everyone who wished to come?*

Of course it could not and cannot. Nevertheless, the good people called in the political power to alleviate the hard lot of these newcomers. What did it do? Its first requirement was that each immigrant should bring with him a certain sum of money. That is to say, it cut off the *most needy* abroad from their sole hope. Later, when the political power in Europe had reduced life to a gloomy hell, but a large number of persons might still have scraped together the requisite sum for admittance to America, the political power here simply cut down admission to a quota. The more desperate the need, the less chance could the political power allow them. Would not many millions in Europe be glad and grateful if they could have even the poorest chance the old system afforded, instead of convict camps, torture cellars, vile humiliations, and violent death?

The sweatshop employer hadn't much capital. He risked the little he had in hiring people. He was accused of doing them a horrible wrong, and his business cited as revealing the intrinsic brutality of capitalism.

The political official is tolerably well-paid, in a permanent job. Risking nothing himself, he gets his pay for thrusting desperate people back from the borders, as drowning men might be beaten back from the sides of a well-provisioned ship. What else can he do? Nothing. Capitalism did what it could; the political power does what it can. Incidentally, the ship was built and stored by capitalism.

As between the private philanthropist and the private capitalist acting as such, take the case of the truly needy man, who is not incapacitated, and suppose that the philanthropist gives him food and clothes and shelter—when he has used them up, he is just where he was before, except that he may have acquired the habit of dependence. But suppose someone with no benevolent motive whatever, simply wanting work done for his own reasons, should hire the needy man for a wage. The employer has not done a good deed. Yet the condition of the employed man has actually been changed.

What is the vital difference between the two actions?

It is that the unphilanthropic employer has brought the man he employed *back into the production line,* on the great circuit of energy; whereas the philanthropist can only divert energy in such manner that there can be no return into production, and therefore less likelihood of the object of his benefaction finding employment.

This is the profound, rational reason why human beings shrink from relief, and hate the very word. It is also the reason why those who perform works of charity under a true vocation do their best to keep it marginal, and gladly yield the opportunity to "do good" in favor of any chance for the beneficiary to work on any half-tolerable terms. Those who cannot avoid going on relief feel and exhibit the results in their physical being; they are cut off from the living springs of self-renewing energy, and their vitality sinks.

The result, if they are kept on relief long enough by the determined philanthropists and politicians in concert, has been described by a relief agent. At first, the "clients" applied reluctantly. "In a few months all that changes. We find that the fellow who wanted just enough to tide him over has settled back to living on relief as a matter of course." The relief agent who said that was himself "living on relief as a matter of course"; but he was a long step lower than his client, in that he did not even recognize his own condition. Why was he able to evade the truth? Because he could hide himself behind the philanthropic motive. "We help to prevent starvation, and we see to it that these people have some sort of shelter and bedding." If the agent were asked, do you grow the food, do you build the shelter, or do you give the money out of your own earnings to pay for them, he would not see that that made any difference. He has been taught that it is right to "live for others," for "social aims" and "social gains." As long as he can believe he is doing that, he will not ask himself what he is necessarily doing *to* those others, nor where the means must come from to support him.

If the full roll of *sincere* philanthropists were called, from the beginning of time, it would be found that all of them together by their strictly philanthropic activities have never conferred upon humanity one-tenth of the benefit derived from the normally self-interested efforts of Thomas Alva Edison, to say nothing of the greater minds who worked out the scientific principles which Edison applied. Innumerable speculative thinkers, inventors, and organizers, have contributed to the comfort, health, and happiness of their fellow men—because that was not their objective. When Robert Owen tried to run a factory for efficient production, the process incidentally improved some very unpromising characters among his employees, who had been on relief, and were therefore sadly degraded; Owen made money for himself; and while so engaged, it occurred to him that if better wages were paid, production could be increased, having made its own market. That was sensible and true. But then Owen became inspired with a humanitarian ambition, to do good to everybody. He collected a lot of humanitarians, in an experimental colony; they were all so intent upon doing good to others that nobody did a lick of work; the colony dissolved acrimoniously; Owen went broke and died mildly crazy. So the important principle he had glimpsed had to wait a century to be rediscovered.

The philanthropist, the politician, and the pimp are inevitably found in alliance because they have the same motives, they seek the same ends, to exist for, through, and by others. And the good people cannot be exonerated for supporting them. Neither can it be believed that the good people are wholly unaware of what actually happens. But when the good people do know, as they certainly do, that three million persons (at the least estimate) were starved to death in one year by the methods they approve, why do they still fraternize with the murderers and support the measures? Because they have been told that the lingering death of the three millions might ultimately benefit a greater number. *The argument applies equally well to cannibalism.*

CHAPTER XXI

Our Japanized Educational System

The boast of the humanitarian era, extending over the past century or more, is that it has effected a fundamental change in the methods and purposes of education. The favored system is called progressive education. Any exact definition may be challenged, because the advocates of this system have never given an exact definition; but let it be described in the most amiable terms, open to correction. Say that progressive education seeks to make schooling a pleasurable experience; it forbids positive punishment; aims at once to encourage self-expression in the youngest children and social-mindedness in older pupils; and that it claims to teach the child to think by experimental projects and by presenting debatable current topics for general discussion, without dogmatic principles.

In contrast, the old-fashioned education said there was no royal road to learning. It gave the teacher sufficient authority for any necessary discipline. It imparted positive facts and positive principles. It discouraged immature self-expression, sought to strengthen character by self-control against the social impulse; and attached personal responsibility to any degree of emancipation from the rule of obedience for children. It taught the child to think by the use of formal logic on impersonal examples; while contemporary issues were kept out of the schoolroom as far as possible.

Which is in reality the most modern type of education?

Forty years ago, Lafcadio Hearn described the educational principles and methods of Japan, in contrast to those of the Western world. Traditionally, Hearn said, Western education began in early childhood "with the repressive part of moral training. . . . It is important to inculcate the duties of behavior, the 'must' and the 'must not' of individual obligation, as soon as possible. Later on, more liberty is allowed. The well-grown boy is made to understand that his future will depend upon his personal effort and capacity; and he is therefore left, in great measure, to take care of himself, being occasionally admonished or warned, as seems needful. . . . Throughout the whole course of mental and moral training, competition is not only expected but required. . . . The aim is the cultivation of individual ability and personal character— the creation of an independent and forceful being."

"Japanese education has always been conducted on the reverse plan. Its object has never been to train the individual for independent action, but to train him for co-operative action. . . . Constraint among us begins with childhood, and gradually relaxes; constraint in Far Eastern training begins later, and thereafter gradually tightens; and it is not a constraint imposed directly by parents and teachers. . . . Not merely up to the age of school life, but considerably beyond it, a Japanese child enjoys a degree of liberty far greater than is allowed to Occidental children. . . . The child is permitted to do as he pleases. . . . He is guarded but not constrained; admonished, but rarely compelled." If punishment becomes absolutely necessary, "by ancient custom, the entire household, servants and all, intercede for the offender; the little brothers and sisters begging in turn to bear the penalty instead. At school, the discipline begins . . . but there is no punishment beyond a public admonition. *Whatever restraint exists is chiefly exerted on the child by the common opinion of his class;* and a skillful teacher is able to direct that opinion. . . . The ruling power is always the class sentiment. . . . In the middle schools, class opinion attains a force to which the teacher himself must bend; as it is quite capable of expelling him for any attempt to over-ride it. . . . It is always the rule of the many over the one; and the power is formidable." *

* JAPAN: An interpretation. By Lafcadio Hearn. Macmillan. (1894.)

The further objective is found in the Japanese social ideal. For over a thousand years, at least, the Japanese have been taught the purest altruism, in the communal cult. "The mere idea of the right to do as one pleases could not enter into the Japanese mind. . . . No man's time or effort can be considered exclusively his own. His right to live rests solely upon his willingness to serve the community. . . . The individual was completely sacrificed to the community. . . . Every member of a community must carefully watch the conduct of his fellow members." That there might be no possibility of personal initiative or choice, all work was absolutely controlled by guilds; and all goods were allotted by authority, in that the amount and kind of possessions anyone could have was minutely determined. A parent might not even buy an extra paper doll for a child. Any deviation in conduct was instantly and ruthlessly punished. Even the language reflected this altruistic code of ethics, by avoiding the use of personal pronouns, and modifying them to a social meaning.

The result, in adult life, is "the sinister absence of moral freedom—the absence of the right to act according to one's own convictions of justice." Indeed, there can be no concept of justice, if the sole authority is that of the mass, of the collective, of the government in the ultimate resort. And the present behavior of the Japanese in war, including their attitude toward prisoners, is fully consistent with their tradition. Whatever they do to their enemies—and they determine who is an enemy, and begin the attack—is no more than they have imposed on themselves "for the good of society."

Since Hearn made these observations, Western education has moved steadily toward the Japanese basis; that is its "progressive" tendency. Class activities, group interests, social influences have become predominant. And the prevailing philosophy with which pupils are indoctrinated is that of "instrumentalism," which denies that there can be any universal or permanent moral values or standards. The most striking result in the pupils is precisely that "sinister absence of moral freedom." Neither evidence nor logic penetrates the fog in which they have been reared. It is difficult to bring one to any conclusion, when detached from the group. They will say, "Well, I just don't think so," as if there could be no facts or connected mental processes, which should lead to one opinion rather than another, or distinguish a conviction from a taste. They have an impression that "everything is different now" from anything that may have been in the past; though they have no idea how or why. Do not two and two make four? Does not a lever operate on exactly the same principle today as it did for Archimedes? They do not quite know. They may say, "Oh, I don't agree with you," but they can give no reason for dissent. They are "not quite convinced," but they can offer no argument in rebuttal. That is to say, when called upon to think, they cannot, because they have been trained to accept the class, the group, or the "social trend," as the sole authority. As far as it can be done, they have been reduced to "ganglions," neural processes in a collective "body," instead of persons.

The Orientalizing of teaching methods in the West has taken effect even in detail. The great use and value of a phonetic alphabet, as distinguished from pictographic writing (hieroglyphs or Chinese characters) is that the pupil is put in possession of the tools very quickly. In English, a child need learn only twenty-six letters, and grasp the principle of their combination, as indicating sounds; and he knows how to read. The phonetic alphabet is one of the greatest labor-saving devices ever invented. With Chinese characters or any other picture writing, thousands of signs have to be learned; scholarship is largely wasted on the mere drudgery of memorization; and further, abstract thought is severely handicapped. Yet it is advocated, as a "modern" method of teaching a child to read, that it shall learn by visual memorizing of words, without learning the alphabet. This method is credited to Bronson Alcott: "There was no primer class, trying painfully to identify A or maybe S. Instead, the little ones were grouped around the schoolmaster, who had a picture in his hand. They looked at the pictures of the animals, and down at the words —dog, cat, cow—until soon they knew which word went with which animal." This is to teach pictograph reading. As far as possible, the advantage of the phonetic alphabet is nullified, including the systematization of knowledge by references under an index. Another "advanced" educational method does not mark examination papers for their accuracy; instead, grades are given indicating that the child has done well in relation to his capacities. That is, the teacher assumes divine omniscience, and pretends to know the child's innate capacities absolutely, by some supernal means, instead of judging the specific result of a specific examination. The negligent child is advantaged, and the diligent, clever, and conscientious child is deprived of an earned benefit. Aside from that, the intrinsic idea that an answer is either correct or incorrect is obscured; and the task itself is made to appear senseless. So in every way the natural outlet of energy in human beings, which in childhood is properly directed toward the development of intelligence and character, is choked down and subverted: the purpose of study is not to learn things which are true in themselves nor to develop independence through such knowledge, but to please and conform to arbitrary authority.

The positive fact that the United States public schools are under the political power is not recognized. Because the schools were started with quite separate organizations, by districts having no connection with each other or with any other political agency, empowered to levy a separate tax which could not be expended for any other object than the local school, nobody realized that the primary field of freedom had been invaded to the utmost extent. There can be no greater stretch of arbitrary power than is required to seize children from their parents, teach them whatever the authorities decree they shall be taught, and expropriate from the parents the funds to pay for the procedure. If this principle really is not understood, let any parent holding a positive religious faith consider how it would seem to him if his children were taken by force and taught an opposite creed. Would he not recognize tyranny naked? But it is objected, religion is not taught in the schools at all. That does not alter the principle involved; though it did obscure the issue in the beginning. The majority of parents were quite willing to pay a school tax, and glad to send their children to school. They tried to keep the teaching strictly secular. Further, when school districts were mostly small, and schoolboards composed of local residents known to everybody, it was quite possible for the parents to know just what was being taught; and to have their wishes consulted in the engagement or retention of teachers and the choice of textbooks. The intrinsic nature of the power authorized was so little realized that this was called "free education," the most absolute contradiction of facts by terminology of which the language is capable. Everything about such schools is compulsory, not free; and the true nature of the institution has developed so fully along its own lines with the passage of time that parents are now helpless when it is admitted by a schoolboard that a small number of teachers are mentally unbalanced. The parents must still deliver their children into the power of those teachers, on penalty of a fine. The teachers have "security of tenure." They can't be discharged.

One of the early "cases" by which "security of tenure" was made to seem plausible for teachers indicates the utter confusion of thought on the subject, arising from failure to recognize the political power in operation. A teacher in California, of excellent character and teaching ability, was dismissed by a corrupt school board for no good reason. The case was taken into court. The teacher was reinstated, on the proper grounds that she had a contract for the term and had not defaulted on it. This was thought a sufficient reason for urging measures by which a teacher must be considered as engaged indefinitely, for that is the only meaning "of security of tenure"; though this is absolutely irrelevant to the original issue (enforcement of contract), and nullifies the contractual right of the employer. That is to say, because the teacher had suffered an injustice which the law was competent to remedy and did remedy, it was proposed and subsequently carried into effect that parents must suffer the same injustice without remedy.

Again, the famous Scopes case, the "monkey" trial in Dayton, Tennessee, was discussed with equal heat and ignorance on both sides. The state passed a law that no instructor in the public schools could impart to his pupils the Darwinian theory of evolution, under penalty. A teacher contravened the law, and was prosecuted. Of course the law was absolutely improper; but it was attacked on the ground that the Darwinian theory of evolution is true, and that the Tennesseeans were uninformed yokels.

But what if Darwinian evolution had been generally taught in the public schools of Tennessee, and a parent had tried to withhold his school taxes and refused to send his children to school *because he did not want them taught that theory;* how many of the ardent champions of Mr. Scopes would have defended such a parent? It is safe to say, not one. All they wanted was that the state should prescribe that their own particular scientific doctrine must be taught, rather than an unorthodox creed. They were not in the least concerned with freedom of thought, speech, or person. They had no conception of personal rights or just authority. They did not ask whether a teacher could have a peculiar moral prerogative to teach his pupils what their parents did not want them to be taught.

In short, they did not question the political control of education; they only wanted to use it themselves. They did not inquire whether such political control is not, by its nature, bound to legislate against statements of both facts and opinion, in prescribing a school curriculum, in the long run. The most exact and demonstrable scientific knowledge will certainly be objectionable to political authority at some point, because it will expose the folly of such authority, and its vicious effects. Nobody would be permitted to show the nonsensical absurdity of "dialectical materialism" in Russia, by logical examination. Nobody is permitted to discuss biology impartially in Germany. And if the political authority is deemed competent to control education, that must be the outcome in any country.

Educational texts are necessarily selective, in subject matter, language, and point of view. Where teaching is conducted by private schools, there will be a considerable variation in different schools; the parents must judge what they want their children taught, by the curriculum offered. Then each must strive for objective truth; and as there is no public authority to control opinion, adults must be supposed to exercise the final judgment on what they learned in school, after they have graduated. Nowhere will there be any inducement to teach the "supremacy of the state" as a compulsory philosophy. But every politically controlled educational system will inculcate the doctrine of state supremacy sooner or later, whether as the divine right of kings, or the "will of the people" in "democracy." Once that doctrine has been accepted, it becomes an almost superhuman task to break the stranglehold of the political power over the life of the citizen. It has had his body, property, and mind in its clutches from infancy. An octopus would sooner release its prey.

A tax-supported, compulsory educational system is the complete model of the totalitarian state.

The extent of the power exercised, and its final implications are not yet recognized in the United States, because parents are *allowed* to send their children to private schools, or to educate them at home—although they must still pay the school tax. But when that permission is granted, and the educational standard is prescribed, it is revocable; it is no longer a right, but a permission. In Russia, in Germany, it is no longer permitted.

Undoubtedly the good people will ask, out of artless perplexity and a short memory, how are children to be educated if there are no tax-supported compulsory public schools? The answer is, by private schools. Anyone who wished could open a school, to which parents could send their children on payment of the necessary fees, which would naturally vary a good deal. Primer education could be given at home, as it generally was in the United States up to fifty years ago; most children could read, write, and perform simple addition before they started school. The *standard* of education in New England was much higher a hundred and fifty years ago than it is now. Nine-tenths of the useful knowledge the average person possesses is certainly acquired out of school. Who taught the population of the United States to drive motor cars? It was not done in school, and could not have been. The practical skill by which the average man gets a living is not learned in school. There is no reason to suppose that children would remain untaught. Before the Civil War, some of the Southern states passed laws making it a crime to teach a slave to read or write. Then the desire to learn, and the readiness to impart knowledge, are so spontaneous and universal that they can be restrained only by legal penalties, even when the social gulf is that between master and bondsman.

But would not some children remain illiterate? They might, as some do now, and as they did in the past. The United States has had one president who did not learn to read and write until after he was not only a grown man, but married and earning his own living. The truth is that in a free country any person who remains illiterate might as well be left so; although simple literacy is not a sufficient education in itself, but the elementary key to an indispensable part of education in civilization. But that further education in civilization *cannot be obtained at all* under full political control of the schools. It is possible only to a certain frame of mind in which knowledge is pursued voluntarily; and this is true even in technical education when it may be presumed that exactly the same technology is taught. A prominent geologist, whose work has been largely in the world's oil-fields, was struck by the fact that "only Americans find oil," * abroad as at home. Why should that be, he asked himself; for he met geologists of equally high natural ability and technical equipment among other nationalities; and they didn't strike oil even when they were walking over it, so to speak. He was forced to the conclusion that "oil must be sought first of all in our minds. Where oil really is, in the final analysis, is in our own heads." It is in "the state of mind of the social order"—the *free* mind. The free mind has persisted in the United States, in spite of the steady intrusion of the political power into the primary field of freedom in education, because choice and personal effort were still the governing factors in getting an advanced education, whether classical or technical; the student whose parents could not easily afford to send him to college had to make a serious decision and effort on his own account, and pursue such studies as he had selected on his own initiative. And when he got through school he had to take his chance of making a living as best he could, probably getting a varied experience of using both his hands and his head, with no ineradicable class distinction to cut off his speculative intelligence from practical application.

That also may be completely changed before long. The final step toward making American education wholly Japanese has been suggested; it is to select the most promising pupils in the public schools, pay their way through the various colleges or universities with Federal funds, and route them into military and bureaucratic positions.

The Germans are notably literate; and they had very fine technical schools. Their literacy enabled them to read "Mein Kampf," and their technology enabled them to build up a war machine which must destroy them. That is what education under the political power must do, once it has obtained full control. It routes human energy into the dead-end political channels.

The most vindictive resentment may be expected from the

* OIL IN THE EARTH. By Wallace E. Pratt. University of Kansas Press.

pedagogic profession for any suggestion that they should be dislodged from their dictatorial position; it will be expressed mainly in epithets, such as "reactionary," at the mildest. Nevertheless, the question to put to any teacher moved to such indignation, is: Do you think nobody would *willingly* entrust his children to you to pay you for teaching them? Why do you have to extort your fees and collect your pupils by compulsion?

CHAPTER XXII

The Energy Circuit
in Wartime

War is a large scale demonstration of the nature of government as mechanism and its relation to the flow of energy. The main reason why government is identified with power is that the authorization and conduct of war is reserved to the political agency; but if this impression is examined as a proposition in physics, it will be found to be the reverse of the truth. Government is repressive structure and expropriative mechanism, by which in peacetime the energy of the citizens is backed up from the fighting channel, to be released, not originated or created, when war is begun. The head of power lies back of the dam. It is not in the army but in the nation, for it consists of surplus production, in both personnel and materials. An army in being is withdrawn from production, and can function only on a continuous supply from the civil life of the nation. It is an end-appliance. Hence nations and empires of long duration are always those of a civilian character, and always *seem* to be unready for war.

Military science as such considers only the action of the end-appliance, and is at a loss when armies become ineffective. The war strength of a nation is generally computed in man-power and armament, including stationary defense works. It is on such calculations that projects for world conquest by force of arms are undertaken; and though they always fail, the inherent reason why they must fail is not perceived.

Though production is the true measure of military power, a gross or total estimate may be even more fatally misleading. Production is the flow of energy. It indicates the available striking force if the connection between the civil order and the army is correct; otherwise, it reveals only the potential scope of disaster.

The correct relation depends upon the mode of conversion of energy in use. In a primitive economy, the available force is a simple percentage. The savage warrior is also the fighter; he is self-subsistent and self-regulating, equating in himself the belligerent impulse and the control. There is no external organization or command. This also holds good for the no-mad pastoral society; the fighting men must maintain their own source of supply and the supply lines, for they are also the producers. In either case, it is obvious that the tribe can-not expend its man-power in a ratio exceeding natural re-placements, over a given term of years, without absolute de-feat by extinction.

In settled agricultural communities with a handicraft cul-ture, some degree of specific military organization becomes practicable. But the appropriate type of organization is de-termined by the extent to which trade is developed. In this respect, the Roman republic was a more advanced economy than that of strict feudalism. The feudal society was a fully organized agrarian economy; and the narrow limit of lia-bility to military service was determined by the scanty margin of surplus production. A feudal seigneury was re-quired to furnish only a certain number of men, approxi-mating to the land-holding, who were expected to keep the field only for a few weeks in the year. It would have been useless to demand more; the economy could not equip nor subsist them, with its meager food supply and short-range transport facilities. The fighting men, knights, squires, and grooms, did not do much productive work, so they could easily be spared, as they had to be supported in peace no less than in war. The producers were practically exempt from military service. Though the feudal fighting men were at the call of the overlord or king, and under his nominal command in war, the real control was local; it answered to the supplies from home. So the rules of war were made accordingly. In its military resources, the Roman republic was five hundred years ahead of feudalism; there was just enough trade and money to permit centralized command, and a wider radius of action. It was possible to take a greater percentage of man-power; therefore every able-bodied citizen was liable to service in emergency. Conscription remained practicable because the radius was still limited, and it was also consonant with the *patria potestas* in the moral order.

When the national revenue is derived mainly from trade, as in the Roman empire and the British empire, conscription ceases to be practicable. The army is a co-efficient of the commercial system; its effectiveness is found in proportion to its mobility, speed, discipline, and constant readiness, rather than its size. This requires a professional army, a minimum always in service instead of a maximum called out for a short term on special occasions. Conscription was abandoned, of necessity, in Rome as in England, precisely when those nations became empires. Money is the medium of a contract society; and it calls for a consonant relation of the army to the nation.

The workable conditions of a military state, organized for "total war," have been perfectly exemplified just once in history, and its limits shown, by Sparta. Production was extorted from slaves, which kept the economy on the lowest subsistence level. All the male citizens (non-slaves) were soldiers; but they could not go far from home to fight, having no lateral facilities—no trade, no money, no transport. The Spartan model was flawless of its dreadful kind. It survived for a considerable period in a static condition; but when it tried to expand—being supplied by the mercantile Greek states for warfare over an extended radius—it fell to pieces. No such state can make good a conquest over a nation of higher production; it will be undone by victory if not by defeat. Any military state which tries to utilize a machine economy will suffer even more rapid dissolution.

Military theory is largely meaningless because it deals with the conduct of armies in being, regardless of the civil order from which they are drawn. Even though the strategy, tactics, and technology may be theoretically identical, a professional army, a mercenary army, and a citizen army fight upon different principles, in accordance with their relation to the civil order.

The professional army, though devoutly loyal to its own country, must fight for its own preservation as an army, as much as for immediate victory. The intermittent object is a particular victory; the specific object is to win a war; but the constant object is to keep the army in being indefinitely. This does not mean that the troops will lack courage at any time; on the contrary, they must never fail in resolution, and any part of the army may be required to take the brunt at any time, at the utmost cost to the detachment. The most demoralizing condition for a professional army is to be involved or used, or to believe that it is being used, by internal factions of its own country. A professional army is an instrument of constituted authority: its hook-up for energy is with the central or trunk line; its normal interest is that of the whole country through the government; and the private interest of the soldiers is confined to their profession. When it is used by a part of the nation against a part of the nation, there is a short circuit; hence even the employment of the army for extraordinary police duty may be a dubious expedient.

A mercenary army fights for its own hand; its interest is in extortion, and can be gauged only by a series of short views. When strictly mercenary armies existed, they were open to offers from any side and were unlikely to do any more fighting than would pay them. Generally they were as dangerous to their employers as to the enemy. They could hardly be demoralized, beyond their ordinary condition; when they exist, it indicates the lack of a normal civil order in the nations which employ them. They were the outcome of a trading economy which had no adequate political structure, no regional bases.

A citizen army fights for the interest of the soldiers as citizens, looking to the consequences of the actual war in which they are engaged. The most positive incentive for a citizen army to fight is the desire to go home; but this means that the soldier must expect to find at home the objective for which he is fighting. The interest of the citizen soldier is that of a producer, a man who has left a job and property. The most demoralizing condition for a citizen army is the knowledge or suspicion that the rights of the individual soldiers as citizens are being impaired under cover of the war. The citizen army fights for a definite cause, which is thought to be attainable by the war; and *if the cause disappears,* the army dissolves. The citizen soldier is sustained on the energy of the private production line of his civilian life, which is temporarily cut in to the military outlet; the civilian line carries the load. If the civilian energy circuit is cut or tampered with, the peak load cannot be maintained. Hence the fact, of historic record, that it is always the largest army a nation can raise which suddenly melts away. And however it may be raised, organized or commanded, an army which is very large in proportion to the size of its nation has the character of a citizen army. It fights with matchless energy when it does fight; and crumbles to nothing when it crumbles, as with the armies of Napoleon, of the Czar, and of Germany at the end of the first World War.

The weakness of purely military theory is evident when it is applied to any war of the past. By the formal rules, the American Revolution should have been lost before it was well begun, and a dozen times afterward. Confronted by these technical impossibilities, the theorists go wild and speculate on what might have happened if Washington had received more adequate support from Congress; if conscription had been resorted to; and so on—whereas if either Americans or Englishmen had been amenable to conscription at that time, there could have been no Revolutionary War at all; nor would there have been any such war if a Congress with definite federal authority had been in existence previously, because such a government must have pertained to an already independent nation. Again, theorists have suggested that the Civil War might have been won by the Federal government in the first campaign if there had been a sufficient standing army to begin with. But the Confederate forces were led by a soldier who had resigned his Federal commission on secession; a large standing army would have been divided in its allegiance. Wars have to be fought in whatever conditions obtain at the time. They spring from those conditions. But in all and any circumstances, the indispensable condition for ultimate victory is that the producers shall retain control of the production system, so that only the end-product may be taken off for military purposes.

The reason this condition is not understood is that in reckoning military effectiveness time is not considered as a factor; no distinction is drawn between short term and long term results. Napoleon is esteemed a master of the art of war because he won numerous battles and over-ran a wide territory during a period of less than twenty years; but at the end, the nation he commanded was exhausted and occupied by its enemies. He had command of the total resources of the nation. Since his time, France has steadily declined in military power, while faithfully maintaining the system used by Napoleon. How did that particular sequence occur—a burst of overwhelming energy followed by a long decline? It was not only that Napoleon emptied the reservoir of surplus energy, but that the sluice gate was left open, with general peacetime conscription, so that the full head of power could never form again. Subsequently Germany followed the same course, with the same attendant phenomena, to the same end, in somewhat accelerated tempo. France was unified by Louis XIV, who won numerous victories and over-ran Europe, to end in defeat; bankruptcy and collapse ensued shortly; the process was repeated in the Revolution and the regime of Napoleon. Bismarck "unified" the German principalities and won victories; Germany over-ran Europe in 1914, was defeated, collapsed in bankruptcy; and has repeated the process in the present world war. These "men of power" are in reality mere scraps of wreckage, floating rubbish in a flood, distinguished by their lack of productive ability and responsibility.

Widespread misery must ensue whenever an army is supplied from a source—whether internal or external—over which the producers have no control. This is a recurrent possibility; it occurs when the kinetic energy has undercut the political bases. It causes wars of the most terrible type, in which nobody is able to make peace. The Hundred Years War, the Wars of the Roses, and the Thirty Years War were of this kind. The break in control is most apparent in the Thirty Years War. The authority of the Holy Roman Emperor was nominally valid for raising an army; but the emperor's direct revenues were inadequate to sustain large forces in the field, for any length of time. The emperor therefore authorized an aristocratic soldier of fortune, Count Wallenstein, to recruit soldiers and subsist them by loot or forced tribute. Other sovereigns, for their own ends, contributed cash subsidies to Wallenstein from time to time. In consequence, there was no effective control over Wallenstein's army; the emperor could not disband it when he wished to; the soldiers roamed about like bands of wolves, eating the country bare and committing ghastly atrocities. When peace came, it was the peace of desolation, the army itself being starved out and the countryside almost depopulated. That was practically the finish of the Holy Roman Empire. Now the effect would have been precisely the same if the Emperor had been in a position to seize the total resources of his subjects for military use; in either case, the situation is that the military agency is not under control of the productive element. Europe at present is in a war of the same type. The governments have taken over the total resources of their nations. All the armies are fighting on the diminishing returns of their capital resources and some subsidies from America. They cannot hope to return to civil life because there is no civil life; neither are they professional soldiers; so they must fight for no objective. The obscure problem is concealed by the apparent problem, for the obscure problem is that there is no control over the armies. (When a motor car cannot be stopped by the people in it, it is out of control.) The nominal commanders of the armies of Europe dare not let them go home. The armies are immense portions of dislocated mass crashing against one another by momentum; and the soldiers are cut off from both past and future, because the production circuit of Europe has been cut through and destroyed. For nations in this situation, not even the cessation of fighting can bring relief, because their governments cannot disband such monstrous armies in any case. They must remain on a war footing. The fact is acknowledged, since the only course proposed is an indeterminate "armistice" under armies of occupation.

Machine production cannot be developed or sustained in any planned economy, even in peacetime, because the dynamo operates on a very long circuit of energy, the connections being made by free exchange. The first charge upon any energy circuit must be for maintenance and replacement throughout the complete circuit. This is obvious in a local energy circuit, where it is a plain question of the producer getting food and clothes and shelter out of his product; even though slave labor is used, the most brutal master can hardly deceive himself into the belief that a slave can continue working if his rations are inadequate to sustain life. But the long circuit is a money economy; and apparently many men do imagine that they can abstract a little more and a little more energy from the money transmission line without consequences to the continuing flow.

The military state is the final form to which every planned economy tends rapidly. But military force consists of energy drawn from production, and yielding no return. Then if the level of general production is lowered, the head of power must be correspondingly lessened. Energy flowing through the channels of private civilian life is self-sustaining, self-augmenting, and self-renewing. Energy flowing into the military channel is used up; it produces nothing, not even maintenance of its own transmission lines. An army may occasionally seize supplies from the enemy, in loot or indemnities, but these are quickly consumed.

Therefore long-term military effectiveness, the survival of a nation through the recurrent hazards of war, generation after generation—and that is what a nation must do if it is to survive at all—depends absolutely on the preservation of capital resources, taking off only the surplus for military use as an end-product. It is doubtful if capital can safely be depleted at all; the superficial appearance is not to be trusted in this respect, for it will be found, on examination of the record, that nations of long survival have never permitted their capital to be impaired even in their greatest military exertions. What they really did was to increase general production. In the Napoleonic wars, it is estimated that the British came through with *general production* fifty per cent higher than when they went in. Napoleon tried to embargo Europe, while the British traded with anyone who would trade, including the French themselves. In the American Civil War, the North certainly increased its general production; while the South insanely *began* the war by laying an embargo on its own cotton, thus paralyzing Southern credit abroad.

The present day theory that "sacrifices" will win a war is the ultimate of irrationality. When a motor truck is needed, one cannot ride around in a sacrifice. The object must be produced, and it can be produced only on the complete circuit, with free men using private property freely. If war takes more than the surplus production over a given length of time, even an unbroken series of victories must bring the nation ever nearer to irremediable defeat, on the ultimate cessation of supplies.

The mistake of a nation which makes war at capital cost, thinking to win before its reserves are exhausted, is that it has undertaken an incalculable expenditure from a limited quantity. It has cut off the dynamo and is running on the battery;

but the power in a battery is a fixed quantity, while the future time a war will last, and the consequent expenditure of energy it will call for through time, *can never be known in advance.* The one certainty is the ratio which such calculations ignore, the fact that if capital is being depleted, more energy taken from the circuit than it produces in surplus, it is a losing formula; the nation must constantly become weaker. If the military force is no more than the surplus energy provides, it is at least a permanent power, extending to infinity, and can therefore hold out for ultimate victory over an indefinite period.

Time is on the side of the nation which increases its general production. Time is neutral to the nation which maintains general production at its previous level. Time is mortal to the nation which fights on its capital resources.

Consequently, with a high energy system, the one thing that must make ultimate victory impossible would be the organization of the whole nation as a military establishment, thus withdrawing it from production. The manufacture of war materials does not constitute a production circuit; they are nothing but end-product. Incidentally, such a military organization will even conflict with itself internally, on the question of where the energy is to be expropriated from the personnel and materials existing at the time it takes over. The "obscure problem" has been completely overlooked; and the "apparent problem" splits into a dozen fallacious problems. This can be understood only if the obscure problem is defined, the real military necessity.*

The real military problem of a nation is to find where the energy for war should be taken off the circuit to obtain the maximum sustained striking force in the end appliance. The dynamo functions on a very long and complex system of transmission lines, from raw material sources to the focal points,

* The distinction between an "apparent problem," that is, a misleading superficial symptom or effect, and the real, "obscure problem," which is the cause, was drawn by Mr. Charles F. Kettering.

tributaries feeding into trunk lines, to be redistributed in end-products. Power is stepped-up all along the line.

And it is not simply a *geometrical progression,* a multiple of man-power, at the end; it is a *transcendent power.*

For convenience in viewing the real problem, let it be assumed that one hundred men * in general production can provide their own subsistence, and over and above that, a *surplus* sufficient to provide the sustenance of one hundred more men with the machinery, materials, and everything necessary to make an airplane of the maximum speed or cruising range, equipped with the maximum armament; and to keep that plane in the air during its effective term of use. So there are two hundred men altogether employed in both the main production circuit and the end production circuit, at the end of which a plane is made available for military use. But once the plane is made, equipped, and in operation, the whole number of men employed throughout the process, with the raw materials they used, would be wholly defenseless *against* the weapon they have made, with its small trained crew. The machine they have made is not merely a multiple of their natural power; it transcends the power that went into it. All of their military effectiveness for modern war has gone into that plane, because they work on the high potential long circuit of energy.

The maximum sustained striking force available from a high energy system, a free economy using its own weapons, is *infinitely greater* than a simple sum by addition or even a multiple of the man-power of the nation. If the two hundred men engaged in the whole process of which the plane is an end-product were taken out of the production line and sent to the front, the strength of two hundred men would not be

* The subsistence of men in production must include the subsistence of everyone incidentally engaged throughout the economy with their families or other dependents. But subsistence for high production also means maintenance and replacement and improvement of the capital assets of the nation—machinery, buildings, farm equipment, livestock and reserve supplies of all kinds, incidental to the system.

added to the army. On the contrary, the striking force they had been supplying would be completely lost, ceasing altogether.

Thus the ratio or percentage of men useful in an army for a high energy nation, to obtain the maximum sustained striking force, is very much *less*, in proportion to the simple manpower of the nation, than it would be with a lower energy system. The higher the potential of energy used in the production system, the smaller the army should be *in proportion* to the simple man-power of the nation. If it does take two hundred men to produce the transcendent power for ten men to use in the end-appliance on the fighting line, then only five per cent of the national man-power can be effective *in the armed forces*. To take more than that percentage of men is to weaken the striking force by inverse ratio.*

But that is what conscription does, taking simple man-power in vast numbers, which means expropriating the energy of the nation precisely at the level where it is ineffective for war, and wasting it to an incalculable extent. The theory of "total war," which must signify general conscription and a "planned economy," with the whole working power of the nation under restrictions and prohibitions, tied to assigned jobs or moved about arbitrarily, cuts the production line at the source. The

* No implication is intended here that airplanes alone constitute a complete effective military force for a high energy nation. The dynamo is the product and means of production of the private property free enterprise capitalist economy. It affords the highest known potential and flow of energy; consequently it has made possible the invention of armament—battleships, tanks, artillery, bombs, airplanes— of unprecedented force, speed, and range. Varying conditions and circumstances must determine the most effective combination, proportion, and dominant or auxiliary relation of these different forms of armament, with the concomitant personnel or military man-power. This is necessarily a matter for judgment by the political and military authorities. They will not be infallible, but the authority must be confided to them because that is the only place it can rest. The airplane is mentioned here as the latest development of the transcendent power in war, but not as excluding the use of other armament. So far, it can only be said that the airplane is *indicated* as peculiarly adapted, by its speed, for the protection of the lines of a long circuit of energy. It is also the armament of a peaceful nation, since by itself it is not a means of conquest but of defense and proper reprisal.

transcendent power from general production can be obtained
only by free men choosing their own jobs of their own volition, for whatever reward the work will bring. The creative
man must find for himself the place and employment in which
he can function; he must have a continuous choice of what he
will do with his faculties, his time and his means. If a man is
put to forced labor, all that can be got out of him is his muscular power. If he is tied to an assigned job, all that can be
got out of him is what the prescribed task permits. When he
works as he chooses, finding for himself the market for his
talent, there is absolutely no telling to what extent he may
increase production. If Charles F. Kettering or Thomas Alva
Edison or Henry Ford had been put to work digging ditches
under duress, one could calculate approximately how much
energy or work could have been got out of them. Left to
their own devices, as they were, it is impossible to say how
much energy they actually released into production. Likewise
the money which accrued to them in salaries or profits, which
gave them greater scope to try out whatever they had in mind,
and went back into production through them, became an infinite or transcendent power; whereas an equal sum divided into
day's wages for ordinary labor would have produced just that
sum in energy. (If taken in taxes, and paid to government
officials, all it does is to increase the dead load.) Hence the
proposed limitation of salaries to productive men would be a
serious restriction on high production; if they were cut low
enough, the effect would be to stop high production altogether.

Now this incalculable or infinite possibility, the transcendent
power, is needed even more urgently in war than in peace; but
*it cannot be made available unless men are free to find their
own employment, and have private control of the means of
production.* Only when personal freedom and private property
are unimpaired can general production increase during wartime, with a concomitant increase of the surplus available for
military use.

The lesson is that energy for military use must be taken off the circuit only as end-product, to attain the maximum sustained striking force. Further, a man is not in himself either a means or a product; his skill in a high technology is self-developed; therefore it can be made effectively available only of his own volition. Can men be conscripted and ordered to step into airplanes and fly? It is impossible. A high production system provides in civilian life most of the training for the use of high technology in war, just as it provides the inventions, the material, the machinery, and the organization for manufacturing high power armament, with the flow of energy to sustain the military forces; and these must be used on the same terms as they are created, that is, by a volunteer personnel, to obtain the maximum striking force. The most comprehensive and fatal error that can be made in war is to take off most of the nation's energy at the level of simple manpower and in money to be expended at the same level for subsistence of a mass army. Then there is nothing left to draw on but the stockpile of raw materials, the machinery of production in existence, which must wear out rapidly, and an inadequate remainder of production personnel who can only go on working on these depreciating capital assets until they are exhausted. That is what Europe has done.

A production system does not determine the moral relations of society. The moral relations create the production system. Free men created the dynamo; and it will not operate except in the private property, free enterprise society of contract. An army is not in correct relation to the civil order unless it is organized on the same moral principles. It is not true that "nobody wins a war." When a nation is attacked, though the cost of the war must be a loss, the nation that preserves itself and its institutions from destruction by defeating the enemy has won the war. A free economy invariably wins against a closed or status economy or "totalitarian state." *But it must fight as a free economy.*

The destruction wrought by the dictator nations of Europe in the present war has given a wholly misleading impression of the real problem involved in making war when the product of a high energy system is used. Those nations prepared for war by filling their storage batteries while they were still on the end of the great world circuit of energy created and maintained by the free economies. Russia contributed nothing to that system creatively. But there are gold mines in Russia; and Russia exported gold, sold bonds abroad, and also squeezed enough out of its own miserable subsistence economy —at the cost of actual starvation of its own populace—to exchange for machinery, and to hire technologists from the free economies. Germany inherited a technology, trained technologists, machinery, and industrial organization from its previous condition of comparative freedom. Germany also used every fraudulent device of currency inflation, huge loans obtained abroad, and foreign credit—deliberate embezzlement over a period of twenty years—to get goods produced by the free economies. Japan sold bonds abroad to buy armaments.* On these storage batteries of energy, Russia, Germany, and Japan plunged into war, and got some more supplies by loot. They are fighting on the reserves of Europe, produced by the previous free economy; and on the product of the American energy circuit. Going around the world both ways, the energy from America met itself at Stalingrad, in a short-circuit. American energy is still supplying Russia, and is its only effective force. In lesser quantity, American energy has also gone into China, to encounter American energy previously supplied to Japan. American energy has literally blown up the civilized world, *because* it was thrown into the political channels in Germany, Russia, and Japan.

The historic relation of Russia to Europe can be indicated only briefly, but it remains unchanged in the present war from what it has been during the past three hundred years. In the life of a nation, decentralization is the formula of duration;

* The late Dwight Morrow related complacently how many Japanese bonds were sold in one California town! The energy transferred by those bonds came down in bombs at Pearl Harbor and Manila.

but this may occur either by design, with a sound political structure, or by default, the complete absence of structure. Given certain conditions, nations of wide expanse may retain a more or less continuous entity by inertia. This is true of China and Russia. Both countries consist largely of vast plains, cut off from adjoining nations by natural barriers of mountain and desert, marsh and landlocked waters and northern ice. They are the end of the trade routes of the old world. Neither of them ever achieved political structure. Only the physical configuration, the plane surface, tended to bring the population of each country under monarchy by aggregation, as movable objects will roll together uneasily in a shallow bowl. Their economies were extremely localized, with only a thin trickle of trade. Up to the rise of the Muscovite monarchy, Russia was a loose aggregation of shifting and disconnected communities. The rural communities were pure democracies. In the old village communes "every question must be settled unanimously"; so dissentients were "belabored until they abandoned their opposition." (Such is the inherent contradiction of the democratic theory.) Barbarian incursions consolidated them under a despotism by pressure. But the central despotism had to leave the local economies to function autonomously, except for taxation.

When a nation with a higher energy system invades a large area containing only local rural economies or energy circuits, it encounters the problem of high energy dissipating in space. While Napoleon was conquering Europe, he could cut in his army on the energy circuit of the nations he occupied, by exacting money indemnities and using the money to draw on the civil production system. In Russia there was no way for him to cut his army in on the production line. The Russian civil population could not have supplied him if they had tried to; they did not have the necessary transport or general organization. Therefore Napoleon's army advanced rapidly to the end of its own supply line, and then halted, as a spent bullet falls to the ground.

In the present war the Germans have encountered the same space problem, and there was no way for them to solve it. They could not bring up enough supplies for their armies to advance indefinitely, because transport requirements increase by geometrical ratio; and they could not get adequate supplies out of the conquered territory. It has been said truly that the failure of Stalin's Five Year Plan ruined Hitler. Likewise Japan invaded China with borrowed energy from the free economies, but it could not get adequate supplies out of China to maintain its mechanized armies. When supplies from America were stopped by embargo, Japan must either withdraw from China at a loss, or declare war on the Western powers in order to seize the outpost supply stations of the Western energy circuit in the Orient, such as the Dutch oil wells and refineries in the East Indies. How long Japan can maintain its high energy military equipment while cut off from the Western production circuit is a question which could only be answered by specific knowledge of its replacement needs and of the raw materials seized. In the long run, the Japanese military power would certainly collapse, just as the machine equipment of Germany and Russia must wear out and pass into desuetude if either or both were permanently out of contact with free economies elsewhere. If freedom were extinguished everywhere in the world, the whole high energy production system must break down and cease to function. No despotism can maintain independently and indefinitely a machine economy or a mechanized army. But until the batteries are completely exhausted, a despotism can do enormous damage; and Japan is in a position to wreak such damage on the Orient and to some extent on the Western world with its present reserves. It is not negligible while it lasts. Nevertheless, *all the fighting force of Japan was drawn from the West.*

Then if the free economies cut their own energy circuits internally by imposing the political power on production, from what source are they to draw the necessary energy to function and to fight? The United States cannot borrow, beg, copy, embezzle, or loot from any other nation in the world, whether for peace or for war. How then can America imitate the "totalitarian" nations? The thing is impossible. Freedom for Americans is not a luxury of peace, to be "sacrificed" in wartime. It is a necessity at all times, but above all in war; then it becomes an instant matter of life or death.

CHAPTER XXIII

The Dynamic Economy and the Future

Primitive savages know how to start a fire by friction. They must have discovered the process tens of thousands of years ago. Yet as lately as the middle of the eighteenth century scientists were still debating whether or not heat was a material element (an "indestructible substance"), though they were already experimenting with the steam engine. So a principle may be put in practice long before it is understood or defined. Therefore it is not strange if the obvious fact that a high production system works on a long circuit of energy has not been perceived and the general laws governing its creation and maintenance have not been formulated. Even the definition of energy stood in the way of understanding the conditions of its extended use by human beings for their own benefit. The definition is confined to measure by its effects; and no practicable design for mechanical apparatus can be conceived except in accordance with such measure. Nevertheless, it obscures the major problem of the utilization of energy throughout a production system; because man himself enters into the energy circuit he uses, and thus introduces a factor which does not answer to measure. As man has a triple function in the circuit, his intervention is triply confusing. Part of the energy is converted and transmitted literally by his physical body, in measurable quantity, as when a man pushes a wheelbarrow; but in the long circuit, or high energy system, this part is small compared to the quantity converted and used through inanimate materials. Another function of man in the energy circuit uses an extremely variable and practically non-measurable quantity of energy, in the intellectual effort of invention or discovery of devices to tap the universal energy; the returns from this are incommensurable with any possible estimate of the energy applied. Then the third function of man in his energy circuit comes into play, to cause even more confusion of thought on the subject. What man does in his third relationship to the energy circuit is to *route* the energy he has tapped and brought under control. The man pushing a wheelbarrow routes it by the same action, his mind sending the command directly through his muscles along with the force applied. There is an imponderable, but it cannot be separated from the ponderable direct force. When energy is routed on the long circuit, it is done by actions in which the force expended is not merely incommensurable to the result, but does not enter into the specific physical sequence of transmission at all.

This is what happens by the use of money, or by credit or other contractual agreements. There is a real, material, unbroken sequence of physical energy carried through in the long circuit of production, which is visible and easily traced. A farmer grows food; he sells most of his product and buys what else he needs, perhaps a tractor. The food has supplied energy to other men who dig ore, make steel, manufacture motors, build and run railways; innumerable other products enter into the sequence; but it is a physical succession of material objects in motion and in process of the conversion of energy, completing a circuit which brings back the tractor to the farmer, or maybe coffee from Brazil or tea from China or gasoline from Texas oil wells. There is no break in the line. But the continuity of the flow is not absolutely and precisely like that of a stream of water running downhill. Left to itself, the water would never run uphill; it must flow down. Yet man may intervene, with engineering devices, by which the full force of the stream is utilized to send a moiety of the water upward again. Likewise in the production circuit a train of cars is hauled uphill, against gravity, by energy which man has brought under control for that purpose. The train stops at stations, because man cuts the flow temporarily. It would never have run in that particular channel "of itself," nor would it start again or continue in the production line without man in the circuit.

When the farmer sells his produce or buys a tractor, using real money, the imponderable is *represented* separately. The weight of the gold does not correspond to the weight of the tractor, nor does the energy exerted in handing over the gold correspond to the energy of the tractor in motion. If a check is given, so that the real existence of the gold may be overlooked, the nature of the transaction is still further obscured. But what occurs is that the energy in the continuous physical sequence is *routed* in a direction specified by a representative parallel action. Perhaps the easiest way to perceive the process is by assuming a production circuit much shorter and simpler than it could ever be in fact. Imagine the farmer, the miner, the steel maker, the tractor manufacturer, etc., standing in a circle, each passing his own product forward on his right, in one direction; while money is passed back on the left in the opposite direction, making payment at each transfer. The physical energy which constitutes the circuit is never in the money; it is in the goods and transport facilities. Further, the intervention of man in the circuit introduces a factor by which more energy is produced (or picked up) en route than is consumed (lost or dissipated). This cannot occur in any specific flow of energy which is not under human control; inanimate nature contains nothing equivalent to the action of man's mind, or to the parallel actions by which man routes such a flow. Nor can these functions be built into a piece of machinery. Forever they must require human intelligence and volition.

Though it is always morally wrong, slavery is possible in a low energy system and impracticable in a high energy system. The reason is evident if the methods of production are compared. A chattel slave is treated as a machine, driven by force; he may neither choose nor quit his work. Then take a job with high-power machinery, involving the utmost responsibility, where the consequences would be most disastrous if the worker did quit at the wrong time; in just that job it is most necessary that he should choose to undertake it and be free to quit it when and as he pleases. To drive a locomotive, a man must first exercise intelligence and volition to qualify himself. He is then engaged on the free judgment of another man as employer. Thereafter, while at work, the engine driver must *at every moment* act on his own judgment. He will not quit while the engine is in motion, but if his judgment failed there could be no way to *prevent* him. On stopping at a station, if the driver should leave the cab and refuse to finish the run, it would be insane to compel him to go on. His decision must be accepted. Likewise, if the engine driver should appear to be unfit, the judgment of his employer (by deputy) must be accepted as sufficient to take the driver off the run. This is the nature of contract. The engine driver receives a schedule, which he follows as a rule, but if it were absolutely impossible for him to act otherwise, there would not be a railroad in operation within six weeks. For the very reason that the action of inanimate machinery is predetermined, the men who use it must be free. No other arrangement is feasible for a high energy circuit, in which services as well as goods are in exchange; and contract is the only relation which admits that arrangement. This is the meaning of the parallel representative sequence of actions, proceeding in reverse direction to the physical energy circuit; these actions carry on the succession of voluntary agreements by which the energy is routed. Hence the inevitable breakdown of the long circuit in a "planned economy," which necessarily requires rationing, restriction, and compulsion.

An engineer cannot and does not attempt to alter or abrogate the laws of physics in utilizing energy; he works with them, to achieve his purpose. And in his inanimate mechanical design he can take into account only the strictly physical function of man. A wheelbarrow must be of such form and size as to be usable by muscle power. A motor car must have the necessary apparatus to start, steer, or stop it. The further functions exercised by human beings who use the machinery in production do not affect the design of specific machines.

But all three functions must be taken into account in the organization of the long circuit; and since this is also a sequence of energy in action, it constitutes a problem of engineering of a peculiar kind. Human beings who enter into that circuit for general production *must* have their physical sustenance out of it; otherwise the circuit will break down. If men tried to do without food, they would not thereby be able to devote to end-use the energy supplied by the food; they would merely drop out of production. For this reason, it is absurd to assume that "sacrifice" is equivalent to production. The prevention of waste is another matter. But since the function of man in the circuit is not merely that of a physical body, the mere allotment of a subsistence measure of energy to be ingested by workers on compulsory jobs cannot maintain the circuit either, because it does not allow for the second and third functions which must be performed by man—invention or discovery, and routing the energy.

For the exercise of intelligence, on invention and discovery, a man must have some surplus materials, time, and energy, at his personal disposal, with freedom to seek whatever employment he prefers.

For the exercise of volition, to route the energy in such channels that production will be maintained, every exchange of goods and labor must be made by free contract.

The engineering problem then is to organize the long circuit for *free men*. The hook-up must be such that every man may change his place and occupation as he pleases within the whole range of possible choice, which is infinite. This calls for distribution of the product by a like method of exchange on agreement at each transfer. Given these conditions, the condition prerequisite to man's physical function in the circuit will prevail; the men engaged can get their livelihood from it by free exchange.

The whole problem is solved by observing throughout the

principle of contract; and it can be solved in no other way. Contract is the principle of the true *dynamic economy*.

The one problem which may be said to have arisen from the dynamic economy is what is called the labor problem. Because the dynamic economy creates unprecedented means of mobility and a fair prospect of finding a livelihood almost anywhere, the great majority of people have forgotten the need of a physical base for security. It is not only the "workingman" who overlooks this primary and unalterable relationship of man to the earth, the function of private ownership in land—which goes back to the simple fact that a human body is a solid object—the technologists, clerical workers, plenty of urban employers, and people living on inherited incomes, are in the same position and equally unaware of it. It may be that these others outnumber the workingmen; but with large industrial centers, the workingmen compose a more obvious group, which is more readily distinguishable by the existence of labor unions and by the fact that, when industry slows down, the workingmen are most visibly affected. They are dislocated mass. But it must be understood that a millionaire could belong in that category, if his millions were entirely in paper securities; he has no base either. There is absolutely no solution for this except individual land ownership by the great majority, and the use of real money. It is not necessary that everyone should own a farm; but enough people must own their homes and have a reserve for "hard times." In the United States, if industry is allowed to follow its natural tendency to decentralize, it rests with individuals whether or not they will provide for their own security; but, in any event, there is no other way. There may be merit in proposals that the employees of industry should have some ownership-interest in it; but this does not meet the need of a base; the miller cannot stand on the running stream.

Whether intended to favor labor or to restrain it, labor legislation is worse than useless. The Wagner Act did not give any power to labor. No law can give power to private persons;

every law transfers power from private persons to government.* But beyond a certain point, such transfer of power may
actually render government helpless, by making it pick up a
load it cannot handle. That is what the Wagner Act did, and
what any legislation attempting to control industrial labor
must do. It attached an instrument of government to dislocated mass; and whenever that mass is disturbed, it must wrest
the instrument out of control and thus nullify its function.
(An army out of control does the same thing; it may tear the
whole mechanism of government apart.) *Dislocated mass cannot be controlled*, unless by opposition on all sides with an
equal force. That is absolutely impossible with industrial labor,
unless it should be always confronted by an army of equal
force; which would reduce the nation to slavery.

But labor may be brought under compulsion—which still
will not be control, and will only create a new danger—by
restrictions nominally imposed *first* on the employer, reaching
the employee indirectly. If an employer is forbidden to hire
anyone who has not obtained *permission* to leave a previous
job, the movements of the worker are restricted precisely as if
he were forbidden to quit a job. The effect on the energy circuit is to cut down production in equal degree.

The main present cause of confusion in political theorizing
also arises from the fact that energy in the long circuit is
routed by parallel representative action. Voting is such an action; but its effect is still less easily discernible, because it is a
relay signal. When a country has a formal political organization, taxation is already authorized; the channel is there, to
divert energy from production into government expenditure.

* Labor leaders mistakenly thought they had gained a victory when what they
called "yellow dog contracts" were outlawed. They do not understand the nature
of law. The "yellow dog" contract was an agreement among employers not to deal
with labor unions. However distasteful the classification may be to unionists, the
fact remains that this is *the same kind of an agreement* as the closed shop contract;
and if the law can forbid that type of agreement, then the closed shop contract can
be outlawed. Contracts made by unions and employers have already been nullified
by this power, against the will of both the union and the employer concerned.

The channel is designated by custom or a constitution. Theoretically a constitution might specify the sum or the percentage to be taken in taxes; but such a limitation is unlikely to be maintained, least of all by the central government which necessarily has the conduct of war. While the structure is sound, stipulations will be observed as to the several fields of taxation for federal, state, and local authorities. The regional interests will tend to preserve this limitation and to keep the rate of taxation reasonable, as long as they have the proper structural relation to the central government. But taxes will be collected no matter what party or persons hold office. Therefore the vote of the citizen does not route the energy. What it does is to designate officials who shall by like representative action determine the quantity of energy to be taken in taxes and then apportion and route it into the various political channels of expenditure.

Because two representative actions occur, it is not generally realized that they give the signal for the impounding and release of real energy; and further, that such energy *can be turned directly against the voter.*

His only safety is to retain for himself at all times a fixed standing ground on which he may resist firmly; and there is no such standing ground except land he owns himself. Otherwise his vote actually deprives him of his natural power, instead of enabling him to exercise it. This is what happens in democracy; it releases force in such manner that there can be no control. For the government has no control either in a democracy. The theory that everyone "participates" in government in a democracy, if everyone votes, does not take into account the nature of physical force and the necessary relation of all physical mass and movement to a solid base. Most abstract theory of government in modern times is completely erroneous because it ignores *physical reality.* Probably the fallacy becomes plausible because the ballot is only a piece of paper, or a touch on a voting machine; no physical energy is transferred in the *act* of voting; it appears to be no more than an expression of opinion. Then if the representative takes office simply on a formal expression of opinion, or signal, it is thought he must be amenable to subsequent opinion in like form. On the contrary, since the representative is permitted to release *real physical energy*, no further signal will be obeyed *unless the voters retain in their private control a corresponding but preponderant power of resistance to any misapplication of the power delegated to their representatives.* The representative parallel actions must always *represent real energy.*

There is also a prevalent fallacy today, which is brought up in denial of the necessity of *individual* free action to create and maintain a high energy system. In some comparatively free economies, such as Denmark and Sweden, much of the economic organization consists of co-operative associations. But these are marginal to the dynamic economies. Semi-socialistic colonies, such as New Zealand and Australia, are even more dependent on individualism elsewhere. They originated none of the machinery by which they obtain production at a level of comfort; they have contributed no inventions or improvements; they sell their surplus product in the free market. The connection enables them to attain a moderately high standard of living, but the level is fixed by the dynamic circuit they draw on. Superficial observers pretend that co-operative associations can supply the primary dynamic function of high production. They cannot; they are only supplementary. Local conditions will indicate the extent of their practical utility; but it is always marginal.

A completely "planned" economy, which is a slave economy, can take in some high-power machinery, running it with diminishing returns for a limited time, into a war. The slave economies of Soviet Russia and Germany have done this; but neither of them can maintain their mechanical equipment without continual replacements from free nations. With a complete factory for the production of motor cars, every part made in the United States shipped to Russia, and assembled there in efficient order by American engineers, the output was less than half the normal production from a similar set-up in the United States. Russia, Germany, and other planned economies are static. When high energy is thrown into them, it can only cause incalculable disturbance in unpredictable ways, like the tremors and subsidences of earthquake terrain; but the damage will be much *less*, if the high energy is admitted only by exchange—that is, if payment is duly exacted by the free economies for loans or sales of goods to the static economies—than if money or machinery or other goods are obtained by the static economies without payment. Since by the nature of the free economy, its product is in the market, it is imperative that the bills should be collected. When money, credit, and goods are handed to the static economies for nothing, whether as a gift or by allowing default, the result is certain, a world war on a commensurate scale, with increased and hopeless oppression of the people of the static economy. Nothing else made the German outbreak possible. Nothing else could have ruined Europe. If the sums of money loaned by America to Europe since 1914, and never repaid, were added up, the total would give the force of the explosive charge which burst in the present war. Loans from governments to governments * are peculiarly and inevitably destructive; but defaulted private loans are also wholly harmful. This holds true to the amount involved of American investments abroad which have been confiscated by foreign governments; the force is then thrown against whatever private economy that foreign nation had, to smash it; the government has obtained supplies over which the producers have no control. Just on that formula, disturb-

* Loans made by one government to another do not answer to any of the proper conditions of credit. The money lent belongs to the people of the lending nation, not to the officials who grant the loan; and it becomes a charge upon the people of the borrowing nation, not upon the officials who negotiate the loan and spend the money. There is no collateral, and no means of collection by civil action. If the debt is not paid, war or the threat of war is the only recourse. Meantime private production is wrecked; the economy of the lending nation has to meet the capital loss; while the economy of the borrowing nation is loaded with the dead weight of government projects (buildings, armies, etc.) for which the money is spent. It is an infallible formula for disaster.

ance and devastation could be charted in advance. Nations in habitual default are invariably nations in habitual convulsion. The one real service a dynamic nation can render to a static nation is to exact prompt collections in full for every penny or scrap of goods supplied. If that is done, the static nation may advance toward freedom. If it is not—the result is before our eyes.

The theory of "historic necessity," on which collectivist argument relies, has no support in fact or principle. The theory is that economic development occurs in an inevitable succession of phases, by which an industrial society, inventing machines on a basis of private property, must then pass into Communism, with public ownership, while retaining the machines for production. So it was prophesied that Germany and England, being highly industrialized, must be the first to turn communistic. Instead, the most backward nation in Europe, Russia, which had never fully emerged from Communism, lapsed back into it; and meantime the United States had outstripped Europe industrially. A feeble excuse was patched up, which had no more sense than the original theory.

As long as this universe lasts, the conditions in which a machine economy can be created and maintained are unalterable; and they exclude collectivism. One variation of the "historic necessity" theory is that "human nature can be changed." If that were true in the vital characteristic, so that men lost the right of liberty and the desire for it, those "changed" ex-human beings would thereby become incapable of inventing and operating machines. The inventions of man are of the spirit, not of materialism; and it is a crime against humanity to take the products of that divine endowment and throw them to the slave-drivers of Communism, to be trampled in the filth of a barracoon.

Because man is not deterministic, there can be no set order of his discoveries. Progress is always possible, but it depends upon the unpredictable use of intelligence. From the known record, it does not appear that men have ever wholly lost any important body of knowledge once attained; though it might lie unused for a time, until the moral principles were affirmed by which material science could be applied beneficially. The precedence of the moral order is clear, since useful discoveries occur only when men secure liberty by restraint of the political power. Such discoveries were made at various times and places, and brought together; but the principles involved are universals. They do not change with "history." Whenever and wherever they are understood and applied they will work, always in the same way. If they are forgotten or ignored, nothing can be achieved. There is no "wave of the future"; humanity shapes its future by moral purpose and the use of reason. Faith in the benevolent omnipotence of government is pure superstition, an aggregate residue of all the "magical" practices of primitive man. As in nature a savage does not know what makes the salmon run in spring, or why game is scarcer one year than another, it is not extraordinary that he should have sought to propitiate some power in nature, expecting a return without a rational cause. This vague expectation of benefit from an invisible power persuaded by *words of magic* has been transferred to the idea of an abstract agency placed above the individual, and amenable to *words*, for the gift of material benefits. But it is actually a complete retrogression, in one gigantic stride, toward darkness and extinction.

The most extreme fallacy is to believe that nothing can be done, that we must drift to disaster and accommodate ourselves to it. If that were true, we must die in heaps, with a miserable remnant reverting to savagery; for there is no compromise. But it is not true.

Everything can be done for a living future, if men take the long view by which the long circuit of energy is created. Not even disaster by temporary negligence need be final. With the establishment of the Republic of the United States of America, a great landmark in secular history was erected. The most profound scholar of the past century, Lord Acton, who devoted his life to study of the history of human liberty, said it "was that which *was not,* until the last quarter of the eighteenth century in Pennsylvania." The event he denoted was unique in that it was the first time a nation was ever founded on reasoned political principles, proceeding from the axiom that man's birthright is freedom. And as long as those principles were maintained, it succeeded beyond all precedent. Until then, nations were formed by chance and circumstance and doubtful experiment; then if a nation sank, it was impossible to reconstruct it. No matter how often a democracy might be tried, it must shortly collapse into despotism. Or if an aristocracy or monarchy developed, and subsequently broke down, another could not be created to take its place, since men could not go back in time to secure the line of descent. But a federal republic with no hereditary element in the political structure can always be reconstituted by design on the same principles and bases.

Whoever is fortunate enough to be an American citizen came into the greatest inheritance man has ever enjoyed. He has had the benefit of every heroic and intellectual effort men have made for many thousands of years, realized at last. If Americans should now turn back, submit again to slavery, it would be a betrayal so base the human race might better perish. The opportunity is equally great to justify the faith which animated that long travail, and bequeathed them such a noble and happy heritage.

APPENDIX:

Paterson's Annotations to
The God of the Machine

Isabel Paterson was concerned that her work be accurate in detail as well as in outline. This concern is demonstrated by the annotations she made in two copies of *The God of the Machine*: a leatherbound presentation copy given her by the publisher, and a copy in normal binding. Paterson's annotations (clearly penciled, like virtually all her other notes in books) correct some typographical errors, refine some wording, and record afterthoughts and questions about historical facts. The dates of the annotations are unknown, but the formality of some of them—one of which is even signed (*"IMP"*)—may indicate that Paterson was mindful of future readers, not known to her personally.

Paterson seems never to have commented on the fact that the last chapter of *The God of the Machine* bears two slightly different titles. The title that appears on the first page of that chapter is "The Dynamic Economy and the Future"; the title in the table of contents and the running heads is "The Dynamic Economy of the Future." In her *Herald Tribune* column of 5 February 1939, Paterson confessed that her long experience in correcting newspaper proof sheets had convinced her that even an army of proofreaders would be likely to overlook "some peculiarly glaring mistake, probably in the front-page headline." If she noticed the error in her chapter title, perhaps she regarded it as one more piece of evidence for her "conviction that there is an irreducible minimum of pure error in all human affairs."

In the following record of Paterson's annotations to *The God of the Machine*, each passage marked by Paterson is identified by page and line number in the text of the original (1943) edition, which is reproduced in this volume. Where Paterson distinguishes particular words for annotation or correction, her note or corrected reading is preceded by a quotation of the relevant passage from the 1943 edition. The two copies of *The God of the Machine* in which Paterson made her notes are cited as C1 (her leatherbound presentation copy) and C2 (her other copy).

15.11	Their activity] Their material activity [C1]
23.8	permission.] permission from the Senate. [C1]
27.9	rights] rights as a Roman citizen, [C1]
28.21	approximately] *deleted;* synchronize [C1]
28.27	entity] *deleted;* form [C1]
28.33	principle] principle and consonant structure [C1]
29.2	ashlar] *deleted; note:* (mistaken term = ashlar is merely dressed (cut) stone. I *meant* the style of masonry which overlaps, or as masons say, breaks the joints) [C1]
35.5	principle] strict principle [C1]
35.5	succession.] *note:* A minor heir could not have performed his function; an incompetent heir was liable to be murdered, that is, scrapped and replaced. [C1]
35.29	the waterwheel] *underlined, followed by inserted question mark; note:* ? Probably an error implied here. Don't think they had the waterwheel? [C1]
35.29	the waterwheel] *circled; note:* Seems to be a mistake—did they have the waterwheel?

	apparently not; no record of it. Must have been a later invention. [C2]
35.33	*note*: Egypt an exception; grain for the dole; government monopoly. [C1]
37.17	strictly] *underlined*; *note*: preponderantly [C1]
38.8	fossilized] *note*: (-not the best term—static? [C1]
38.35	residual] *lined through* [C1]
45.32	heavy-road] heavy-load [C1]
67.5	*note, evidently intended as a replacement for the sentence beginning on this line*: the subordinate condition of the slave, which he cannot rise above by his own volition and efforts, is status. But he is bought and sold by contract between masters. [C2]
109.1-5	*note*: This needs correction, for in fact at that time some law or ordinance or prerogative existed by which the possessions or fortune of any Jew, on his decease, passed to the Crown; apparently this is how the king obtained such notes or mortgages. *IMP* [C1]
109.2-30	*note*: This part is not entirely correct historically. Should be verified and corrected. Instead of the interpretation given here, it seems that the fact was, the estate left by a few ment [sic] to the crown by law, and that was how a "debt" might "fall into the hands" of the king. I don't know in what way the king had been taking more than "the chattel contained in the bond." [C2]
109.3-4	collections difficult, especially] *underlined* [C2]
109.5	been discounting their notes] *underlined*; *note*: Probably this is an erroneous deduction. [C2]
109.14	process] *underlined* [C1]

109.16-18   *note*: On the death of Louis XIV, there was a shakedown of the tax farmers and financiers by the Regent's government. [C1]

112.29-36   *note*: much condensed, had to omit mention of the peculiar effect on later history of John's extensive sale of charters to towns and mercantile interests as an expedient to raise money—an ultimate extension of liberties as a result of an attempted despotism. [C1]

113.28-29   *note*: All this is much condensed, omitting mention of the previous claim of the Pope against William of Normandy for feudal homage and dues, which William positively denied. [C1]

130.15-27   *bracketed by line in left margin* [C2]

133.12   verdict] *underlined*; *note*: should be "decision," or judgment [C1]

133.19-20   Judicial review *is not* concerned with deciding whether] *passage underlined* [C1]

133.19-26   Judicial review . . . in the Constitution.] *note:* This passage as it stands is incorrect, a[?] confusion of the question of Constitutional limitations and of the general "police power" (note from Judge Guy L. Fake.) Needs revision. [C1]

138.34   or strain] *circled*; *note*: and the distributed stresses [C2]

139.27   a point] *caret between "a" and "point"*, with line to words in right margin:
variable
uncompensated [C2]

142.2   house.] house and the inhabitants acted as they did in the panic of desperation. [C2]

149.24   Burke] *underlined*; *note*: Was this Burke's saying? or was it Chateaubriand? or both? [C1]

158.18	verdict] *circled; note*: decision [C2]
158.29	plead] plead in court [C2]
159.24	border.] national border. [C2]
261.6	to pay] or pay [C1]

Index*